**??????????????????
CHECK YOURSELF OUT
??????????????????**

??????????????? CHECK YOURSELF OUT ???????????????

The Complete Book of Self-Testing

Edited by Craig T. Norback

Times
BOOKS

Published by TIMES BOOKS, a division
of Quadrangle/The New York Times Book Co., Inc.
Three Park Avenue, New York, N.Y. 10016

Published simultaneously in Canada by
Fitznenry & Whiteside, Ltd., Toronto

Copyright © 1980 by Craig T. Norback

All rights reserved. No part of this book may
be reproduced in any form or by any electronic
or mechanical means including information storage
and retrieval systems without permission in writing
from the publisher, except by a reviewer who may
quote brief passages in a review.

Library of Congress Cataloging in Publication Data

Main entry under title:

Check yourself out.

   1. Success—Testing.   2. Psychological tests.

I. Norback, Craig T.
BF637.S8C46   1980   158′.028′7   80-5143
ISBN 0-8129-0935-6

Design, typography, and layout by
THE BOOKMAKERS, INCORPORATED

Editorial, Design, Graphic, and Production Services to the Publishing Industry

Set in type by Robert E. Mebane Communications,
Forty Fort, Pa. and
Design Systems, Wilkes-Barre, Pa.

Manufactured in the United States of America.

??????????
Contents
??????????

Acknowledgments **vii**
Introduction **ix**

APTITUDE
The Mensa Test 3
The Thinker's Test 6
How Resourceful Are You? 9
Reading Speed Test 53
How Well Do You Listen? 56

PERSONALITY
Your Lifestyle Profile 61
Can You Control Your Jealousy? 64
The Friendship Test 67
How Tolerant Are You? 71
The Honesty Test 75
How Assertive Are You? 78
What Does Your Handwriting Reveal about You? 81
How Do Your Manners Measure Up? 85
Your Weather Sensitivity Risk-Factor Profile 88
Are You Disorganized? 89

GENERAL
Should Your Return to School? 93
The National Cooking Institute Cooking Test 96
How Smart a Traveler Are You? 99
How Good a Driver Are You? 103
Testing Your Traffic Safety Knowledge 106
How Well Do You Know Your Car? 108
Can You Survive in the Outdoors? 111

PERSONAL RELATIONSHIPS
Are You Marriage Material? 117
Singles Lifestyle: Can It Work for You? 119
How Romantic Are You? 121
Are You Thinking about Parenthood? 123
How Do You Rate as a Single Parent? 125
Test Yourself: How Good a Parent Are You? 135

HEALTH/BEAUTY
What's Your Nutritional IQ? 143
Are You Naturally Healthy? 146
Are You Taking Care of Your Body? 150
Can You Distinguish the Facts from the Myths in Diets? 152
Do You Need Psychotherapy? 156
Can You Administer First Aid? 160
Do You Know What to Do When You Get a Headache? 163
Schedule of Recent Experience (SRE) 166
Stress: Are You Coping? 169
Do You Have Trouble Sleeping? 171
What Are the Signs of Alcoholism? 173

FINANCES
Are You a Good Money Manager? 177
What's Your Credit Rating? 179
Are You a Smart Shopper? 183
Do You Need a Tax Accountant? 186
Are You Financially Prepared for Retirement? 189
Is Your Worth Insured? 193

HOME
Are You Ready to Buy Your Own Home? 199
Do You Know Your Rights as a Tenant? 203
Are You Energy Conscious? 205
How Good Is Your Decorating Ability? 208
Are You Safety Conscious? 211

JOB/CAREER
How Good Is Your Job Interview Technique? 215
The Harrington/O'Shea System for Career Decision Making 218
Does Your Job Have Good Growth Potential? 224
How Good Are Your Business Communications Skills? 227
Are You Ready for a Promotion? 231
Are You about to Be Fired? 233
What Can You Expect as a Working Mother? 235
Are You a Workaholic? 237
Do You Have What It Takes to Start Your Own Business? 239
Women: Is Your Wardrobe Working for You? 241
Men: Is Your Wardrobe Working for You? 244

Acknowledgments

The editor wishes to express his gratitude and thank the following people and organizations for their assistance and cooperation in compiling information for this book. These people and organizations are: Anne Hebenstreit; Mensa; *Construction and Use of Written Simulations,* by permission, copyright © 1975, 1976 by The Psychological Corporation; *Reading Drills,* © 1975 by Edward B. Fry, published by Jamestown Publishers, Providence, Rhode Island, and reprinted with their permission; Sperry Corporation; Reprinted from the *Journal of American Insurance,* Winter 1979-80; © 1974, LHJ Publishing, Inc., reprinted with permission of *Ladies' Home Journal*; Excerpted with permission from *Understanding Yourself* by Christopher Evans, © 1977 A & W Publishers, Inc., and Phoebus Publishing Company; The American Association of Handwriting Analysts; from *Weathering: How the Atmosphere Conditions Your Body, Your Mind, Your Moods—And Your Health* by Stephen Rosen, copyright © 1979 by Stephen Rosen, reprinted with permission of the publisher, M. Evans and Company, Inc., New York; National Cooking Institute, Englewood, and Denver, Colorado; Eric Friedheim, editor and publisher, *The Travel Agent*; Warren Rumsfield, North American Professional Driver Education Association; National Safety Council; National Alliance for Optional Parenthood; © Copyright, 1980, Parents Without Partners, Inc., Washington, D.C.; © Parents Magazine Enterprised, reprinted from *Parents* by permission; The American Natural Hygiene Society, Inc.; Copyright © 1979, Lean Line, Inc. South Plainfield, New Jersey; Reprinted from May 19, 1978, issue of *Family Circle Magazine,* © 1978, The Family Circle, Inc.; Copyright © 1979 by Thomas H. Holmes, M.D., Department of Psychiatry and Behavioral Sciences, University of

ACKNOWLEDGMENTS

Holmes, M.D., Department of Psychiatry and Behavioral Sciences, University of Washington School of Medicine, Seattle, Washington School of Medicine, Seattle, Washington; Consumer Credit Counseling Service, New York, New York; © Copyright 1980, Career Planning Associates, Inc.; National Council on Alcoholism; Karl Albrecht, Ph.D. and Dr. Kenneth E. Everard.

??????????????? Introduction ??????????????

How well do you know yourself? How aware are you of your abilities, talents, and limitations? Are you realistic about your hopes, dreams, and goals?

People have always made an effort to delve into their own psyches, to find new dimensions to their own personalities, to discover new and fascinating aspects of themselves, and to satisfy an insistence on coming face-to-face with their inner, secret self.

Check Yourself Out: The Complete Book of Self-Testing will reveal your true personality. Each test is complete in itself, and together the more than fifty tests will help you discover and rediscover the person you really are.

?????????
APTITUDE
?????????

??????????????????
The Mensa Test
??????????????????

Founded in 1954 by Roland Berrill and Dr. L.L. Ware, Mensa is an international organization with over 28,000 active members in fourteen countries. While the purpose of Mensa is to provide contact between members to help stimulate research in psychology and social science, it is the intellectual makeup of the group that fascinates the 30,000 people who annually apply for membership. To qualify you must score higher than 98 percent of the general population would on intelligence tests created by the organization. Here is a sample test that will help you determine whether you might be one of that elite 2 percent.

?

1. Write in the brackets a word that means the same thing as the left-hand word in one sense, and the same thing as the right hand word in another sense.
   example: Globule (Drop) Fall
   Hire (_____)Betroth

2. In the square below, there is a rule of arithmetic that applies across and down. Find the rule and figure the missing number.
   example: 2 7 9   6 2 4
             5 4 9   2 ? 0
             7 11 18   4 0 4

3. Which word does not belong?
   a. car   b. moon   c. fish
   d. happy e. belief

4. Complete the series: 3, 7, 19, 55, 163,_____.

5. Underline the item within the brackets that belongs to the following series:

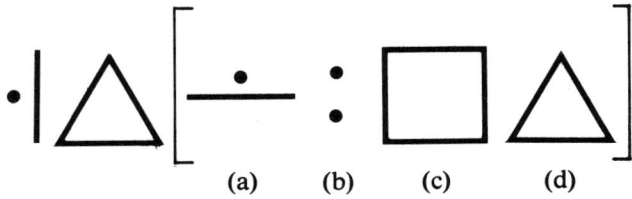

   (a)   (b)   (c)   (d)

6. Insert the same number in both brackets that completes the equation:
   $$\frac{3}{(\_\_\_)} = \frac{(\_\_\_)}{27}$$

7. "Don't trade horses when crossing a stream" means:
   a. You might fall off and get wet.
   b. Don't attempt something until you are fully prepared.
   c. Decide what you are going to do before you do it.
   d. Don't change plans when something is half completed.

8. "Mountain" is to "land" as "whirlpool" is to "_____".
   (fluid, wet, sea, sky, shower)

9. Underline the two words most *opposite* in meaning:
   intense, extensive, majority, extreme, diffuse

APTITUDE

10. Underline the two words most *similar* in meaning:
    attract, lure, entice, persuade, please

11. Write the missing middle number:
    example: 3 (12) 4   4 ( ) 5

12. Fill in the missing number:
    example: 3, 6, (9), 12   65, 33, ( ), 9

13. Which one of the diagrams on the right can be turned over or rotated to become the same as the diagram on the left?

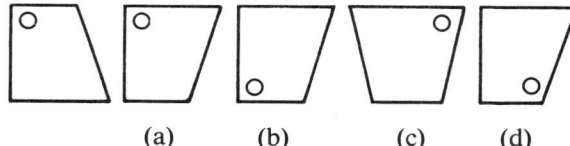

    (a)   (b)   (c)   (d)

14. X is larger than Y
    Z is smaller than Y
    Therefore:
    a. Z is smaller than X
    b. Z is larger than X
    c. Z is equal to X

15. What number, multiplied by 4, is equal to three-fourths of 112?

16. A house is 36 feet long and 27 feet wide. How wide would a house of the same proportions be if it were 68 feet long?

17. M is above N and O
    N is above O and below P
    Therefore:
    1. M is not above O and P
    2. O is above N
    3. P is above O
    4. O is above P

18. Fill in the missing letter:
    B, E, I, N, _____.

19. Fill in the missing number:
    46, 39, 30, 19, _____.

20. 27 is to 3 as 343 is to _____. (The answer is a whole number.)

21. Underline the symbol in the brackets that has the characteristic held in common by the first three symbols.

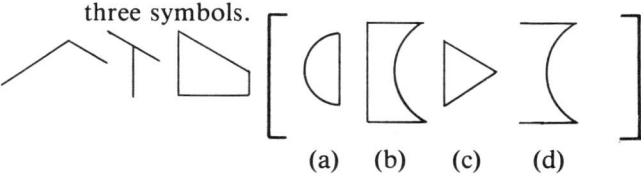

    (a)   (b)   (c)   (d)

22. If she turns either left or right at the stop sign she will run out of gas before she reaches a service station. She has already gone too far past a service station to turn around and return to it before she runs out of gas. She does not see a service station lying ahead of her. Therefore:
    a. She may run out of gas.
    b. She will run out of gas.
    c. She should not have taken this route.

23. a is to i as i is to   (j, e, o, h, u)

24.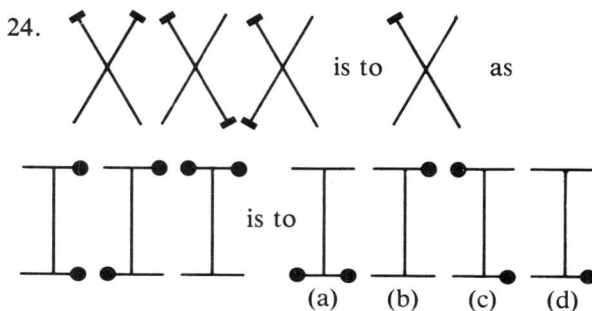

25. Complete the analogy by writing one word in the spaces, ending with the letters printed.
    example: high is to low as sky is to
                /e/a/r/t/h.
               skull is to brain as shell is to
                / / /l/k.

ANSWERS

1. engage
2. 2
3. happy
4. 487
5. c
6. 9
7. d
8. sea
9. intense, diffuse

10. lure, entice
11. 20
12. 17
13. b
14. a
15. 21
16. 51 feet
17. 3
18. T

19. 6
20. 7
21. c
22. a
23. u
24. b
25. /y/o/l/k/

THE MENSA TEST

SCORING

Give yourself one point for each correct answer. You receive an additional four (4) points if you completed the test in less than 15 minutes; three (3) points if you completed the test in less than 20 minutes; two (2) points if you completed the test in less than 25 minutes; and one (1) point if you completed the test in less than 30 minutes.

If you scored:

25-29 points: You are quite intelligent—a perfect candidate for Mensa.

20-24 points: This should put you in the high upper percent of the population—certainly a Mensa candidate.

16-19 points: An honorable score. You might want to try the Mensa test.

Less than 16 points: Forget about joining Mensa, but you're in good company. Many world famous figures (writers, businessmen, artists, etc.) don't have exceptional IQs either.

What's the verdict? If you think you may be Mensa material or if you'd like to receive membership information, write to Mensa, Dept. CN, 1701 West Third Street, Brooklyn, New York 11223. If you send them a check or money order for $6.00, they'll send you an IQ test you can complete in the privacy of your home.

?

??????????????????????
The Thinker's Test
??????????????????????

Karl Albrecht, Ph.D., a consultant in management and organization development, is the author of *Brain Power*. He devised this test as a measure of logical powers. Take it and see how powerful *your* brain is.

People who have learned to organize their ideas into sequence or chains of logic can usually reason their way effectively through confused or complicated situations in the business of living. Here's a quiz well calculated to challenge that particular thinking skill and its everyday companion skills—and set you thinking about thinking.

If Tom is shorter than Dick, and Harry is taller than Dick, is Tom taller or shorter than Harry?

Do you find thinking puzzles like this one easy, hard, or somewhere in between? However you find them, they can help you assess and improve your practical thinking skills. If you answered that Tom is shorter than Harry, you've just shown your ability at a skill which psychologists call *sequential thought*.

Are you hungry for mental stimulation? The following Thinker's Test will challenge and exercise a variety of practical thinking skills, so you can identify your strongest ones as well as those that need further development. Before going through the questions, consider these useful strategies: Approach each question with a playful, flexible, and exploratory attitude. Draw thinking diagrams—sketches or "models"—to help organize your thoughts. Think out loud. Put your thoughts into words. Use names, labels, and verbal relationships to clarify and add structure to your thought processes.

In the answers, you'll find a discussion of the various kinds of thinking skills they call forth. Don't feel discouraged if you haven't managed to get every question right—most people don't. There is no scoring system, so it's more important to think about thinking—and your relative strengths and weaknesses—than to wind up with the right answer.

QUESTIONS

1. Bob, Carol, Ted and Alice are sitting around a table discussing their favorite sports.
    a. Bob sits directly across from the jogger.
    b. Carol sits to the right of the racquetball player.
    c. Alice sits across from Ted.
    d. The golfer sits to the left of the tennis player.
    e. A man sits on Ted's right.

    What sport does each of the four prefer?

2. Find the pattern that governs this familiar sequence, and figure out the next letter: O, T, T, F, F, S, S, E?

3. If three days ago was the day before Friday, what will the day after tomorrow be?

4. Six drinking glasses stand in a row, with the first three full of water and the next three empty. By handling and moving only one glass, how can you arrange the six glasses so that no

THE THINKER'S TEST

full glass stands next to another full one, and no empty glass stands next to another empty one?

5. Excavating in England, an archeologist found a Roman coin dated "44 B.C." and bearing a likeness of Julius Caesar. Another archeologist correctly identified the coin as a fake. How did he know?

6. How can you arrange the numbers from 1 to 9 to form a 3 x 3 square array, such that each row, each column, and the two diagonals will all total exactly 15?

7. In five minutes, write down as many unusual uses as you can for a paper clip.

8. Three playing cards lie face down on the table, in a row. We know that:
   a. To the right of the Jack is a Diamond.
   b. To the left of the Diamond is a Club.
   c. To the right of the Heart is a Jack.
   d. To the left of the King is an Ace.

   Match up each card with its suit and position.

9. Solve this problem in your mind, without using a diagram or model. Imagine that you put two pieces of typing paper on your desk with a piece of carbon paper between them, as if you wanted to write something in duplicate. Now, imagine that you fold this assembly in half with the crease running from left to right, bringing the lower half back under the top.

   If you write your name on the top half of the top sheet, how many copies will you make, where will they appear (front, back, top, bottom, first sheet, second sheet), and how will they be oriented?

ANSWERS

1. Bob plays tennis, Carol jogs, Ted plays golf and Alice plays raquetball. This question challenges your skill at *organizing information* and *making logical inferences*.

2. The next letter is "N," the first letter of the word "Nine." This series consists of the initials of the counting numbers. To answer this one correctly, you had to use your *pattern recognition* skills.

3. If you answered Tuesday, you have exercised your skill at *sequential thinking*. To solve it, you must "find the end of the rope," first figuring out what day today is, and then proceed to establish the day after tommorrow. Drawing a thinking diagram, such as a list of the days of the week in sequence, can help here.

4. Pick up the middle one of the full glasses and, after pouring its water into the middle empty glass, put it back in its original position. This one helped you to assess your *mental flexibility*. The ability to *categorize your options* (push, pull, lift, slide, pour, etc.) is also involved here.

5. The archeologist realized that, since the dating system based on "B.C." and "A.D." originated after the birth of Christ, a coinmaker before that time couldn't have known about it, and therefore would not have stamped this date on a coin.

6. One arrangement of the numbers has 2, 9, and 4 across the first row, 7, 5, and 3 in the second row, and 6, 1, and 8 in the third row. The diagonals become (reading from the left corners) 2, 5, and 8, and 6, 5, and 4.

   This puzzle assesses the extent to which you approach problems by *strategic attack*, instead of simple trial-and-error. A careful reasoning process before you start writing down any numbers can reduce the matter to just a few possibilities. For example, we can focus on the center number of the matrix, which gets added to every other number in some combination or other. We realize we can't use 9 for the center, because adding it to 8 would overshoot the target sum of 15. By the same reasoning process, we can disqualify 8, 7 and 6. We can also eliminate 1, 2, 3 and 4 as too small to make sums of 15 in all directions. When we realize that only 5 will fill the bill for the center position, we can quickly figure out the rest of them.

7. Count the number of uses you listed. Less than ten implies a bit of "mental arthritis." More than 20 suggests you find it easy to think of lots of possibilities and points of view in a situation—a sign of what psychologists consider *creative thinking*.

APTITUDE

8. From left to right, the Ace of Hearts, Jack of Clubs, and King of Diamonds. (The "d" clue does *not* say "to the immediate left...") Solving this one requires careful *deductive reasoning*.
9. First, copies can only appear on the face of the second sheet, because no matter how you fold the package, the ink side of the carbon paper will contact only the second sheet. You will have produced *two copies* of your name on the front of the second sheet, one of them on the upper half and a mirror-image version on the lower half, with the letters upside down. This puzzle stresses your skill at *visualization* and *spatial reasoning*.

EVALUATION

Now to review the results. Which problems did you find easiest, which hardest? Did you find any trend or pattern in your results? Once you've identified the skills you are weak in, you can improve them by consciously challenging and using them.

To develop your thinking skills, treat yourself to a book of thinking puzzles and games and work them through. Use the techniques of organizing information, drawing thinking diagrams, and thinking sequentially in everyday situations like balancing your checkbook, working out a vacation plan, or making an important decision.

If you have children, develop your thinking skills by playing games together. Look around for practical-thinking courses at a community college or university extension.

When you realize what a wonderful resource that biological computer of yours really is, and how precious it is to you, you'll begin to respect it, use it and develop it more. By thinking about thinking, and by seeking mental exercise rather than avoiding it, you can steadily increase your brain power all through your life.

Originally appeared in the April 1980 *Reader's Digest*. Copyright © 1980 by The Reader's Digest Assn., Inc.

???????????????????
How Resourceful Are You?
???????????????????

Christine H. McGuire, Lawrence M. Solomon, and Philip G. Bashook designed the following test as part of the book, *Construction and Use of Written Simulations* (The Psychological Corporation). The book was written to help simulate and stimulate the decision-making process.

A simulation, basically, is any model that exactly recreates all the essential elements of a situation or phenomenon to be analyzed. In engineering, for example, it is possible to feed all the specifications of an automobile to a computer which can then calculate (and even display on a TV screen) exactly what would happen when that automobile struck a wall at a given rate of speed.

"The Traveler" is a psychological simulation designed primarily to test your skill at problem solving. But there are other revelations about your personality lurking in the test as well. To start, read the next section and imagine that you are the Traveler.

?

THE TRAVELER

OPENING SCENE

In celebration of having landed your first real job—teaching school—you are traveling alone on your first trip to Europe. You have just three days left on your 21-day excursion fare and you plan to spend them in Warsaw. Since your family originally came from Poland, you naturally wish to visit all the sights and have therefore planned very full days of sightseeing. Because you do not understand Polish, you do anticipate some difficulty in getting around.

The trip is a present from your wealthy but slightly eccentric uncle, who emigrated from Poland in 1932. Before leaving the United States you promised that you would try to obtain for him as much information as you could about a Mr. Kowalski of Warsaw from whom he had last heard three years ago. Your uncle wants you to locate him and determine his relationship with your family; he thinks the man may be a cousin. In addition to a photograph of Mr. Kowalski, you have the following information about him:

Name: J. Kowalski
Address: Karolkowa 18, Warsaw
Phone: 49-64-21

When last heard from, Mr. Kowalski was working for an import-export company that specialized in exporting amber products.

This is your first day in Warsaw and you are staying at the Hotel Bristol. You are studying the available map and planning your day, while having breakfast. Since you want to get your uncle's business out of the way with a minimum of time and expense, you have asked the hotel operator to phone the number your uncle gave you. Just as you are finishing breakfast, the waiter brings you a phone message which reads: "No one at 49-64-21 by the name of Kowalski. No one there speaks English. Do you want help with other calls?"

Before going on to Section A, read the instructions.

?

INSTRUCTIONS

As you will see when you look at Section A, it lists just about all of the options open to you—ranging from a number of steps you could take to find Mr.

APTITUDE

Kowalski to forgetting the whole thing and having a pleasant time sightseeing.

In the book from which this test is taken, the Answer Section is completely blank until the user rubs each answer with a special marker to bring out the answer. This approach is impractical here, so you're on your honor not to peek. Each time you refer to the Answer Section, it will either tell you what happens next or where to turn. Everything that you, the Traveler, could find in any sequence (and you control this) and at any expenditure of time or money is *somewhere* in Sections A through O.

To start out, read the instructions in your diary, look at the description and map of Warsaw, and review if you like the opening scene. Then on to Section A.

??

DIARY

In the spaces below, record the amount of time taken in each section, as directed. Note that, in the three days you have to spend in Warsaw, you MAY SPEND UP TO 35½ HOURS in search of J. Kowalski. Whenever you are directed to record time in the diary, note the time in the left-hand space, add the time to elapsed time, and record the NEW elapsed time in the right-hand space. For example, suppose that after an elapsed time of 2 hr. 30 min. you take an action that requires 30 min.

Time Spent	Elapsed Time
	2 hr. 30 min.
30 min.	3 hr.

If and when your total elapsed time equals 35 hr. 30 min., STOP and record here _____ the LETTER of the section you are in. Then, turn to Section M and follow instructions.

Time Spent	Elapsed Time	Time Spent	Elapsed Time	Time Spent	Elapsed Time
___	___	___	___	___	___
___	___	___	___	___	___
___	___	___	___	___	___
___	___	___	___	___	___
___	___	___	___	___	___
___	___	___	___	___	___
___	___	___	___	___	___
___	___	___	___	___	___
___	___	___	___	___	___
___	___	___	___	___	___
___	___	___	___	___	___
___	___	___	___	___	___

DO NOT record time on the following page unless specifically instructed to do so. If you ARE instructed to do so, begin at "0" time and continue to a total of 28½ hours.

HOW RESOURCEFUL ARE YOU?

If you again run out of time before locating J. Kowalski, follow response 316 to obtain further instructions.

Time Spent	Elapsed Time	Time Spent	Elapsed Time	Time Spent	Elapsed Time
_____	_____	_____	_____	_____	_____
_____	_____	_____	_____	_____	_____
_____	_____	_____	_____	_____	_____
_____	_____	_____	_____	_____	_____
_____	_____	_____	_____	_____	_____
_____	_____	_____	_____	_____	_____
_____	_____	_____	_____	_____	_____
_____	_____	_____	_____	_____	_____
_____	_____	_____	_____	_____	_____

???

SIGHTSEEING IN WARSAW

OLD WARSAW ROUTE starts from the Castle Square and leads through the Old Town and New Town, which form a beautiful historical whole, completely reconstructed after the war devastations.

The sightseeing starts from Swietojanska Street. Here stands the Gothic Cathedral of St. John; next to it is the Jesuit Church, dating from the beginning of the 17th century. The Old Town Market Square is a jewel of 17th- and 18th-century architecture. Quaint small shops sell products of various arts and crafts. There are also attractive cafes and restaurants. Next we see Nowomiejska Street, with defense walls and the Barbican (15th century)—reconstructed from the very foundations and one of the few structures of this type still existent in Europe—giving an example of medieval fortifications. Freta Street leads to the New Town Market Square, where stands the handsome baroque Church of Sisters of the Blessed Sacrement (17th century).

The ROYAL ROUTE also starts from the Castle Square. Here rises King Sigismund Column, erected in 1644, and we see the ruins of the royal castle, completely destroyed during the last war. Krakowskie Przedmiescie, emerging from the Square, is one of Europe's most beautiful streets and has many old churches and palaces: St. Anne's Church (1454), Radziwill Palace (now housing the Presidium of the Council of Ministers) with the monument of Prince Joseph Poniatowski, and Potocki Palace (17th century)—the seat of the Ministry of Culture and Art.

Warsaw University occupies the rebuilt Kazimierzowski Palace and also Tyszkiewicz and Uruski Palaces. Opposite the University stands the Fine Arts Academy, in the former Czapski Palace. In the Church of St. Cross (17th century) there is an urn containing the heart of Frederic Chopin. In front of Staszic Palace (19th century) stands the statue of Nicolaus Copernicus, the great Polish astronomer (1473–1543), carved by the famous Danish sculptor Thorvaldsen.

The continuation of Krakowskie Przedmiescie—Nowy Swiat Street—is known as one of the most pleasant streets in the capital. It was entirely rebuilt after the war, according to its 19th-century design. Ujazdowskie Avenue, called Warsaw's "summer salon," is lined with small historical palaces housing various foreign embassies. Lazienki is the capital's loveliest park, founded in the 17th century, and contains valuable monuments of architecture and art, such as the Island Palace. This was built in the 18th century by two architects, Merlini and Kamsetzer, for the last of the Polish Kings—Stanislaus Augustus Poniatowski.

Further sightseeing information is available from:

Polish Travel Office (ORBIS)
13, Krakowskie Przedmiescie
tel. 26-16-67

APTITUDE

PROBLEM SECTION

SECTION A: FIRST STEP

You would now (Choose ONLY ONE, unless otherwise directed in the Answer Section):

1. Try to get some expert assistance from individuals or special agencies
2. Visit Karolkowa 18
3. Check the alphabetical telephone directory for a new listing for J. Kowalski
4. Locate a city directory of Warsaw residents
5. Take the sightseeing trip you have planned and, when you get home, explain to your uncle what has happened
6. Return to your hotel room and have the operator phone 49-64-21 again while you are on the line
7. Check the telephone directory to get a list of Warsaw business firms that deal in amber products
8. Check the telephone directory to get a list of Warsaw companies engaged in the import-export business

SECTION B: SIGHTSEEING

You spend two hours to return to your hotel room by a slightly roundabout way so you can see some of the sights on your list. After a half hour for coffee and blintzes at a restaurant near the Bristol, you are ready to start out again. Record 2½ hours in your diary and continue with this section.

You would now (Choose ONLY ONE, unless otherwise directed in the Answer Section):

9. Try to get some expert assistance from individuals or special agencies, if you have not already done so
10. Check the alphabetical telephone directory for a new listing for J. Kowalski, if you have not already done so
11. Locate a city directory of Warsaw residents, if you have not already done so
12. Take the sightseeing trip you have planned and, when you get home, explain to your uncle what has happened
13. Return to your hotel room and have the operator phone 49-64-21 again while you are on the line, if you have not already done so
14. Check the telephone directory to get a list of Warsaw business firms that deal in amber products, if you have not already done so
15. Check the telephone directory to get a list of Warsaw companies engaged in the import-export business, if you have not already done so
16. During the day, visit some of the Kowalskis you have located
17. In the evening, visit some of the Kowalskis you have located
18. Phone some of the Kowalskis you have located

SECTION C: EXPERT ASSISTANCE

You approach the hotel clerk, who tells you that the consulate and tourist agencies offer such help. Furthermore, employers have information on their employees and the *milicja* (police) have a city directory of Warsaw residents. You would now contact (Select AS MANY AS you consider USEFUL and estimate 30 minutes for each encounter):

19. A special investigator
20. The *milicja*
21. The Foreign Tourists Office
22. ORBIS (Polish Travel Office)
23. The U.S. consulate
24. An English-speaking taxi driver
25. An airline representative

Record in your diary the time spent and continue with this section.

You would now (Choose ONLY ONE, unless otherwise directed in the Answer Section):

29. Visit Karolkowa 18, if you have not already done so
30. Check the alphabetical telephone directory for a new listing for J. Kowalski, if you have not already done so
31. Locate a city directory of Warsaw residents, if you have not already done so

HOW RESOURCEFUL ARE YOU?

32. Take the sightseeing trip you have planned and, when you get home, explain to your uncle what has happened
33. Return to your hotel room and have the operator phone 49-64-21 again while you are on the line, if you have not already done so
34. Check the telephone directory to get a list of Warsaw business firms that deal in amber products, if you have not already done so
35. Check the telephone directory to get a list of Warsaw companies engaged in the import-export business, if you have not already done so
36. During the day, visit some of the Kowalskis you have located
37. In the evening, visit some of the Kowalskis you have located
38. Phone some of the Kowalskis you have located

SECTION D: EVENING VISITS

Names and addresses of Kowalskis you have located are listed below. If you wish to make an evening visit to any one of them, follow the appropriate response (Select AS MANY AS you WISH and estimate one hour for each visit):

39. 44-19-26 Kowalski, Adam
    Wawelska 12
40. 19-21-12 Kowalski, Bernard
    mgr. inz. arch.
    Waleoznych 5
41. 45-20-03 Kowalski, Bogdan
    dr. med.
    Grojecka 219
42. 34-88-91 Kowalski, Cezary
    Buczka 43
43. 34-00-17 Kowalski, Czestaw
    Okopowa 27A
44. 29-21-63 Kowalski, Edmund
    mgr. prawa
    Warecka 2
45. 26-22-48 Kowalski, Edward
    art. muzyk
    Swigtokrzyska 12
46. 22-27-47 Kowalski, Eugeniusz
    Zwyciezcow 44
47. 43-40-11 Kowalski, Eugeniusz
    Pl. Narutowioza 18
48. 43-92-88 Kowalski, Grzegóry
    ul Karolkowa 93
49. 25-92-88 Kowalski, Grzegorz
    Al. Niepodleglosci 184
50. 35-36-72 Kowalski, Ignacy
    mgr. inz.
    Stawki 8
51. 37-33-51 Kowalski, Ignazy
    mgr. inz.
    Stawki 8
52. -- -- -- Kowalski, Jadwiga
    Chmielna 21
53. -- -- -- Kowalski, Jadwiga
    ul Minska 19A
54. 81-62-03 Kowalski, Jadwiga
    Leszno 280
55. 28-65-31 Kowalski, Jadwiga
    ul Obroncow 24
56. -- -- -- Kowalski, Jadwiga
    Kopernika, 29
57. 44-93-36 Kowalski, Jadwiga
    Nowowiejska 37
58. -- -- -- Kowalski, Jan
    ul Mredzynarodowa 9
59. -- -- -- Kowalski, Jan
    ul Minska 19
60. 43-93-36 Kowalski, Jan
    ul Karolkowa 91
61. -- -- -- Kowalski, Jan
    ul Obroncow 51
62. 27-52-69 Kowalski, Jan
    lek. dent.
    Pl. Grzybowski 21
63. 45-12-19 Kowalski, Jan
    narzedzia ogrodnicze
    Czerniakowska 218
64. 17-55-33 Kowalski, Jan
    prof. dr.
    Al. Waszyngtona 134
65. 26-66-16 Kowalski, Jan E.
    Hibnera 12
66. 25-63-69 Kowalski, Jan Stefan
    Chmielna 35
67. 43-77-00 Kowalski, Josef
    doc. dr. med.
    Filtrowa 63

APTITUDE

68. 26-17-92 Kowalski, Josef
              Em. Plater 56
69. 32-28-18 Kowalski, Jozef
              inz.
              Konwiktorska 77
70. 28-65-35 Kowalski, Jozef
              Poksal 16
71. 25-48-84 Kowalski, Jozef
              Kopernika 25
72. 26-74-98 Kowalski, Jozef
              lekarz, chor. wewn.
              Rutkowskiego 9
73. 44-53-57 Kowalski, Jozef
              inz. rolnik
              Biatobrzeska 93
74. -- -- -- Kowalski, Jozef
              Czerniakowska 200
75. 28-66-61 Kowalski, Jozef
              ul Lucka 13
76. -- -- -- Kowalski, Jozef
              Rutkowskiego 19
77. 35-07-16 Kowalski, Konstanty
              Niska 69

Record in your diary the time spent.

UNLESS OTHERWISE DIRECTED IN THE ANSWER SECTION, FOLLOW RESPONSE 316 TO OBTAIN FURTHER INSTRUCTIONS

SECTION E: PHONE CALLS

Names, addresses, and phone numbers of Kowalskis in the most recent telephone directory are listed below. You will have repeated opportunities to return to this section to make any additional calls you wish. Take Answer A to the first call to an individual; use Answer B for any subsequent call *to the same person*. If you wish to call anyone, follow the appropriate response (Select AS MANY AS you WISH and estimate 10 minutes for each call):

78. 44-19-26 Kowalski, Adam
              Wawelska 12
79. 19-21-12 Kowalski, Bernard
              mgr. inz. arch.
              Waleoznych 5
80. 45-20-03 Kowalski, Bogdan
              dr. med.
              Grojecka 219
81. 34-88-91 Kowalski, Cezary
              Buczka 43
82. 34-00-17 Kowalski, Czestaw
              Okopowa 27A
83. 29-21-63 Kowalski, Edmund
              mgr. prawa
              Warecka 2
84. 26-22-48 Kowalski, Edward
              art. muzyk
              Swigtokrzyska 12
85. 22-27-47 Kowalski, Eugeniusz
              Zwyciezcow 44
86. 43-40-11 Kowalski, Eugeniusz
              Pl. Narutowioza 18
87. 25-92-88 Kowalski, Grzegorz
              Al. Niepodleglosci 184
88. 35-36-72 Kowalski, Ignacy
              mgr. inz.
              Stawki 8
89. 44-93-36 Kowalski, Jadwiga
              Nowowiejska 37
90. 27-52-69 Kowalski, Jan
              lek. dent.
              Pl. Grzybowski 21
91. 45-12-19 Kowalski, Jan
              narzedzia ogrodnicze
              Czerniakowska 218
92. 17-55-33 Kowalski, Jan
              prof. dr.
              Al. Waszyngtona 134
93. 26-66-16 Kowalski, Jan E.
              Hibnera 12
94. 25-63-69 Kowalski, Jan Stefan
              Chmielna 35
95. 43-77-00 Kowalski, Josef
              doc. dr. med
              Filtrowa 63
96. 26-17-92 Kowalski, Josef
              Em. Plater 56
97. 32-28-18 Kowalski, Jozef
              inz.
              Konwiktorska 77
98. 28-65-35 Kowalski, Jozef
              Poksal 16
99. 25-48-84 Kowalski, Jozef
              Kopernika 25

HOW RESOURCEFUL ARE YOU?

100. 26-74-98   Kowalski, Jozef
                  lekarz, chor. wewn.
                  Rutkowskiego 9
101. 44-53-57   Kowalski, Jozef
                  inz. rolnik
                  Biatobrzeska 93
102. 35-07-16   Kowalski, Konstanty
                  Niska 69

Record in your diary the time spent and continue with this section.

You would now (Choose ONLY ONE EACH TIME you are directed to this section):

103. Try to get some expert assistance from individuals or special agencies, if you have not already done so
104. Visit Karolkowa 18, if you have not already done so
105. Check the alphabetical telephone directory for a new listing for J. Kowalski, if you have not already done so
106. Locate a city directory of Warsaw residents, if you have not already done so
107. Take the sightseeing trip you have planned and, when you get home, explain to your uncle what has happened
108. Return to your hotel room and have the operator phone 49-64-21 again while you are on the line, if you have not already done so
109. Check the telephone directory to get a list of Warsaw business firms that deal in amber products, if you have not already done so
110. Check the telephone directory to get a list of Warsaw companies engaged in the import-export business, if you have not already done so
111. During the day, visit some of the Kowalskis you have located
112. In the evening, visit some of the Kowalskis you have located
113. Go on a three-hour sightseeing tour and plan to complete your calls later

SECTION F: CITY DIRECTORY

Names and addresses of Kowalskis from the city directory, but not listed in the most recent telephone directory, are shown below. If you wish further information about any of them from the *milicja* (police), follow the appropriate response (Select AS MANY AS you WISH and estimate 10 minutes for each inquiry):

114. 43-92-88   Kowalski, Grzegory
                  ul Karolkowa 93
                  inz. rolnik
115. 37-33-51   Kowalski, Ignazy
                  Stawki 8
                  mgr. inz.
116. -- -- --   Kowalski, Jadwiga
                  Chmielna 21
117. -- -- --   Kowalski, Jadwiga
                  ul Minska 19A
                  robotnik
118. 81-62-03   Kowalski, Jadwiga
                  Leszno 280
119. 28-65-31   Kowalski, Jadwiga
                  ul Obroncow 24
                  robotnik
120. -- -- --   Kowalski, Jadwiga
                  Kopernika, 29
121. -- -- --   Kowalski, Jan
                  ul Mredzynarodowa 9
                  urzednik
122. -- -- --   Kowalski, Jan
                  ul Minska 19
                  kierowca
123. 43-93-36   Kowalski, Jan
                  ul Karolkowa 91
                  inz. rolnik
124. -- -- --   Kowalski, Jan
                  ul Obroncow 51
                  urzednik
125. -- -- --   Kowalski, Jozef
                  Czerniakowska 200
                  narzedzia ogrodnicze
126. 28-66-61   Kowalski, Jozef
                  ul Lucka 13
                  lekarz
127. -- -- --   Kowalski, Jozef
                  inz.
                  Rutkowskiego 19

APTITUDE

Record in your diary the time spent and continue with this section.

You would now (Choose ONLY ONE, unless otherwise directed in the Answer Section):

128. Try to get some expert assistance from individuals or special agencies, if you have not already done so
129. Visit Karolkowa 18, if you have not already done so
130. Check the alphabetical telephone directory for a new listing for J. Kowalski, if you have not already done so
131. Take the sightseeing trip you have planned and, when you get home, explain to your uncle what has happened
132. Return to your hotel room and have the operator phone 49-64-21 again while you are on the line, if you have not already done so
133. Check the telephone directory to get a list of Warsaw business firms that deal in amber products, if you have not already done so
134. Check the telephone directory to get a list of Warsaw companies engaged in the import-export business, if you have not already done so
135. During the day, visit some of the Kowalskis you have located
136. In the evening, visit some of the Kowalskis you have located
137. Phone some of the Kowalskis listed in the city directory

SECTION G: PHONE CALLS

Names and addresses of Kowalskis from the city directory, but not listed in the most recent telephone directory, are shown below. If you wish to phone anyone listed, follow the appropriate response (Select AS MANY AS you WISH and estimate 10 minutes for each call):

138. 43-92-88 Kowalski, Grzegory
     ul Karolkowa 93
139. 37-33-51 Kowalski, Ignazy
     Stawki 8
140. -- -- -- Kowalski, Jadwiga
     Chmielna 21
141. -- -- -- Kowalski, Jadwiga
     ul Minska 19A
142. 81-62-03 Kowalski, Jadwiga
     Leszno 280
143. 28-65-31 Kowalski, Jadwiga
     ul Obroncow 24
144. -- -- -- Kowalski, Jadwiga
     Kopernika, 29
145. -- -- -- Kowalski, Jan
     ul Mredzynarodowa 9
146. -- -- -- Kowalski, Jan
     ul Minska 19
147. 43-93-36 Kowalski, Jan
     ul Karolkowa 91
148. -- -- -- Kowalski, Jan
     ul Obroncow 51
149. -- -- -- Kowalski, Jozef
     Czerniakowska 200
150. 28-66-61 Kowalski, Jozef
     ul Lucka 13
151. -- -- -- Kowalski, Jozef
     Rutkowskiego 19

Record in your diary the time spent and continue with this section.

You would now (Choose ONLY ONE, unless otherwise directed in the Answer Section):

152. Try to get some expert assistance from individuals or special agencies, if you have not already done so
153. Visit Karolkowa 18, if you have not already done so
154. Check the alphabetical telephone directory for a new listing for J. Kowalski, if you have not already done so
155. Take the sightseeing trip you have planned and, when you get home, explain to your uncle what has happened
156. Return to your hotel room and have the operator phone 49-64-21 again while you are on the line, if you have not already done so
157. Check the telephone directory to get a list of Warsaw business firms that deal in amber products, if you have not already done so
158. Check the telephone directory to get a list of Warsaw companies engaged in the import-export business, if you have not already done so

HOW RESOURCEFUL ARE YOU?

159. During the day, visit some of the Kowalskis you have located
160. In the evening, visit some of the Kowalskis you have located
161. Phone some of the Kowalskis listed in the most recent telephone directory

SECTION H: AMBER FIRMS

Names, addresses, and phone numbers of Warsaw firms dealing in amber products are listed below. If you do *not* wish to phone any firms, continue with items 172 and following. If you do wish to phone any of them, follow the appropriate response (Select AS MANY AS you WISH and estimate 10 minutes for each call):

Amber and Amber Products (cooperatives)
162. Buczka
     Grojecka 74
     Phone 22-62-13
163. Bursztyn
     Roszynska 67
     Phone 27-16-50
164. Exportor
     Grojecka 60
     Phone 63-72-58

Amber and Amber Products (shops)
165. Bizuteria Ozodobna
     Krakowskie Przedmiescie 27
     Phone 41-25-03
166. Galanteria
     Middowa 2
     Phone 47-62-73
167. Jantar
     Krakowskie Przedmiescie 32
     Phone 71-83-20
168. Orno
     Mariensztat 3
     Phone 51-26-10

Amber and Amber Products (state enterprise)
169. Amboro
     Jerozolimskie 25
     Phone 26-31-02
170. Arka
     Marszarkowska 54
     Phone 37-05-11

171. Centromor
     Novy Swiat 67
     Phone 26-06-71

Record in your diary the time spent and continue with this section.

You would now (Choose ONLY ONE, unless otherwise directed in the Answer Section):

172. Try to get some expert assistance from individuals or special agencies, if you have not already done so
173. Visit Karolkowa 18, if you have not already done so
174. Check the alphabetical telephone directory for a new listing for J. Kowalski, if you have not already done so
175. Locate a city directory of Warsaw residents, if you have not already done so
176. Take the sightseeing trip you have planned and, when you get home, explain to your uncle what has happened
177. Return to your hotel room and have the operator phone 49-64-21 again while you are on the line, if you have not already done so
178. Visit some of the amber firms you have located in the directory
179. Check the telephone directory to get a list of Warsaw companies engaged in the import-export business, if you have not already done so
180. During the day, visit some of the Kowalskis you have located
181. In the evening, visit some of the Kowalskis you have located
182. Phone some of the Kowalskis you have located

SECTION I: VISITS TO AMBER FIRMS

The names and addresses of Warsaw firms dealing in amber products are listed below. If you wish to visit any of these firms, follow the appropriate response (Select AS MANY AS you WISH and estimate one hour for each visit):

APTITUDE

Amber and Amber Products (cooperatives)

183. Buczka
 Grojecka 74
 Phone 22-62-13
184. Bursztyn
 Roszynska 67
 Phone 27-16-50
185. Exportor
 Grojecka 60
 Phone 63-72-58

Amber and Amber Products (shops)

186. Bizuteria Ozodobna
 Krakowskie Przedmiescie 27
 Phone 41-25-03
187. Galanteria
 Middowa 2
 Phone 47-62-73
188. Jantar
 Krakowskie Przedmiescie 32
 Phone 71-83-20
189. Orno
 Mariensztat 3
 Phone 51-26-10

Amber and Amber Products (state enterprise)

190. Amboro
 Jerozolimskie 25
 Phone 26-31-02
191. Arka
 Marszarkowska 54
 Phone 37-05-11
192. Centromor
 Novy Swiat 67
 Phone 26-06-71

Record in your diary the time spent and continue with this section.

You would now (Choose ONLY ONE, unless otherwise directed in the Answer Section):

193. Try to get some expert assistance from individuals or special agencies, if you have not already done so
194. Visit Karolkowa 18, if you have not already done so
195. Check the alphabetical telephone directory for a new listing for J. Kowalski, if you have not already done so
196. Locate a city directory of Warsaw residents, if you have not already done so
197. Take the sightseeing trip you have planned and, when you get home, explain to your uncle what has happened
198. Return to your hotel room and have the operator phone 49-64-21 again while you are on the line, if you have not already done so
199. Check the telephone directory to get a list of Warsaw companies engaged in the import-export business, if you have not already done so
200. During the day, visit some of the Kowalskis you have located
201. In the evening, visit some of the Kowalskis you have located
202. Phone some of the Kowalskis you have located

SECTION J: IMPORT-EXPORT COMPANIES

Names, addresses, and phone numbers of all import-export companies in the Warsaw area are listed below. If you do *not* wish to phone any firms, continue with items 213 and following. If you do wish to phone any of them, follow the appropriate response (Select AS MANY AS you WISH and estimate 10 minutes for each call):

203. ABC Export
 Chalubinskiego 62
 Phone 72-58-66
204. Buczka
 Grojecka 74
 Phone 22-62-13
205. Centromor
 Novy Swiat 67
 Phone 26-06-71
206. Cepelia
 Marchlewskiego 17
 Phone 42-40-17
207. Coopexim
 Novy Swiat 54
 Phone 26-37-55
208. Dalmon
 Chalubinskiego 54
 Phone 72-30-16

HOW RESOURCEFUL ARE YOU?

209. Im. Marchlewskiego
 Jerozolimskie 103
 Phone 67-13-28
210. Rozewie
 Novy Swiat 71
 Phone 26-10-17
211. Universum
 Piekna 2
 Phone 29-73-88
212. Varimex
 Tawarowa 93
 Phone 63-39-78

Record in your diary the time spent and continue with this section.

You would now (Choose ONLY ONE, unless otherwise directed in the Answer Section):

213. Try to get some expert assistance from individuals or special agencies, if you have not already done so
214. Visit Karolkowa 18, if you have not already done so
215. Check the alphabetical telephone directory for a new listing for J. Kowalski, if you have not already done so
216. Locate a city directory of Warsaw residents, if you have not already done so
217. Take the sightseeing trip you have planned and, when you get home, explain to your uncle what has happened
218. Return to your hotel room and have the operator phone 49-64-21 again while you are on the line, if you have not already done so
219. Check the telephone directory to get a list of Warsaw business firms that deal in amber products, if you have not already done so
220. Visit some of the import-export firms that you have located
221. During the day, visit some of the Kowalskis you have located
222. In the evening, visit some of the Kowalskis you have located
223. Phone some of the Kowalskis you have located

SECTION K: VISITS TO IMPORT-EXPORT COMPANIES

The names and addresses of all import-export companies operating in the Warsaw area are listed below. If you wish to visit any of them, follow the appropriate response (Select AS MANY AS you WISH and estimate one hour for each visit):

224. ABC Export
 Chalubinskiego 62
 Phone 72-58-66
225. Buczka
 Grojecka 74
 Phone 22-62-13
226. Centromor
 Novy Swiat 67
 Phone 26-06-71
227. Cepelia
 Marchlewskiego 17
 Phone 42-40-17
228. Coopexim
 Novy Swiat 54
 Phone 26-37-55
229. Dalmon
 Chalubinskiego 54
 Phone 72-30-16
230. Im. Marchlewskiego
 Jerozolimskie 103
 Phone 67-13-28
231. Rozewie
 Novy Swiat 71
 Phone 26-10-17
232. Universum
 Piekna 2
 Phone 29-73-88
233. Varimex
 Tawarowa 93
 Phone 63-39-78

Record in your diary the time spent and continue with this section.

You would now (Choose ONLY ONE, unless otherwise directed in the Answer Section):

234. Try to get some expert assistance from individuals or special agencies, if you have not already done so

APTITUDE

235. Visit Karolkowa 18, if you have not already done so
236. Check the alphabetical telephone directory for a new listing for J. Kowalski, if you have not already done so
237. Locate a city directory of Warsaw residents, if you have not already done so
238. Take the sightseeing trip you have planned and, when you get home, explain to your uncle what has happened
239. Return to your hotel room and have the operator phone 49-64-21 again while you are on the line, if you have not already done so
240. Check the telephone directory to get a list of Warsaw business firms that deal in amber products, if you have not already done so
241. During the day, visit some of the Kowalskis you have located
242. In the evening, visit some of the Kowalskis you have located
243. Phone some of the Kowalskis you have located

SECTION L: REPEAT PHONE CALL

After 30 minutes, the operator phones your room to say that she has the party on the line. With the hotel operator serving as interpreter, you confirm that this is indeed the right number but that the person you are talking to is Professor S. Jus and that his address is Karolkowa 72. He, his wife, and two children have lived at this address for two years. There is no one else in the household, and he doesn't know anything about the previous tenants. He does know two J. Kowalskis but neither ever lived here and neither is in the import-export business. Record 45 minutes in your diary and continue with this section.

You would now (Choose ONLY ONE, unless otherwise directed in the Answer Section):

244. Try to get some expert assistance from individuals or special agencies, if you have not already done so
245. Visit Karolkowa 18, if you have not already done so
246. Check the alphabetical telephone directory for a new listing for J. Kowalski, if you have not already done so

247. Locate a city directory of Warsaw residents, if you have not already done so
248. Take the sightseeing trip you have planned and, when you get home, explain to your uncle what has happened
249. Check the telephone directory to get a list of Warsaw business firms that deal in amber products, if you have not already done so
250. Check the telephone directory to get a list of Warsaw companies engaged in the import-export business, if you have not already done so
251. During the day, visit some of the Kowalskis you have located
252. In the evening, visit some of the Kowalskis you have located
253. Phone some of the Kowalskis you have located

SECTION M: EXTENSION OF STAY

You make an urgent call to immigration authorities who advise you they will give you a 12-hour emergency extension of your visa and that, if you will apply in person early tomorrow to the several offices involved, you can *probably* get a three-day emergency extension of your visa. However, it will take you at least half a day to get it and will cost you $360 U.S. extra in air fare to give up your excursion rate. You know that is a lot of money and that your only hope is to have your uncle cable you a loan. He may be willing to do it, but he certainly will not be very pleased about it.

Under these circumstances, you would now (Choose ONLY ONE):

254. Abandon your search, return home as planned, and explain everything to your uncle
255. Risk the displeasure of your uncle, but decide to spend the time and effort to get an extension to continue your search

SECTION N: DAY VISITS

Names and addresses of Kowalskis living in the Warsaw area are shown below. If you wish to visit anyone during the day, follow the appropriate response (Select AS MANY AS you WISH and estimate one hour for each visit):

HOW RESOURCEFUL ARE YOU?

256. 44-19-26 Kowalski, Adam
Wawelska 12

257. 19-21-12 Kowalski, Bernard
mgr. inz. arch.
Waleoznych 5

258. 45-20-03 Kowalski, Bogdan
dr. med.
Grojecka 219

259. 34-88-91 Kowalski, Cezary
Buczka 43

260. 34-00-17 Kowalski, Czestaw
Okopowa 27A

261. 29-21-63 Kowalski, Edmund
mgr. prawa
Warecka 2

262. 26-22-48 Kowalski, Edward
art. muzyk
Swigtokrzyska 12

263. 22-27-47 Kowalski, Eugeniusz
Zwyciezcow 44

264. 43-40-11 Kowalski, Eugeniusz
Pl. Narutowioza 18

265. 43-92-88 Kowalski, Grzegory
ul Karolkowa 93

266. 25-92-88 Kowalski, Grzegorz
Al. Niepodleglosci 184

267. 35-36-72 Kowalski, Ignacy
mgr. inz.
Stawki 8

268. 37-33-51 Kowalski, Ignazy
mgr. inz.
Stawki 8

269. -- -- -- Kowalski, Jadwiga
Chmielna 21

270. -- -- -- Kowalski, Jadwiga
ul Minska 19A

271. 81-62-03 Kowalski, Jadwiga
Leszno 280

272. 28-65-31 Kowalski, Jadwiga
ul Obroncow 24

273. -- -- -- Kowalski, Jadwiga
Kopernika, 29

274. 44-93-36 Kowalski, Jadwiga
Nowowiejska 37

275. -- -- -- Kowalski, Jan
ul Mredzynarodowa 9

276. -- -- -- Kowalski, Jan
ul Minska 19

277. 43-93-36 Kowalski, Jan
ul Karolkowa 91

278. -- -- -- Kowalski, Jan
ul Obroncow 51

279. 27-52-69 Kowalski, Jan
lek. dent.
Pl. Grzybowski 21

280. 45-12-19 Kowalski, Jan
narzedzia ogrodnicze
Czerniakowska 218

280.[a] 17-55-33 Kowalski, Jan
prof. dr.
Al. Waszyngtona 134

281. 26-66-16 Kowalski, Jan E.
Hibnera 12

282. 25-63-69 Kowalski, Jan Stefan
Chmielna 35

283. 43-77-00 Kowalski, Josef
doc. dr. med
Filtrowa 63

284. 26-17-92 Kowalski, Josef
Em. Plater 56

285. 32-28-18 Kowalski, Jozef
inz.
Konwiktorska 77

286. 28-65-35 Kowalski, Jozef
Poksal 16

287. 25-48-84 Kowalski, Jozef
Kopernika 25

288. 26-74-98 Kowalski, Jozef
lekarz, chor. wewn.
Rutkowskiego 9

289. 44-53-57 Kowalski, Jozef
inz. rolnik
Biatobrzeska 93

290. -- -- -- Kowalski, Jozef
Czerniakowska 200

291. 28-66-61 Kowalski, Jozef
ul Lucka 13

292. -- -- -- Kowalski, Jozef
Rutkowskiego 19

293. 35-07-16 Kowalski, Konstanty
Niska 69

Record in your diary the time spent and continue with this section.

You would now (Choose ONLY ONE EACH TIME you are directed to this section):

APTITUDE

294. Try to get some expert assistance from individuals or special agencies, if you have not already done so
295. Visit Karolkowa 18, if you have not already done so
296. Check the alphabetical telephone directory for a new listing for J. Kowalski, if you have not already done so
297. Locate a city directory of Warsaw residents, if you have not already done so
298. Take the sightseeing trip you have planned and, when you get home, explain to your uncle what has happened
299. Return to your hotel room and have the operator phone 49-64-21 again while you are on the line, if you have not already done so
300. Check the telephone directory to get a list of Warsaw business firms that deal in amber products, if you have not already done so
301. Check the telephone directory to get a list of Warsaw companies engaged in the import-export business, if you have not already done so
302. In the evening, visit some of the Kowalskis you have located
303. Phone some of the Kowalskis you have located

SECTION O: WARSAW TELEPHONE DIRECTORY

Below are names, addresses, and phone numbers for Kowalskis listed in the most recent telephone directory.

44-19-26	Kowalski, Adam Wawelska 12
19-21-12	Kowalski, Bernard mgr. inz. arch. Waleoznych 5
45-20-03	Kowalski, Bogdan dr. med. Grojecka 219
34-88-91	Kowalski, Cezary Buczka 43
34-00-17	Kowalski, Czestaw Okopowa 27A
29-21-63	Kowalski, Edmund mgr. prawa Warecka 2
26-22-48	Kowalski, Edward art. muzyk Swigtokrzyska 12
22-27-47	Kowalski, Eugeniusz Zwyciezcow 44
43-40-11	Kowalski, Eugeniusz Pl. Narutowioza 18
25-92-88	Kowalski, Grzegorz Al. Niepodleglosci 184
35-36-72	Kowalski, Ignacy mgr. inz. Stawki 8
44-93-36	Kowalski, Jadwiga Nowowiejska 37
27-52-69	Kowalski, Jan lek. dent. Pl. Grzybowski 21
45-12-19	Kowalski, Jan narzedzia ogrodnicze Czerniakowska 218
17-55-33	Kowalski, Jan prof. dr. Al. Waszyngtona 134
26-66-16	Kowalski, Jan E. Hibnera 12
25-63-69	Kowalski, Jan Stefan Chmielna 35
43-77-00	Kowalski, Josef doc. dr. med Filtrowa 63
26-17-92	Kowalski, Josef Em. Plater 56
32-28-18	Kowalski, Jozef inz. Konwiktorska 77
28-65-35	Kowalski, Jozef Poksal 16
25-48-84	Kowalski, Jozef Kopernika 25
26-74-98	Kowalski, Jozef lekarz, chor. wewn. Rutkowskiego 9
44-53-57	Kowalski, Jozef inz. rolnik Biatobrzeska 93
35-07-16	Kowalski, Konstanty Niska 69

Record 15 minutes in your diary and continue with this section.

22

HOW RESOURCEFUL ARE YOU?

With the information you have, you would now (Choose ONLY ONE, unless otherwise directed in the Answer Section):

304. Try to get some expert assistance from individuals or special agencies, if you have not already done so
305. Visit Karolkowa 18, if you have not already done so
306. Locate a city directory of Warsaw residents, if you have not already done so
307. Take the sightseeing trip you have planned and, when you get home, explain to your uncle what has happened
308. Return to your hotel room and have the operator phone 49-64-21 again while you are on the line, if you have not already done so
309. Check the telephone directory to get a list of Warsaw business firms that deal in amber products, if you have not already done so
310. Check the telephone directory to get a list of Warsaw companies engaged in the import-export business, if you have not already done so
311. During the day, visit some of the Kowalskis you have located
312. In the evening, visit some of the Kowalskis you have located
313. Phone some of the Kowalskis you have located

???

The Visible Traveler

In this Answer Section, the Problem Section is repeated side by side with the answers. The first time around, you should concentrate only on the specific answers you are looking for. After you have finished taking the test, you can look over the problems and solutions simultaneously to see how the simulation was put together.

PROBLEM SECTION

SECTION A: FIRST STEP

You would now (Choose ONLY ONE, unless otherwise directed in the Answer Section):
1. Try to get some expert assistance from individuals or special agencies
2. Visit Karolkowa 18
3. Check the alphabetical telephone directory for a new listing for J. Kowalski
4. Locate a city directory of Warsaw residents
5. Take the sightseeing trip you have planned and, when you get home, explain to your uncle what has happened
6. Return to your hotel room and have the operator phone 49-64-21 again while you are on the line

ANSWER SECTION

1. Turn to Section C.
2. After one hour you arrive at the address to find an empty lot; record one hour in your diary and turn to Section B.
3. Turn to Section O.
4. You are told the *milicja* (police) have such a directory; if you wish to go to the station to look it over, record 30 minutes in your diary and turn to Section F; otherwise make another choice from this section.
5. Follow response 315.
6. Turn to Section L.

APTITUDE

SECTION A: continued

7. Check the telephone directory to get a list of Warsaw business firms that deal in amber products
8. Check the telephone directory to get a list of Warsaw companies engaged in the import-export business

SECTION B: SIGHTSEEING

You spend two hours to return to your hotel room by a slightly roundabout way so you can see some of the sights on your list. After a half hour for coffee and blintzes at a restaurant near the Bristol, you are ready to start out again. Record 2½ hours in your diary and continue with this section.

You would now (Choose ONLY ONE, unless otherwise directed in the Answer Section):

9. Try to get some expert assistance from individuals or special agencies, if you have not already done so
10. Check the alphabetical telephone directory for a new listing for J. Kowalski, if you have not already done so
11. Locate a city directory of Warsaw residents, if you have not already done so

12. Take the sightseeing trip you have planned and, when you get home, explain to your uncle what has happened
13. Return to your hotel room and have the operator phone 49-64-21 again while you are on the line, if you have not already done so
14. Check the telephone directory to get a list of Warsaw business firms that deal in amber products, if you have not already done so
15. Check the telephone directory to get a list of Warsaw companies engaged in the import-export business, if you have not already done so
16. During the day, visit some of the Kowalskis you have located
17. In the evening, visit some of the Kowalskis you have located

SECTION A: continued

7. Turn to Section H.
8. Turn to Section J.

9. Turn to Section C.
10. Turn to Section O.
11. You are told the *milicja* (police) have such a directory; if you wish to go to the station to look it over, record 30 minutes in your diary and turn to Section F; otherwise, make another choice from this section.
12. Follow response 315.
13. Turn to Section L.
14. Turn to Section H.
15. Turn to Section J.
16. Turn to Section N.
17. Turn to Section D.

HOW RESOURCEFUL ARE YOU?

SECTION B: continued

18. Phone some of the Kowalskis you have located

SECTION C: EXPERT ASSISTANCE

You approach the hotel clerk, who tells you that the consulate and tourist agencies offer such help. Furthermore, employers have information on their employees and the *milicja* (police) have a city directory of Warsaw residents. You would now contact (Select AS MANY AS you consider USEFUL and estimate 30 minutes for each encounter):

19. A special investigator

20. The *milicja*

21. The Foreign Tourists Office

22. ORBIS (Polish Travel Office)

23. The U.S. consulate

SECTION B: continued

18. Turn to Section E.

19. The hotel clerk directs you to an English-speaking special investigator who says it will cost at least $50 U.S. in advance, plus expenses, to locate J. Kowalski. If you wish to hire him, follow response 26. Otherwise, continue with items 20 and following.

20. After they have satisfied themselves that your search is legitimate, the *milicja* suggest you try getting Mr. Kowalski's phone number; use the city directory at the station or contact his employer. The English-speaking assistant to the Captain will help you use the phone if you wish.

21. Staff suggests calling Mr. Kowalski or visiting him; they have an English-speaking secretary who will help you; however, if you wish assistance in traveling about the city, there will be a charge of $2.50 U.S. per hour for an interpreter. If you want to hire the interpreter, follow response 27. Otherwise, continue with items 22 and following.

22. Suggest calling Mr. Kowalski or inquiring at his employer; they have an English-speaking guide who will help you; however, if you wish assistance in traveling about the city, there will be a charge of $2.50 U.S. per hour for an interpreter. If you want to hire the interpreter, follow response 27. Otherwise, continue with items 23 and the following.

23. Informs you that the *milicja* (police) have a directory listing everyone in the city; mentions that employers keep a rather extensive file on employees, but doubts that they

APTITUDE

SECTION C: continued

24. An English-speaking taxi driver

25. An airline representative

would let you see it; informs you that at present they can't free up anyone to help you locate Mr. Kowalski, but please let them know if they can be of any other assistance; staff is always glad to help.

24. The driver asks $2 U.S. per hour for his services, plus cab fare. If you wish to hire him, follow response 28. Otherwise, continue with items 25 and following.

25. Suggests you see the *milicja* (police) or visit Mr. Kowalski at his home.

26. You tell the investigator he must locate J. Kowalski before you leave. You spend the remainder of your stay enjoying the sights. Just before you are to leave Warsaw, the investigator reports back indicating he has located J. Kowalski, but the information will cost you an additional $450 U.S. You barely have time to visit the person he has located. If you wish to buy the information, follow response 314; if not, turn to Section M.

27. Your interpreter is very helpful and willing to follow your instructions. Follow response 317 for a glossary of Polish terms and then continue with this section.

28. The cab driver agrees to drive you wherever you wish to go and serve as your interpreter if you wish to talk to anyone. Follow response 317 for a glossary of Polish terms and then continue with this section.

Record in your diary the time spent and continue with this section.

You would now (Choose ONLY ONE, unless otherwise directed in the Answer Section):

29. Visit Karolkowa 18, if you have not already done so

30. Check the alphabetical telephone directory for a new listing for J. Kowalski, if you have not already done so

31. Locate a city directory of Warsaw residents, if you have not already done so

32. Take the sightseeing trip you have planned and, when you get home, explain to your uncle what has happened

29. After one hour you arrive at the address to find an empty lot; record one hour in your diary and turn to Section B.

30. Turn to Section O.

31. You are told the *milicja* (police) have such a directory; if you wish to go to the station to look it over, record 30 minutes in your diary and turn to Section F; otherwise, make another choice from this section.

32. Follow response 315.

HOW RESOURCEFUL ARE YOU?

SECTION C: continued

33. Return to your hotel room and have the operator phone 49-64-21 again while you are on the line, if you have not already done so
34. Check the telephone directory to get a list of Warsaw business firms that deal in amber products, if you have not already done so
35. Check the telephone directory to get a list of Warsaw companies engaged in the import-export business, if you have not already done so
36. During the day, visit some of the Kowalskis you have located
37. In the evening, visit some of the Kowalskis you have located
38. Phone some of the Kowalskis you have located

33. Turn to Section L.

34. Turn to Section H.

35. Turn to Section J.

36. Turn to Section N.

37. Turn to Section D.

38. Turn to Section E.

SECTION D: EVENING VISITS

Names and addresses of Kowalskis you have located are listed below. If you wish to make an evening visit to any one of them, follow the appropriate response (Select AS MANY AS you WISH and estimate one hour for each visit):

39. 44-19-26   Kowalski, Adam
               Wawelska 12
40. 19-21-12   Kowalski, Bernard
               mgr. inz. arch.
               Waleoznych 5
41. 45-20-03   Kowalski, Bogdan
               dr. med.
               Grojecka 219
42. 34-88-91   Kowalski, Cezary
               Buczka 43
43. 34-00-17   Kowalski, Czestaw
               Okopowa 27A
44. 29-21-63   Kowalski, Edmund
               mgr. prawa
               Warecka 2
45. 26-22-48   Kowalski, Edward
               art. muzyk
               Swigtokrzyska 12
46. 22-27-47   Kowalski, Eugeniusz
               Zwyciezcow 44
47. 43-40-11   Kowalski, Eugeniusz
               Pl. Narutowioza 18

39. Already answered your questions over phone.
40. Already answered your questions over phone.
41. Already answered your questions over phone.
42. Already answered your questions over phone.
43. Already answered your questions over phone.
44. Already answered your questions over phone.
45. Already answered your questions over phone.
46. Already answered your questions over phone.
47. Already answered your questions over phone.

APTITUDE

SECTION D: continued

48. 43-92-88 Kowalski, Grzegory
   ul Karolkowa 93

49. 25-92-88 Kowalski, Grzegorz
   Al. Niepodleglosci 184

50. 35-36-72 Kowalski, Ignacy
   mgr. inz.
   Stawki 8

51. 37-33-51 Kowalski, Ignazy
   mgr. inz.
   Stawki 8

52. -- -- -- Kowalski, Jadwiga
   Chmielna 21

53. -- -- -- Kowalski, Jadwiga
   ul Minska 19A

54. 81-62-03 Kowalski, Jadwiga
   Leszno 280

55. 28-65-31 Kowalski, Jadwiga
   ul Obroncow 24

56. -- -- -- Kowalski, Jadwiga
   Kopernika, 29

57. 44-93-36 Kowalski, Jadwiga
   Nowowiejska 37

58. -- -- -- Kowalski, Jan
   ul Mredzynarodowa 9

59. -- -- -- Kowalski, Jan
   ul Minska 19

60. 43-93-36 Kowalski, Jan
   ul Karolkowa 91

61. -- -- -- Kowalski, Jan
   ul Obroncow 51

62. 27-52-69 Kowalski, Jan
   lek. dent.
   Pl. Grzybowski 21

63. 45-12-19 Kowalski, Jan
   narzedzia ogrodnicze
   Czerniakowska 218

64. 17-55-33 Kowalski, Jan
   prof. dr.
   Al. Waszyngtona 134

65. 26-66-16 Kowalski, Jan E.
   Hibnera 12

66. 25-63-69 Kowalski, Jan Stefan
   Chmielna 35

67. 43-77-00 Kowalski, Josef
   doc. dr. med.
   Filtrowa 63

48. Have no relative in America.

49. Already answered your questions over phone.

50. Already answered your questions over phone.

51. No correspondence with anyone in U.S.A.

52. Have no relative in America.

53. No correspondence with anyone in U.S.A.

54. No correspondence with anyone in U.S.A.

55. Ignore instructions at end of this section; instead, follow response 314.

56. Have no relative in America.

57. Already answered your questions over phone.

58. No correspondence with anyone in U.S.A.

59. Have no relative in America.

60. Have no relative in America.

61. No correspondence with anyone in U.S.A.

62. Already answered your questions over phone.

63. Already answered your questions over phone.

64. Already answered your questions over phone.

65. Already answered your questions over phone.

66. Already answered your questions over phone.

67. Already answered your questions over phone.

HOW RESOURCEFUL ARE YOU?

SECTION D: continued

68.	26-17-92	Kowalski, Josef Em. Plater 56	68.	Already answered your questions over phone.
69.	32-28-18	Kowalski, Jozef inz. Konwiktorska 77	69.	Already answered your questions over phone.
70.	28-65-35	Kowalski, Jozef Poksal 16	70.	Already answered your questions over phone.
71.	25-48-84	Kowalski, Jozef Kopernika 25	71.	Already answered your questions over phone.
72.	26-74-98	Kowalski, Jozef lekarz, chor. wewn. Rutkowskiego 9	72.	Already answered your questions over phone.
73.	44-53-57	Kowalski, Jozef inz. rolnik Biatobrzeska 93	73.	Already answered your questions over phone.
74.	-- -- --	Kowalski, Jozef Czerniakowska 200	74.	No correspondence with anyone in U.S.A.
75.	28-66-61	Kowalski, Jozef ul Lucka 13	75.	Have no relative in America.
76.	-- -- --	Kowalski, Jozef Rutkowskiego 19	76.	No correspondence with anyone in U.S.A.
77.	35-07-16	Kowalski, Konstanty Niska 69	77.	Already answered your questions over phone.

Record in your diary the time spent.

UNLESS OTHERWISE DIRECTED IN THE ANSWER SECTION, FOLLOW RESPONSE 316 TO OBTAIN FURTHER INSTRUCTIONS

SECTION E: PHONE CALLS

Names, addresses, and phone numbers of Kowalskis in the most recent telephone directory are listed below. You will have repeated opportunities to return to this section to make any additional calls you wish. Take Answer A to the first call to an individual; use Answer B for any subsequent call *to the same person*. If you wish to call anyone, follow the appropriate response (Select AS MANY AS you WISH and estimate 10 minutes for each call):

78.	44-19-26	Kowalski, Adam Wawelska 12	A78. B78.	No J. Kowalski known at this address. No J. Kowalski known at this address.
79.	19-21-12	Kowalski, Bernard mgr. inz. arch. Waleoznych 5	A79. B79.	A nephew named Jan Kowalski lived with us two years ago but left Warsaw; new address unknown. Nothing to add to previous conversation.

APTITUDE

SECTION E: continued

80.	45-20-03	Kowalski, Bogdan dr. med. Grojecka 219	A80. Doctor very busy; says call back later. B80. No J. Kowalski known at this address.
81.	34-88-91	Kowalski, Cezary Buczka 43	A81. No J. Kowalski known at this address. B81. No answer.
82.	34-00-17	Kowalski, Czestaw Okopowa 27A	A82. No J. Kowalski known at this address. B82. Annoyed that you called again; hangs up without giving any information.
83.	29-21-63	Kowalski, Edmund mgr. prawa Warecka 2	A83. No J. Kowalski known at this address. B83. No answer.
84.	26-22-48	Kowalski, Edward art. muzyk Swigtokrzyska 12	A84. No J. Kowalski known at this address. B84. No answer.
85.	22-27-47	Kowalski, Eugeniusz Zwyciezcow 44	A85. No answer. B85. No J. Kowalski known at this address.
86.	43-40-11	Kowalski, Eugeniusz Pl. Narutowioza 18	A86. No answer. B86. No J. Kowalski known at this address.
87.	25-92-88	Kowalski, Grzegorz Al. Niepodleglosci 184	A87. No J. Kowalski known at this address. B87. No answer.
88.	35-36-72	Kowalski, Ignacy mgr. inz. Stawki 8	A88. No answer. B88. No J. Kowalski known at this address.
89.	44-93-36	Kowalski, Jadwiga Nowowiejska 37	A89. No answer. B89. No correspondence with anyone in U.S.A.
90.	27-52-69	Kowalski, Jan lek. dent. Pl. Grzybowski 21	A90. No answer. B90. No correspondence with anyone in U.S.A.
91.	45-12-19	Kowalski, Jan narzedzia ogrodnicze Czerniakowska 218	A91. No correspondence with anyone in U.S.A. B91. Annoyed that you called again and hangs up.
92.	17-55-33	Kowalski, Jan prof. dr. Al. Waszyngtona 134	A92. No answer. B92. No correspondence with anyone in U.S.A.
93.	26-66-16	Kowalski, Jan E. Hibnera 12	A93. No correspondence with anyone in U.S.A. B93. No answer.
94.	25-63-69	Kowalski, Jan Stefan Chmielna 35	A94. A niece named J. Kowalski lived with us last year, but left Warsaw; new address unknown. Don't know about her but no one else corresponded with anyone in U.S.A. B94. Nothing to add to previous conversation.
95.	43-77-00	Kowalski, Josef doc. dr. med Filtrowa 63	A95. Doctor is very busy; asks that you call back. B95. No correspondence with anyone in U.S.A.
96.	26-17-92	Kowalski, Josef Em. Plater 56	A96. No answer. B96. No correspondence with anyone in U.S.A.

HOW RESOURCEFUL ARE YOU?

SECTION E: continued

97.	32-28-18	Kowalski, Jozef inz. Konwiktorska 77	A97. No correspondence with anyone in U.S.A. B97. No answer.
98.	28-65-35	Kowalski, Jozef Poksal 16	A98. No answer. B98. No correspondence with anyone in U.S.A.
99.	25-48-84	Kowalski, Jozef Kopernika 25	A99. No answer. B99. No correspondence with anyone in U.S.A.
100.	26-74-98	Kowalski, Jozef lekarz, chor. wewn. Rutkowskiego 9	A100. No correspondence with anyone in U.S.A. B100. Annoyed that you called again and hangs up.
101.	44-53-57	Kowalski, Jozef inz. rolnik Biatobrzeska 93	A101. No answer. B101. No correspondence with anyone in U.S.A.
102.	35-07-16	Kowalski, Konstanty Niska 69	A102. Does not understand questions and hangs up. B102. No correspondence with anyone in U.S.A.

Record in your diary the time spent and continue with this section.

You would now (Choose ONLY ONE EACH TIME you are directed to this section);

103. Try to get some expert assistance from individuals or special agencies, if you have not already done so

103. Turn to Section C.

104. Visit Karolkowa 18, if you have not already done so

104. After one hour you arrive at the address and find an empty lot; record one hour in your diary and turn to Section B.

105. Check the alphabetical telephone directory for a new listing for J. Kowalski, if you have not already done so

105. Turn to Section O.

106. Locate a city directory of Warsaw residents, if you have not already done so

106. You are told the *milicja* (police) have such a directory; if you wish to go to the station to look it over, record 30 minutes in your diary and turn to Section F; otherwise, make another choice from this section.

107. Take the sightseeing trip you have planned and, when you get home, explain to your uncle what has happened

107. Follow response 315.

108. Return to your hotel room and have the operator phone 49-64-21 again while you are on the line, if you have not already done so

108. Turn to Section L.

109. Check the telephone directory to get a list of Warsaw business firms that deal in amber products, if you have not already done so

109. Turn to Section H.

110. Check the telephone directory to get a list of Warsaw companies engaged in the import-export business, if you have not already done so

110. Turn to Section J.

APTITUDE

SECTION E: continued

111. During the day, visit some of the Kowalskis you have located

112. In the evening, visit some of the Kowalskis you have located

113. Go on a three-hour sightseeing tour and plan to complete your calls later

111. Turn to Section N.

112. Turn to Section D.

113. Record 3 hours in your diary and continue with your calls. For each call, follow the appropriate response in Column A or B. If you do not locate the right Mr. Kowalski, record in your diary the additional time spent and make another choice from this section.

SECTION F: CITY DIRECTORY

Names and addresses of Kowalskis from the city directory, but not listed in the most recent telephone directory, are shown below. If you wish further information about any of them from the *milicja* (police), follow the appropriate response (Select AS MANY AS you WISH and estimate 10 minutes for each inquiry):

114. 43-92-88   Kowalski, Grzegory
                     ul Karolkowa 93
                     inz. rolnik

115. 37-33-51   Kowalski, Ignazy
                     Stawki 8
                     mgr. inz.

116. -- -- --   Kowalski, Jadwiga
                     Chmielna 21

117. -- -- --   Kowalski, Jadwiga
                     ul Minska 19A
                     robotnik

118. 81-62-03   Kowalski, Jadwiga
                     Leszno 280

119. 28-65-31   Kowalski, Jadwiga
                     ul Obroncow 24
                     robotnik

120. -- -- --   Kowalski, Jadwiga
                     Kopernika, 29

121. -- -- --   Kowalski, Jan
                     ul Mredzynarodowa 9
                     urzednik

122. -- -- --   Kowalski, Jan
                     ul Minska 19
                     kierowca

123. 43-93-36   Kowalski, Jan
                     ul Karolkowa 91
                     inz. rolnik

114. Wife: Jadwiga.

115. Kawaler (unmarried man).

116. Wdowa (widow); Cezary killed in war.

117. Panna (unmarried woman).

118. Wdowa (widow); husband, Edward, died last month—had been dr. med.

119. Wdowa (widow); Jozef died two years ago—had been urzednik (clerk) for Centromor.

120. Panna (unmarried woman).

121. Wife: Anna.

122. Wife: Maria.

123. Wdowiec (widower); Anna died last year.

HOW RESOURCEFUL ARE YOU?

SECTION F: continued

124.	-- -- --	Kowalski, Jan ul Obroncow 51 urzednik	124. Wife: Alicja.
125.	-- -- --	Kowalski, Jozef Czerniakowska 200 narzedzia ogrodnicze	125. Wife: Matgorzata.
126.	28-66-61	Kowalski, Jozef ul Lucka 13 lekarz	126. Kawaler (unmarried man).
127.	-- -- --	Kowalski, Jozef inz. Rutkowskiego 19	127. Wife: Halina.

Record in your diary the time spent and continue with this section.

You would now (Choose ONLY ONE, unless otherwise directed in the Answer Section):

128. Try to get some expert assistance from individuals or special agencies, if you have not already done so

    128. Turn to Section C.

129. Visit Karolkowa 18, if you have not already done so

    129. After one hour you arrive at the address to find an empty lot; record one hour in your diary and turn to Section B.

130. Check the alphabetical telephone directory for a new listing for J. Kowalski, if you have not already done so

    130. Turn to Section O.

131. Take the sightseeing trip you have planned and, when you get home, explain to your uncle what has happened

    131. Follow response 315.

132. Return to your hotel room and have the operator phone 49-64-21 again while you are on the line, if you have not already done so

    132. Turn to Section L.

133. Check the telephone directory to get a list of Warsaw business firms that deal in amber products, if you have not already done so

    133. Turn to Section H.

134. Check the telephone directory to get a list of Warsaw companies engaged in the import-export business, if you have not already done so

    134. Turn to Section J.

135. During the day, visit some of the Kowalskis you have located

    135. Turn to Section N.

136. In the evening, visit some of the Kowalskis you have located

    136. Turn to Section D.

137. Phone some of the Kowalskis listed in the city directory

    137. Turn to Section G.

APTITUDE

SECTION G: PHONE CALLS

Names and addresses of Kowalskis from the city directory, but not listed in the most recent telephone directory, are shown below. If you wish to phone anyone listed, follow the appropriate response (Select AS MANY AS you WISH and estimate 10 minutes for each call):

138.	43-92-88	Kowalski, Grzegory ul Karolkowa 93	138.	Jadwiga answers and indicates no correspondence with anyone in U.S.A., but suggests you speak with her husband when he gets home from work.
139.	37-33-51	Kowalski, Ignazy Stawki 8	139.	No J. Kowalski known at this address.
140.	-- -- --	Kowalski, Jadwiga Chmielna 21	140.	No phone.
141.	-- -- --	Kowalski, Jadwiga ul Minska 19A	141.	No phone.
142.	81-62-03	Kowalski, Jadwiga Leszno 280	142.	No correspondence with anyone in U.S.A.
143.	28-65-31	Kowalski, Jadwiga ul Obroncow 24	143.	No answer.
144.	-- -- --	Kowalski, Jadwiga Kopernika, 29	144.	No phone.
145.	-- -- --	Kowalski, Jan ul Mredzynarodowa 9	145.	No phone.
146.	-- -- --	Kowalski, Jan ul Minska 19	146.	No phone.
147.	43-93-36	Kowalski, Jan ul Karolkowa 91	147.	No correspondent in U.S.A.
148.	-- -- --	Kowalski, Jan ul Obroncow 51	148.	No phone.
149.	-- -- --	Kowalski, Jozef Czerniakowska 200	149.	No phone.
150.	28-66-61	Kowalski, Jozef ul Lucka 13	150.	No answer.
151.	-- -- --	Kowalski, Jozef Rutkowskiego 19	151.	No phone.

Record in your diary the time spent and continue with this section.

You would now (Choose ONLY ONE, unless otherwise directed in the Answer Section):

152. Try to get some expert assistance from individuals or special agencies, if you have not already done so

152. Turn to Section C.

HOW RESOURCEFUL ARE YOU?

SECTION G: continued

153. Visit Karolkowa 18, if you have not already done so

154. Check the alphabetical telephone directory for a new listing for J. Kowalski, if you have not already done so

155. Take the sightseeing trip you have planned and, when you get home, explain to your uncle what has happened

156. Return to your hotel room and have the operator phone 49-64-21 again while you are on the line, if you have not already done so

157. Check the telephone directory to get a list of Warsaw business firms that deal in amber products, if you have not already done so

158. Check the telephone directory to get a list of Warsaw companies engaged in the import-export business, if you have not already done so

159. During the day, visit some of the Kowalskis you have located

160. In the evening, visit some of the Kowalskis you have located

161. Phone some of the Kowalskis listed in the most recent telephone directory

153. After one hour you arrive at the address to find an empty lot; record one hour in your diary and turn to Section B.

154. Turn to Section O.

155. Follow response 315.

156. Turn to Section L.

157. Turn to Section H.

158. Turn to Section J.

159. Turn to Section N.

160. Turn to Section D.

161. Turn to Section E.

SECTION H: AMBER FIRMS

Names, addresses, and phone numbers of Warsaw firms dealing in amber products are listed below. If you do *not* wish to phone any firms, continue with items 172 and following. If you do wish to phone any of them, follow the appropriate response (Select AS MANY AS you WISH and estimate 10 minutes for each call):

Amber and Amber Products (cooperatives)

162. Buczka
     Grojecka 74
     Phone 22-62-13

163. Bursztyn
     Roszynska 67
     Phone 27-16-50

164. Exportor
     Grojecka 60
     Phone 63-72-58

162. No one by the name of J. Kowalski working here now; personnel clerk refuses to give out further information on the phone.

163. No one by the name of J. Kowalski working here now; personnel clerk refuses to give out further information on the phone.

164. No one by the name of J. Kowalski working here now; personnel clerk refuses to give out further information on the phone.

APTITUDE

SECTION H: continued

Amber and Amber Products (shops)

165. Bizuteria Ozodobna
Krakowskie Przedmiescie 27
Phone 41-25-03

166. Galanteria
Middowa 2
Phone 47-62-73

167. Jantar
Krakowskie Przedmiescie 32
Phone 71-83-20

168. Orno
Mariensztat 3
Phone 51-26-10

Amber and Amber Products (state enterprise)

169. Amboro
Jerozolimskie 25
Phone 26-31-02

170. Arka
Marszarkowska 54
Phone 37-05-11

171. Centromor
Novy Swiat 67
Phone 26-06-71

165. No one by the name of J. Kowalski working here now; personnel clerk refuses to give out further information on the phone.

166. Clerk calls Mr. Kowalski to the phone; he turns out to be Mr. Grzegorz Kowalski.

167. No one by the name of J. Kowalski working here now; personnel clerk refuses to give out further information on the phone.

168. Clerk calls Miss Jadwiga Kowalski to the phone but she has not been corresponding with anyone in America and you are unable to learn whether anyone in her family has been corresponding with such a person.

169. No one by the name of J. Kowalski working here now; personnel clerk refuses to give out further information on the phone.

170. No one by the name of J. Kowalski working here now; personnel clerk refuses to give out further information on the phone.

171. No one by the name of J. Kowalski working here now; personnel clerk refuses to give out further information on the phone.

Record in your diary the time spent and continue with this section.

You would now (Choose ONLY ONE, unless otherwise directed in the Answer Section):

172. Try to get some expert assistance from individuals or special agencies, if you have not already done so

173. Visit Karolkowa 18, if you have not already done so

174. Check the alphabetical telephone directory for a new listing for J. Kowalski, if you have not already done so

175. Locate a city directory of Warsaw residents, if you have not already done so

176. Take the sightseeing trip you have planned and, when you get home, explain to your uncle what has happened

172. Turn to Section C.

173. After one hour you arrive at the address to find an empty lot; record one hour in your diary and turn to Section B.

174. Turn to Section O.

175. You are told the *milicja* (police) have such a directory; if you wish to go to the station to look it over, record 30 minutes in your diary and turn to Section F; otherwise, make another choice from this section.

176. Follow response 315.

HOW RESOURCEFUL ARE YOU?

SECTION H: continued

177. Return to your hotel room and have the operator phone 49-64-21 again while you are on the line, if you have not already done so

177. Turn to Section L.

178. Visit some of the amber firms you have located in the directory

178. Turn to Section I.

179. Check the telephone directory to get a list of Warsaw companies engaged in the import-export business, if you have not already done so

179. Turn to Section J.

180. During the day, visit some of the Kowalskis you have located

180. Turn to Section N.

181. In the evening, visit some of the Kowalskis you have located

181. Turn to Section D.

182. Phone some of the Kowalskis you have located

182. Turn to Section E.

SECTION I: VISITS TO AMBER FIRMS

The names and addresses of Warsaw firms dealing in amber products are listed below. If you wish to visit any of these firms, follow the appropriate response (Select AS MANY AS you WISH and estimate one hour for each visit):

Amber and Amber Products (cooperatives)

183. Buczka
Grojecka 74
Phone 22-62-13

183. There is no J. Kowalski currently working in this firm; the personnel office advises you that after searching their records they can find no record of a J. Kowalski who has worked there in the last five years.

184. Bursztyn
Roszynska 67
Phone 27-16-50

184. There is no J. Kowalski currently working in this firm; the personnel office advises you that after searching their records they can find no record of a J. Kowalski who has worked there in the last five years.

185. Exportor
Grojecka 60
Phone 63-72-58

185. There is no J. Kowalski currently working in this firm; the personnel office advises you that after searching their records they can find no record of a J. Kowalski who has worked there in the last five years.

Amber and Amber Products (shops)

186. Bizuteria Ozodobna
Krakowskie Przedmiescie 27
Phone 41-25-03

186. There is no J. Kowalski currently working in this firm; the personnel office advises you that after searching their records they can find no record of a J. Kowalski who has worked there in the last five years.

187. Galanteria
Middowa 2
Phone 47-62-73

187. There is a Grzegorz Kowalski currently working in this firm; the personnel office advises you that after searching their

APTITUDE

SECTION I: continued

188. Jantar
  Krakowskie Przedmiescie 32
  Phone 71-83-20

189. Orno
  Mariensztat 3
  Phone 51-26-10

Amber and Amber Products (state enterprise)

190. Amboro
  Jerozolimskie 25
  Phone 26-31-02

191. Arka
  Marszarkowska 54
  Phone 37-05-11

192. Centromor
  Novy Swiat 67
  Phone 26-06-71

Record in your diary the time spent and continue with this section.

You would now (Choose ONLY ONE, unless otherwise directed in the Answer Section):

193. Try to get some expert assistance from individuals or special agencies, if you have not already done so

194. Visit Karolkowa 18, if you have not already done so

195. Check the alphabetical telephone directory for a new listing for J. Kowalski, if you have not already done so

196. Locate a city directory of Warsaw residents, if you have not already done so

---

records they can find no record of a J. Kowalski who has worked there in the last five years.

188. There is no J. Kowalski currently working in this firm; the personnel office advises you that after searching their records they can find no record of a J. Kowalski who has worked there in the last five years.

189. There is a Jadwiga Kowalski currently working in this firm. After talking to Jadwiga Kowalski with the help of an English-speaking salesclerk, you are persuaded that she is not the J. Kowalski you wish to locate and that no one in her family has been corresponding with anyone in America.

190. There is no J. Kowalski currently working in this firm; the personnel office advises you that after searching their records they can find no record of a J. Kowalski who has worked there in the last five years.

191. There is no J. Kowalski currently working in this firm; the personnel office advises you that after searching their records they can find no record of a J. Kowalski who has worked there in the last five years.

192. The personnel office informs you that a Jozef Kowalski was employed here as *urzednik* (clerk). However, he died two years ago. Their records show that, at the time of his death, he was living at ul Obroncow 24 with his wife, Jadwiga, and their children.

193. Turn to Section C.

194. After one hour you arrive at the address to find an empty lot; record one hour in your diary and turn to Section B.

195. Turn to Section O.

196. You are told the *milicja* (police) have such a directory; if you wish to go to the station to look it over, record 30 minutes in your

HOW RESOURCEFUL ARE YOU?

SECTION I: continued

197. Take the sightseeing trip you have planned and, when you get home, explain to your uncle what has happened
198. Return to your hotel room and have the operator phone 49-64-21 again while you are on the line, if you have not already done so
199. Check the telephone directory to get a list of Warsaw companies engaged in the import-export business, if you have not already done so
200. During the day, visit some of the Kowalskis you have located
201. In the evening, visit some of the Kowalskis you have located
202. Phone some of the Kowalskis you have located

diary and turn to Section F; otherwise, make another choice from this section.

197. Follow response 315.

198. Turn to Section L.

199. Turn to Section J.

200. Turn to Section N.

201. Turn to Section D.

202. Turn to Section E.

SECTION J: IMPORT-EXPORT COMPANIES

Names, addresses, and phone numbers of all import-export companies in the Warsaw area are listed below. If you do *not* wish to phone any firms, continue with items 213 and following. If you do wish to phone any of them, follow the appropriate response (Select AS MANY AS you WISH and estimate 10 minutes for each call):

203. ABC Export
     Chalubinskiego 62
     Phone 72-58-66
204. Buczka
     Grojecka 74
     Phone 22-62-13
205. Centromor
     Novy Swiat 67
     Phone 26-06-71
206. Cepelia
     Marchlewskiego 17
     Phone 42-40-17
207. Coopexim
     Novy Swiat 54
     Phone 26-37-55

203. No J. Kowalski employed here now; personnel clerk refuses to give any further information over the phone.
204. No J. Kowalski employed here now; personnel clerk refuses to give any further information over the phone.
205. No J. Kowalski employed here now; personnel clerk refuses to give any further information over the phone.
206. No J. Kowalski employed here now.

207. Jan Kowalski is called to the phone, but doesn't know anything about your uncle. No one else there by that name. Personnel office refuses to give out any more information on the phone.

APTITUDE

SECTION J: continued

208. Dalmon
Chalubinskiego 54
Phone 72-30-16

208. Grzegorz Kowalski currently there in shipping department but is on vacation now and is not expected back for two weeks. No one else there by that name. Personnel office refuses to give out any more information on the phone.

209. Im. Marchlewskiego
Jerozolimskie 103
Phone 67-13-28

209. No J. Kowalski employed there now; personnel clerk refuses to give any further information over the phone.

210. Rozewie
Novy Swiat 71
Phone 26-10-17

210. No J. Kowalski employed there now; personnel clerk refuses to give any further information over the phone.

211. Universum
Piekna 2
Phone 29-73-88

211. Jozef Kowalski called to the phone but denies writing any letters to America.

212. Varimex
Tawarowa 93
Phone 63-39-78

212. Ignacy Kowalski called to the phone, and has been writing to a sister in California but never heard of your uncle.

Record in your diary the time spent and continue with this section.

You would now (Choose ONLY ONE, unless otherwise directed in the Answer Section):

213. Try to get some expert assistance from individuals or special agencies, if you have not already done so

213. Turn to Section C.

214. Visit Karolkowa 18, if you have not already done so

214. After one hour you arrive at the address to find an empty lot; record one hour in your diary and turn to Section B.

215. Check the alphabetical telephone directory for a new listing for J. Kowalski, if you have not already done so

215. Turn to Section O.

216. Locate a city directory of Warsaw residents, if you have not already done so

216. You are told the *milicja* (police) have such a directory; if you wish to go to the station to look it over, record 30 minutes in your diary and turn to Section F; otherwise, make another choice from this section.

217. Take the sightseeing trip you have planned and, when you get home, explain to your uncle what has happened

217. Follow response 315.

218. Return to your hotel room and have the operator phone 49-64-21 again while you are on the line, if you have not already done so

218. Turn to Section L.

219. Check the telephone directory to get a list of Warsaw business firms that deal in amber products, if you have not already done so

219. Turn to Section H.

HOW RESOURCEFUL ARE YOU?

SECTION J: continued

220. Visit some of the import-export firms that you have located
221. During the day, visit some of the Kowalskis you have located
222. In the evening, visit some of the Kowalskis you have located
223. Phone some of the Kowalskis you have located

220. Turn to Section K.
221. Turn to Section N.
222. Turn to Section D.
223. Turn to Section E.

SECTION K: VISITS TO IMPORT-EXPORT COMPANIES

The names and addresses of all import-export companies operating in the Warsaw area are listed below. If you wish to visit any of them, follow the appropriate response (Select AS MANY AS you WISH and estimate one hour for each visit):

224. ABC Export
Chalubinskiego 62
Phone 72-58-66

225. Buczka
Grojecka 74
Phone 22-62-13

226. Centromor
Novy Swiat 67
Phone 26-06-71

227. Cepelia
Marchlewskiego 17
Phone 42-40-17

228. Coopexim
Novy Swiat 54
Phone 26-37-55

229. Dalmon
Chalubinskiego 54
Phone 72-30-16

230. Im. Marchlewskiego
Jerozolimskie 103
Phone 67-13-28

224. There is no J. Kowalski currently working at this firm; on checking the records the personnel clerk informs you that they have no record of a J. Kowalski having worked there in the last five years.

225. There is no J. Kowalski currently working at this firm; on checking the records the personnel clerk informs you that they have no record of a J. Kowalski having worked there in the last five years.

226. The personnel office at Centromor informs you that a Jozef Kowalski was employed there as urzednik (clerk). However, he died two years ago. Their records show that at the time of his death he was living at ul Obroncow 24 with his wife, Jadwiga, and their children.

227. No J. Kowalski in the company files.

228. Jan Kowalski can give no further information about any family in America; no other J. Kowalski on company records in past four years.

229. G. Kowalski on vacation; his home address is in a Warsaw suburb. He has lived in Warsaw only two years; no J. Kowalski in company files.

230. J. Kowalski worked here four years ago but emigrated to America two years ago. No other J. Kowalski in company files.

APTITUDE

SECTION K: continued

231. Rozewie
    Novy Swiat 71
    Phone 26-10-17

232. Universum
    Piekna 2
    Phone 29-73-88

233. Varimex
    Tawarowa 93
    Phone 63-39-78

231. J. Kowalski started working there as a temporary clerk about a year ago. He stayed only eight months and left for the country four months ago.

232. Josef Kowalski has not been in touch with anyone in America; no one in his family has. No other Kowalski in company files.

233. Ignacy Kowalski has a 4-year-old daughter named Jadwiga, but she is the only J. Kowalski in company files.

Record in your diary the time spent and continue with this section.

You would now (Choose ONLY ONE, unless otherwise directed in the Answer Section):

234. Try to get some expert assistance from individuals or special agencies, if you have not already done so

235. Visit Karolkowa 18, if you have not already done so

236. Check the alphabetical telephone directory for a new listing for J. Kowalski, if you have not already done so

237. Locate a city directory of Warsaw residents, if you have not already done so

238. Take the sightseeing trip you have planned and, when you get home, explain to your uncle what has happened

239. Return to your hotel room and have the operator phone 49-64-21 again while you are on the line, if you have not already done so

240. Check the telephone directory to get a list of Warsaw business firms that deal in amber products, if you have not already done so

241. During the day, visit some of the Kowalskis you have located

242. In the evening, visit some of the Kowalskis you have located

243. Phone some of the Kowalskis you have located

234. Turn to Section C.

235. After one hour you arrive at the address to find an empty lot; record one hour in your diary and turn to Section B.

236. Turn to Section O.

237. You are told the *milicja* (police) have such a directory; if you wish to go to the station to look it over, record 30 minutes in your diary and turn to Section F; otherwise, make another choice from this section.

238. Follow response 315.

239. Turn to Section L.

240. Turn to Section H.

241. Turn to Section N.

242. Turn to Section D.

243. Turn to Section E.

HOW RESOURCEFUL ARE YOU?

SECTION L: REPEAT PHONE CALL

After 30 minutes, the operator phones your room to say that she has the party on the line. With the hotel operator serving as interpreter, you confirm that this is indeed the right number but that the person you are talking to is Professor S. Jus and that his address is Karolkowa 72. He, his wife, and two children have lived at this address for two years. There is no one else in the household, and he doesn't know anything about the previous tenants. He does know two J. Kowalskis but neither ever lived here and neither is in the import-export business. Record 45 minutes in your diary and continue with this section.

You would now (Choose ONLY ONE, unless otherwise directed in the Answer Section):

244. Try to get some expert assistance from individuals or special agencies, if you have not already done so

245. Visit Karolkowa 18, if you have not already done so

246. Check the alphabetical telephone directory for a new listing for J. Kowalski, if you have not already done so

247. Locate a city directory of Warsaw residents, if you have not already done so

248. Take the sightseeing trip you have planned and, when you get home, explain to your uncle what has happened

249. Check the telephone directory to get a list of Warsaw business firms that deal in amber products, if you have not already done so

250. Check the telephone directory to get a list of Warsaw companies engaged in the import-export business, if you have not already done so

251. During the day, visit some of the Kowalskis you have located

252. In the evening, visit some of the Kowalskis you have located

253. Phone some of the Kowalskis you have located

244. Turn to Section C.

245. After one hour you arrive at the address to find an empty lot; record one hour in your diary and turn to Section B.

246. Turn to Section O.

247. You are told the *milicja* (police) have such a directory; if you wish to go to the station to look it over, record 30 minutes in your diary and turn to Section F; otherwise make another choice from this section.

248. Follow response 315.

249. Turn to Section H.

250. Turn to Section J.

251. Turn to Section N.

252. Turn to Section D.

253. Turn to Section E.

APTITUDE

SECTION M: EXTENSION OF STAY

You make an urgent call to immigration authorities who advise you they will give you a 12-hour emergency extension of your visa and that, if you will apply in person early tomorrow to the several offices involved, you can *probably* get a three-day emergency extension of your visa. However, it will take you at least half a day to get it and will cost you $360 U.S. extra in air fare to give up your excursion rate. You know that is a lot of money and that your only hope is to have your uncle cable you a loan. He may be willing to do it, but he certainly will not be very pleased about it.

Under these circumstances, you would now (Choose ONLY ONE):

254. Abandon your search, return home as planned, and explain everything to your uncle

254. You return home. Your uncle is at first pleased with your devotion to duty and economy, but gradually he begins to mutter about how stupid you are and to issue veiled hints about your "lost heritage."
END OF PROBLEM

255. Risk the displeasure of your uncle, but decide to spend the time and effort to get an extension to continue your search

255. You succeed in extending your visa and in getting a loan from your uncle. Use the lower half of your diary to record spending 5 hours. Return now to the section you left when you ran out of time, and continue with the choices listed there.

SECTION N: DAY VISITS

Names and addresses of Kowalskis living in the Warsaw area are shown below. If you wish to visit anyone during the day, follow the appropriate response (Select AS MANY AS you WISH and estimate one hour for each visit):

256. 44-19-26 Kowalski, Adam
             Wawelska 12

256. No J. Kowalski at this address.

257. 19-21-12 Kowalski, Bernard
             mgr. inz. arch.
             Waleoznych 5

257. No correspondence with anyone in U.S.A.

258. 45-20-03 Kowalski, Bogdan
             dr. med.
             Grojecka 219

258. No one home.

259. 34-88-91 Kowalski, Cezary
             Buczka 43

259. No one home.

260. 34-00-17 Kowalski, Czestaw
             Okopowa 27A

260. No correspondence with anyone in U.S.A.

261. 29-21-63 Kowalski, Edmund
             mgr. prawa
             Warecka 2

261. No one home.

HOW RESOURCEFUL ARE YOU?

SECTION N: continued

262.	26-22-48	Kowalski, Edward art. muzyk Swigtokrzyska 12	262. No one home.
263.	22-27-47	Kowalski, Eugeniusz Zwyciezcow 44	263. No J. Kowalski at this address.
264.	43-40-11	Kowalski, Eugeniusz Pl. Narutowioza 18	264. No J. Kowalski at this address. No correspondence with anyone in U.S.A.
265.	43-92-88	Kowalski, Grzegory ul Karolkowa 93	265. Jadwiga says man from Chicago visited last year. Suggests you return in evening to talk with husband.
266.	25-92-88	Kowalski, Grzegorz Al. Niepodleglosci 184	266. No correspondence with anyone in U.S.A.
267.	35-36-72	Kowalski, Ignacy mgr. inz. Stawki 8	267. No one home.
268.	37-33-51	Kowalski, Ignazy mgr. inz. Stawki 8	268. No one home.
269.	-- -- --	Kowalski, Jadwiga Chmielna 21	269. No one home.
270.	-- -- --	Kowalski, Jadwiga ul Minska 19A	270. No one home. Neighbors indicate she has been away for the summer; they have no idea when she will be back.
271.	81-62-03	Kowalski, Jadwiga Leszno 280	271. No correspondence with anyone in U.S.A.
272.	28-65-31	Kowalski, Jadwiga ul Obroncow 24	272. No one home. One of the neighbors volunteers that the oldest daughter is always threatening to run away to live with a rich cousin in America.
273.	-- -- --	Kowalski, Jadwiga Kopernika, 29	273. No one home. Neighbors are of no help.
274.	44-93-36	Kowalski, Jadwiga Nowowiejska 37	274. No one home.
275.	-- -- --	Kowalski, Jan ul Mredzynarodowa 9	275. No correspondence with anyone in U.S.A.
276.	-- -- --	Kowalski, Jan ul Minska 19	276. No one home. Neighbor volunteers that family has gone to visit relatives in northern Germany. Neighbor has never heard them speak of a relative in the U.S.A.
277.	43-93-36	Kowalski, Jan ul Karolkowa 91	277. No one home. Neighbors refuse to say anything about Jan Kowalski.
278.	-- -- --	Kowalski, Jan ul Obroncow 51	278. No correspondence with anyone in U.S.A.
279.	27-52-69	Kowalski, Jan lek. dent. Pl. Grzybowski 21	279. No correspondence with anyone in U.S.A.

APTITUDE

SECTION N: continued

280.	45-12-19	Kowalski, Jan narzedzia ogrodnicze Czerniakowska 218	280.	No one home.
280.[a]	17-55-33	Kowalski, Jan prof. dr. Al. Waszyngtona 134	280.[a]	No correspondence with anyone in U.S.A.
281.	26-66-16	Kowalski, Jan E. Hibnera 12	281.	No correspondence with anyone in U.S.A.
282.	25-63-69	Kowalski, Jan Stefan Chmielna 35	282.	No one home.
283.	43-77-00	Kowalski, Josef doc. dr. med Filtrowa 63	283.	No correspondence with anyone in U.S.A.
284.	26-17-92	Kowalski, Josef Em. Plater 56	284.	No one home. Neighbors are of no help.
285.	32-28-18	Kowalski, Jozef inz. Konwiktorska 77	285.	No one home.
286.	28-65-35	Kowalski, Jozef Poksal 16	286.	No correspondence with anyone in U.S.A.
287.	25-48-84	Kowalski, Jozef Kopernika 25	287.	No one home.
288.	26-74-98	Kowalski, Jozef lekarz, chor. wewn. Rutkowskiego 9	288.	No correspondence with anyone in U.S.A.
289.	44-53-57	Kowalski, Jozef inz. rolnik Biatobrzeska 93	289.	No correspondence with anyone in U.S.A.
290.	-- -- --	Kowalski, Jozef Czerniakowska 200	290.	No correspondence with anyone in U.S.A.
291.	28-66-61	Kowalski, Jozef ul Lucka 13	291.	No one home. Neighbors say he is away on business; no idea when he will return.
292.	-- -- --	Kowalski, Jozef Rutkowskiego 19	292.	No correspondence with anyone in U.S.A.
293.	35-07-16	Kowalski, Konstanty Niska 69	293.	No one home.

Record in your diary the time spent and continue with this section.

You would now (Choose ONLY ONE EACH TIME you are directed to this section):

294. Try to get some expert assistance from individuals or special agencies, if you have not already done so

294. Turn to Section C.

HOW RESOURCEFUL ARE YOU?

SECTION N: continued

295. Visit Karolkowa 18, if you have not already done so

295. After one hour you arrive at the address to find an empty lot; record one hour in your diary and turn to Section B.

296. Check the alphabetical telephone directory for a new listing for J. Kowalski, if you have not already done so

296. Turn to Section O.

297. Locate a city directory of Warsaw residents, if you have not already done so

297. You are told the *milicja* (police) have such a directory; if you wish to go to the station to look it over, record 30 minutes in your diary and turn to Section F; otherwise, make another choice from this section.

298. Take the sightseeing trip you have planned and, when you get home, explain to your uncle what has happened

298. Follow response 315.

299. Return to your hotel room and have the operator phone 49-64-21 again while you are on the line, if you have not already done so

299. Turn to Section L.

300. Check the telephone directory to get a list of Warsaw business firms that deal in amber products, if you have not already done so

300. Turn to Section H.

301. Check the telephone directory to get a list of Warsaw companies engaged in the import-export business, if you have not already done so

301. Turn to Section J.

302. In the evening, visit some of the Kowalskis you have located

302. Turn to Section D.

303. Phone some of the Kowalskis you have located

303. Turn to Section E.

SECTION O:
WARSAW TELEPHONE DIRECTORY

Below are names, addresses, and phone numbers for Kowalskis listed in the most recent telephone directory.

    44-19-26   Kowalski, Adam
                          Wawelska 12

    19-21-12   Kowalski, Bernard
                          mgr. inz. arch.
                          Waleoznych 5

    45-20-03   Kowalski, Bogdan
                          dr. med.
                          Grojecka 219

    34-88-91   Kowalski, Cezary
                          Buczka 43

APTITUDE

SECTION O: continued

    34-00-17   Kowalski, Czestaw
                     Okopowa 27A

    29-21-63   Kowalski, Edmund
                     mgr. prawa
                     Warecka 2

    26-22-48   Kowalski, Edward
                     art. muzyk
                     Swigtokrzyska 12

    22-27-47   Kowalski, Eugeniusz
                     Zwyciezcow 44

    43-40-11   Kowalski, Eugeniusz
                     Pl. Narutowioza 18

    25-92-88   Kowalski, Grzegorz
                     Al. Niepodleglosci 184

    35-36-72   Kowalski, Ignacy
                     mgr. inz.
                     Stawki 8

    44-93-36   Kowalski, Jadwiga
                     Nowowiejska 37

    27-52-69   Kowalski, Jan
                     lek. dent.
                     Pl. Grzybowski 21

    45-12-19   Kowalski, Jan
                     narzedzia ogrodnicze
                     Czerniakowska 218

    17-55-33   Kowalski, Jan
                     prof. dr.
                     Al. Waszyngtona 134

    26-66-16   Kowalski, Jan E.
                     Hibnera 12

    25-63-69   Kowalski, Jan Stefan
                     Chmielna 35

    43-77-00   Kowalski, Josef
                     doc. dr. med
                     Filtrowa 63

    26-17-92   Kowalski, Josef
                     Em. Plater 56

    32-28-18   Kowalski, Jozef
                     inz.
                     Konwiktorska 77

    28-65-35   Kowalski, Jozef
                     Poksal 16

    25-48-84   Kowalski, Jozef
                     Kopernika 25

    26-74-98   Kowalski, Jozef
                     lekarz, chor. wewn.
                     Rutkowskiego 9

HOW RESOURCEFUL ARE YOU?

SECTION O: continued

    44-53-57   Kowalski, Jozef
                    inz. rolnik
                    Biatobrzeska 93
    35-07-16   Kowalski, Konstanty
                    Niska 69

Record 15 minutes in your diary and continue with this section.

With the information you have, you would now (Choose ONLY ONE, unless otherwise directed in the Answer Section):

304. Try to get some expert assistance from individuals or special agencies, if you have not already done so

305. Visit Karolkowa 18, if you have not already done so

306. Locate a city directory of Warsaw residents, if you have not already done so

307. Take the sightseeing trip you have planned and, when you get home, explain to your uncle what has happened

308. Return to your hotel room and have the operator phone 49-64-21 again while you are on the line, if you have not already done so

309. Check the telephone directory to get a list of Warsaw business firms that deal in amber products, if you have not already done so

310. Check the telephone directory to get a list of Warsaw companies engaged in the import-export business, if you have not already done so

311. During the day, visit some of the Kowalskis you have located

312. In the evening, visit some of the Kowalskis you have located

313. Phone some of the Kowalskis you have located

304. Turn to Section C.

305. After one hour you arrive at the address to find an empty lot; record one hour in your diary and turn to Section B.

306. You are told the *milicja* (police) have such a directory; if you wish to go to the station to look it over, record 30 minutes in your diary and turn to Section F; otherwise, make another choice from this section.

307. Follow response 315.

308. Turn to Section L.

309. Turn to Section H.

310. Turn to Section J.

311. Turn to Section N.

312. Turn to Section D.

313. Turn to Section E.

314. You show Mrs. Kowalski the photograph your uncle had given you. She is very excited; you finally figure out that she recognizes the picture as a photograph of her husband, who died two years ago. Dur-

49

APTITUDE

ing your conversation with Mrs. Kowalski, you learn that her husband and your uncle were related by the fact that her husband's mother was a first cousin to your uncle's aunt. You have an exciting time during your remaining visit in Warsaw, and upon returning to the U.S.A. you report to your uncle. He is most pleased with your finding and suggests that you take the entire summer next year to tour all of Europe at his expense.
END OF PROBLEM

315. You have a wonderful time in Warsaw and feel it is the highlight of your trip. You are eager to tell your uncle because you know he will be pleased that you liked the city and glad you are able to tell him how it looks now. Unfortunately, when you get back to America, he is furious at your "irresponsibility in not bothering to locate Kowalski" and threatens to disinherit you.
END OF PROBLEM

316. You return home without locating your man; your uncle is at first pleased with your devotion to duty and economy, but gradually he begins to mutter about how stupid you are and to issue veiled hints about your "lost heritage."
END OF PROBLEM

317. See Glossary of Polish Terms.

GLOSSARY OF POLISH TERMS

GENERAL

kawaler unmarried man
milicja police
ORBIS Polish Travel Office
panna unmarried woman
wdowa widow
wdowiec widower

OCCUPATIONS

art. muzyk musician
doc. dr. med. assist. professor of medicine
dr. med. medical doctor
inz. engineer
inz. rolnik agricultural engineer
kierowca chauffeur

lekarz physician
lekarz, chor. wewn. physician specializing in internal medicine
lek. dent. dentist
mgr. inz. master engineer
mgr. inz. arch. master architectural engineer
mgr. prawa lawyer
narzedzia ogrodnicze private supplier of agricultural tools
prof. dr. professor
robotnik worker
urzednik clerk

Record in your diary 15 minutes spent for negotiations with your interpreter. Return to Section C and continue with your selections.

HOW RESOURCEFUL ARE YOU?

FEEDBACK

On completing "The Traveler," students would ordinarily receive feedback on their performance. Had the exercise been used for assessment purposes, the report to them might have been in the form of a score or set of scores. Since the exercise is used here for instructional purposes, a different kind of information is appropriate. The following discussion is illustrative of such qualitative feedback.

OBJECTIVE

This exercise was designed to sample your ability to use the resources of a large city, to adapt your data gathering to unfamiliar circumstances, to modify your approach when your initial strategy proves unsuccessful, and to integrate fragmentary information in arriving at a solution. The exercise is also designed to provide some information about your persistence in trying to solve a stubborn problem, your willingness to forego immediate gratification in order to please a member of your family, and the relative importance you attach to your money versus your time.

RECOMMENDED STRATEGY

Since the first strategy you try (phoning the three-year-old telephone number your uncle has given you) does not work, it is reasonable to assume that the number is out-of-date and hence that by consulting a more recent telephone directory you may solve your problem.

Inspection of the directory reveals, however, that Kowalski is a relatively common name in Warsaw. Phoning all those listed in the current directory will take a minimum of 4 hours and 10 minutes; limiting your calls only to the J. Kowalskis will take 2 hours and 10 minutes. Since you cannot be sure you can reach someone at every number, this approach involves considerable time and, in the absence of "lucking out," offers a low probability of success. Similar difficulties attend any effort to extend your search to the additional Kowalskis (or J. Kowalskis) listed in the up-dated city directory at the police station. Any attempt to increase your probable chances of success by visiting all the Kowalskis or J. Kowalskis listed in either the phone or city directory is certain to involve a very substantial time investment, most of which is likely to be wasted. In addition there is no assurance that you will succeed in finding everyone at home during the next three days—even if you devote full time to that type of search. Consequently, it should be obvious that you must give up the search or find a more efficient way of conducting it.

The latter can be accomplished either by obtaining expert assistance or by finding a method of narrowing the field which you personally will search. At this point you can, at a cost of approximately ½ hour and $500, buy the information you need and "enjoy your stay" knowing that you may have to make future sacrifices to replenish your savings. You have one additional clue that may help you to conduct a more focused search; three years ago the J. Kowalski you seek worked for an import-export firm which specialized in amber products. With that piece of information you can cross-check in the classified phone directory to see how many firms would be involved in this type of import-export business. Your cross-check will reveal that there are only two firms which fit the description. Though you are unable to get information over the telephone, these two firms are still your best leads and a visit to them may be helpful.

A maximum investment of two hours in visiting these two firms enables you to focus further inquiry on a single name and address which seems sufficiently promising to merit further investigation. The investment of one hour to make an immediate visit to that address provides you with another encouraging piece of information. The additional, or alternate, decision that the chances are better to find someone at home in the evening should lead you to risk another hour's involvement to visit the address you have been given. This decision rewards you with an immediate solution to your problem.

The critical element in the successful approach to such a problem is the ability to integrate fragments of information, so as to take maximum advantage of data sources in order to accomplish a *systematic narrowing of the field of search* as quickly as possible. Using that approach in this problem assures a solution with a maximum investment of 4 hours and 35 minutes; with a little luck supplementing your logical approach, you could accomplish it in as little as 2 hours.

AN ALTERNATE SOLUTION

If you are unwilling to forego the immediate satisfactions of tourism and are willing to spend $500, you can hire a private investigator to do the work for you. Such a choice indicates that you value your time in Warsaw at $125-$250 per hour. As a young (and presumably not very well-to-do school teacher) this may be an overevaluation of your time that may re-

APTITUDE

quire subsequent sacrifices. Only you can decide if it is worth it. The diagram (or map) below portrays these two alternative methods of solving the problem.

MAP OF "THE TRAVELER"

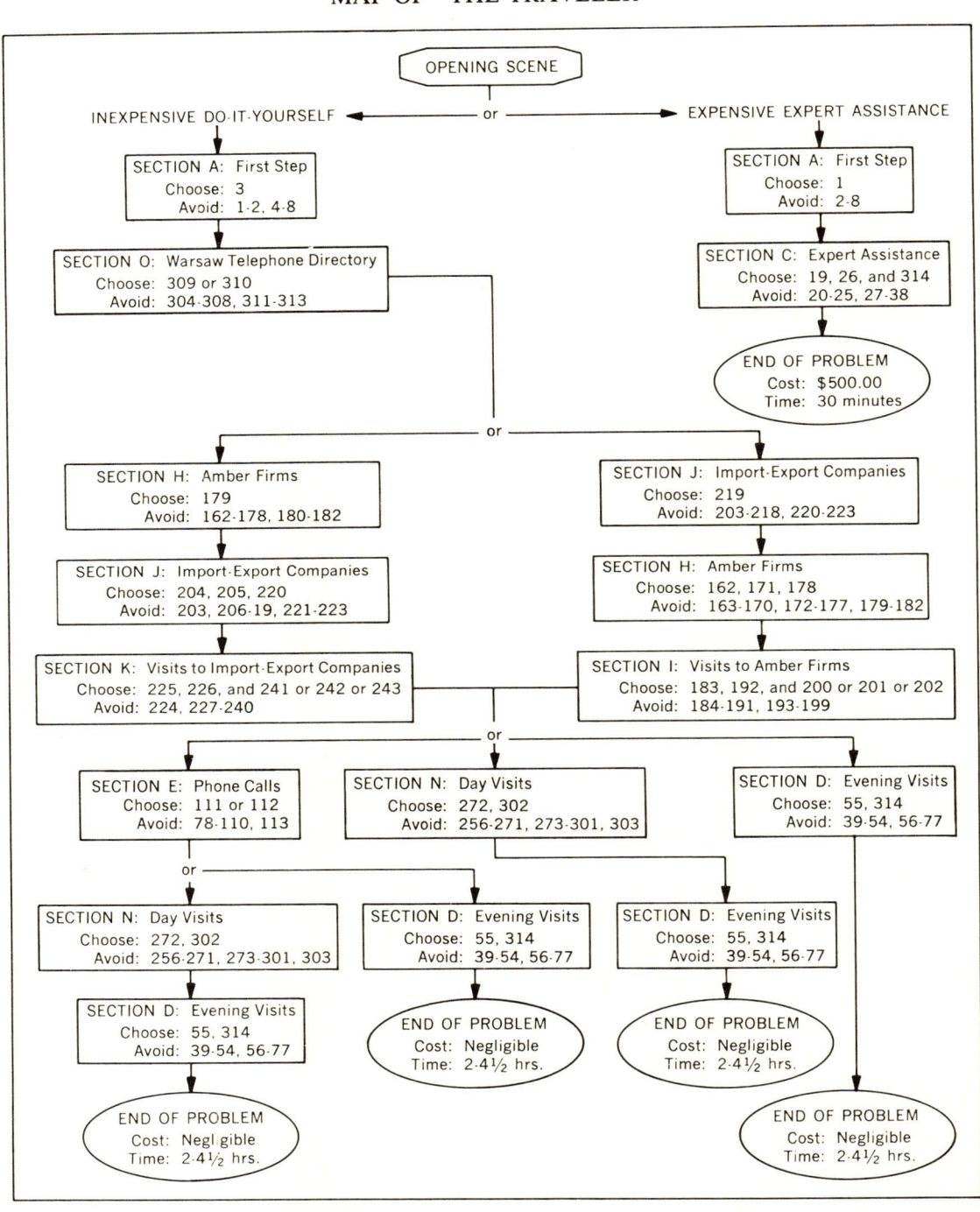

```
                          OPENING SCENE
         INEXPENSIVE DO-IT-YOURSELF  ←— or —→  EXPENSIVE EXPERT ASSISTANCE

         SECTION A: First Step                  SECTION A: First Step
           Choose: 3                              Choose: 1
           Avoid: 1-2, 4-8                        Avoid: 2-8

         SECTION O: Warsaw Telephone Directory   SECTION C: Expert Assistance
           Choose: 309 or 310                     Choose: 19, 26, and 314
           Avoid: 304-308, 311-313                Avoid: 20-25, 27-38

                                                 END OF PROBLEM
                                                   Cost: $500.00
                                                   Time: 30 minutes

                            —— or ——

         SECTION H: Amber Firms                  SECTION J: Import-Export Companies
           Choose: 179                            Choose: 219
           Avoid: 162-178, 180-182                Avoid: 203-218, 220-223

         SECTION J: Import-Export Companies      SECTION H: Amber Firms
           Choose: 204, 205, 220                  Choose: 162, 171, 178
           Avoid: 203, 206-19, 221-223            Avoid: 163-170, 172-177, 179-182

         SECTION K: Visits to Import-Export      SECTION I: Visits to Amber Firms
           Companies                              Choose: 183, 192, and 200 or 201 or 202
           Choose: 225, 226, and 241 or 242       Avoid: 184-191, 193-199
             or 243
           Avoid: 224, 227-240

                            —— or ——

   SECTION E: Phone Calls    SECTION N: Day Visits     SECTION D: Evening Visits
     Choose: 111 or 112        Choose: 272, 302          Choose: 55, 314
     Avoid: 78-110, 113        Avoid: 256-271,           Avoid: 39-54, 56-77
                                 273-301, 303

           —— or ——

   SECTION N: Day Visits     SECTION D: Evening        SECTION D: Evening
     Choose: 272, 302          Visits                    Visits
     Avoid: 256-271,           Choose: 55, 314           Choose: 55, 314
       273-301, 303            Avoid: 39-54, 56-77       Avoid: 39-54, 56-77

   SECTION D: Evening        END OF PROBLEM            END OF PROBLEM
     Visits                    Cost: Negligible          Cost: Negligible
     Choose: 55, 314           Time: 2-4½ hrs.           Time: 2-4½ hrs.
     Avoid: 39-54, 56-77

   END OF PROBLEM
     Cost: Negligible
     Time: 2-4½ hrs.
```

Copyright © 1975 by The Psychological Corporation.

??????????????????????
Reading Speed Test
??????????????????????

Reading isn't just a matter of speed. Yet, if you are a slow reader, you might be spending too much time on comprehension. On the other hand, if you are a fast reader you might not be comprehending all you are reading.

The key to good reading ability is to find the middle ground—where you can understand the material and still maintain a good speed. Your answers to the following Reading Speed Test will tell you where you stand in speed and comprehension.

?

MAGIC

Starting Time: Minutes_____Seconds_____

Magic, or conjuring, is a form of entertainment that is based on pretending to do things which are impossible. The magician is a specially trained actor. He tries to make the audience believe that he has the power to do things which are against the laws of nature.

Magic shows are entertaining as long as the audience does not discover how the tricks are done. The magician always tries to keep his tricks a secret.

The magician usually depends on his skill with his hands, on his knowledge of psychology, and, sometimes, on mechanical devices. Since magic tricks are meant to fool people, the use of psychology is important. The magician must keep people from noticing all the movements of his hands and from thinking about the secret parts of his equipment. He must also lead the audience to draw false conclusions. The magician's success depends on the fact that many things seen by the eye do not register on the mind.

Two basic magic tricks are making objects seem to appear and making objects seem to disappear. A combination of these two tricks makes for some interesting effects. For example, the magician puts a small ball under one of several cups. The ball then seems to jump from one cup to another or to change color. What actually happens is that the magician, employing quick hand movements or a mechanical device, hides one ball. While doing this he talks to the audience and waves a brightly colored cloth with one hand. The audience is too busy watching the cloth and listening to the magician's words to notice that his other hand is hiding the ball.

Another favorite trick is to cut or burn something, and then make it appear whole again. What actually happens is that the magician makes the cut or burned object disappear by quickly hiding it while the audience watches something else. Then he "magically" makes it appear whole again by displaying another object that has not been cut or burned.

There are a number of so-called "mind-reading" tricks in which the magician purports to tell a person what he is thinking about. For some of these tricks the magician has a person write down his thoughts. Then the magician secretly obtains the paper. Another "mind-reading" technique is to have a trained helper blindfold the magician. Then the helper has the audience hand him various objects. The helper can tell the magician what the objects are, without mentioning their names, by using keywords or codewords as he talks to the magician. This trick may take the magician and his helper many months to learn.

A magician's powers are really quite limited, but he makes people believe that he can do most anything by changing or combining several tricks.

Tricks in which the magician apparently cuts people in half or makes them disappear are called illusions. The word illusion derives from the fact that mirrors

APTITUDE

are often used to perform these tricks. A famous illusion trick is to saw a woman in half. The woman is put into a long box with her head sticking out of one end and her feet sticking out of the other end. The magician takes an ordinary wood saw and cuts the box into two halves. The audience is shocked, thinking that perhaps he has killed the woman. A few moments later, however, the magician puts his "magic" cape over the box and the woman comes out. The woman that the audience saw being cut in two was only an image in a mirror—an illusion.

Conjuring is as popular today as it was in ancient times. Records show that over 2,000 years ago magic performances were being given in ancient Egypt, India, Rome, China, and Greece. These early magicians only performed for small groups of people on a street corner or for a king and his friends. The magicians in those days used only small objects that they could carry with them or borrow, such as cups, pebbles, knives, and string.

Early conjurers frequently wore a large apron with many pockets in which they could carry their props. The bag-like apron served as identification and as a place to hide things while performing. Conjurers also carried a small folding table on which to perform their tricks.

About 1400, more elaborate tricks were invented which used larger equipment, such as boxes and barrels with false bottoms. Under these false bottoms the magician could hide a bird, rabbit, plant, or whatever he wanted to make appear suddenly. From one barrel he could make several different liquids pour forth while he told the audience that he was changing the entire contents of the barrel by magic. People of that time knew very little about mechanical devices, so it was easier for the magician to deceive them.

Some conjurers made enough money to buy a donkey, a horse, or even a horse and wagon so that they could carry bigger equipment. Conjurers also began to rent halls or empty stores so that they could give their shows indoors. Some conjurers used a large room in a local inn to give their performances. Others had a large van that could be opened in the rear to make a stage.

The most successful magicians would move only three or four times a year. They decorated their stages with lots of equipment, but used only a small part of it in each show. In this way they could entice the same people back over and over again. Some of their equipment was of no use at all. It was only used to decorate the stage and impress the audience.

Modern magic did not really start until the 1800s. Its father is considered to be Jean Houdin, a Frenchman, who developed rules for conjuring. Houdin was also a highly skilled mechanic and watchmaker. Today modern magicians can perform feats of magic that would have been impossible years ago because they now have better mechanical equipment and greater knowledge of audience psychology.

?

Finishing Time: Minutes_____Seconds_____

COMPREHENSION

Answer the questions without looking back at the passage. When finished, correct your answers by checking with the answer key. Find your words per minute by looking in the chart following this section.

1. The magician pretends to do things that
   ____ a. people like.
   ____ b. are impossible.
   ____ c. are secret.
   ____ d. make people laugh.

2. An important part of a magic trick is that
   ____ a. it does not take too long.
   ____ b. it has a combination of interesting effects.
   ____ c. the audience doesn't discover how it is done.
   ____ d. a bright colored cloth is used.

3. If a magician cuts something, such as a cloth, he usually makes it appear whole again by
   ____ a. displaying a duplicate.
   ____ b. using special glue.
   ____ c. not really cutting it.
   ____ d. showing you only the part not cut.

4. In the 1400s some of the favorite new tricks used
   ____ a. cups and balls.
   ____ b. cloth and knives.
   ____ c. mind reading.
   ____ d. false bottoms.

READING SPEED TEST

5. A mark of a magician's success was that
    - ____ a. he used big equipment.
    - ____ b. he didn't move often.
    - ____ c. he performed in an inn.
    - ____ d. his tricks involved illusions.

6. Psychology is an important part of magic tricks because
    - ____ a. magicians are psychologists.
    - ____ b. there is no such thing as magic.
    - ____ c. it tells you how much people see.
    - ____ d. there is a special branch of psychology devoted to magic.

7. The audience draw false conclusions because
    - ____ a. the magician is smart.
    - ____ b. they are led to believe them by the conjurer.
    - ____ c. they like to be deceived.
    - ____ d. there could be no other explanation.

8. After reading this article, you would conclude that mind reading
    - ____ a. couldn't really work.
    - ____ b. requires much concentration.
    - ____ c. requires a special talent.
    - ____ d. could work only for some people.

9. What is one valid conclusion you can draw from this article?
    - ____ a. Magicians are now extinct.
    - ____ b. People today don't like to be fooled.
    - ____ c. Magic is only for children.
    - ____ d. It is more difficult to be a magician today than it was 400 years ago.

10. Another good title for this article would be
    - ____ a. "Magic Is a Lost Art."
    - ____ b. "How to Fool Your Friends."
    - ____ c. "The First Actors."
    - ____ d. "An Introduction to Conjuring."

?

Comprehension Answers

1-b, 2-c, 3-a, 4-d, 5-b, 6-b, 7-b, 8-a, 9-d, 10-d

From *Reading Drills*, copyright © 1975 by Edward B. Fry. Published by Jamestown Publishers, Providence, Rhode Island, and reprinted by their permission.

Reading Time

Minutes	Seconds	Words per minute

Total number right	Percent

WORDS PER MINUTE

Reading Time	Words per Minute	Reading Time	Words per Minute
1:00	1000	3:20	300
1:05	923	3:25	293
1:10	857	3:30	286
1:15	800	3:35	279
1:20	750	3:40	273
1:25	706	3:45	267
1:30	667	3:50	261
1:35	632	3:55	255
1:40	600	4:00	250
1:45	571	4:05	245
1:50	545	4:10	240
1:55	522	4:15	235
2:00	500	4:20	231
2:05	480	4:25	226
2:10	462	4:30	222
2:15	444	4:35	218
2:20	429	4:40	214
2:25	414	4:45	210
2:30	400	4:50	207
2:35	387	4:55	203
2:40	375	5:00	200
2:45	364	5:05	197
2:50	353	5:10	194
2:55	343	5:15	190
3:00	333	5:20	187
3:05	324	5:25	185
3:10	315	5:30	182
3:15	308		

?

EVALUATION

The key to good reading ability is flexibility and balance. Your speed should not be constant throughout, but should be adjusted from faster to slower depending upon the difficulty of the material to be read.

Optimum score for the Reading Speed Test should be 70 to 80 percent. If you scored above 80 percent you are reading too carefully and too closely; you might want to speed up your reading to cover more material. If you are reading under 70 percent, your comprehension is below average. To better your comprehension, Dr. Fry recommends, train at a local community college or university evening course.

How Well Do You Listen?

Good listening is essential in business. Unfortunately, most of us don't really listen to what is being said. In order to train yourself to be a good listener, there are four major steps: 1) building an awareness of the importance of listening in business; 2) increasing your understanding of the nature of listening and its impact on the total communications process; 3) diagnosing your listening abilities and practices; and 4) developing skills and techniques to improve listening effectiveness.

Because listening is important to success and a great strength in the marketplace, Sperry Corporation has made an extra effort to improve the listening and responding skills of their employees. The following test (devised by Dr. Lyman K. Steil, Chairman of the Speech-Communication Division, Department of Rhetoric at the University of Minnesota in St. Paul and special consultant to Sperry Corporation) has been instituted at all five divisions of the Sperry Corporation and the success of the program proves that it is important to be a good listener.

?

Here are three tests in which we'll ask you to rate yourself as a listener. Your responses will extend your understanding of yourself as a listener. And highlight areas in which improvement might be welcome . . . to you and to those around you.

When you've completed the tests, please turn to the evaluation to see how your scores compare with those of thousands of others who've taken the same tests before you.

Quiz #1

A. Circle the term that best describes you as a listener.
Superior   Excellent   Above Average   Average   Below Average   Poor   Terrible

B. On a scale of 0 to 100 (100 = highest), how would you rate yourself as a listener?

_____
(0 - 100)

?

Quiz #2

How do you think the following people would rate you as a listener? (1 - 100)
Your Best Friend _____
Your Boss _____
Business Colleague _____
A Job Subordinate _____
Your Spouse _____

?

Quiz #3

As a listener, how often do you find yourself engaging in these ten bad listening habits? First, check the appropriate columns. Then tabulate your score using the key on the following page.

HOW WELL DO YOU LISTEN?

Listening Habit	Almost always	Usually	Sometimes	Seldom	Almost never	Score*
1. Calling the subject uninteresting						
2. Criticizing the speaker's delivery or mannerisms						
3. Getting overstimulated by something the speaker says						
4. Listening primarily for facts						
5. Trying to outline everything						
6. Faking attention to the speaker						
7. Allowing interfering distractions						
8. Avoiding difficult material						
9. Letting emotion-laden words arouse personal antagonism						
10. Wasting the advantage of thought speed (daydreaming)						
TOTAL SCORE						

*Key

For every "Almost always" checked, give yourself a score of 2
For every "Usually" checked, give yourself a score of 4
For every "Sometimes" checked, give yourself a score of 6
For every "Seldom" checked, give yourself a score of 8
For every "Almost never" checked, give yourself a score of 10

???

EVALUATION

This is how other people have responded to the same questions that you've just answered.

Quiz #1
A. 85% of all listeners questioned rated themselves as *Average* or less. Fewer than 5% rate themselves as *Superior* or *Excellent*.

B. On the 0–100 scale, the extreme range is 10–90; the general range is 35–85; and the *Average* rating is 55.

Quiz #2
When comparing the listening self-ratings and projected ratings of others, most respondents believe that their best friends would rate them highest as a listener. And that rating would be higher than the one they gave themselves in Quiz #1 . . . where the average was a 55.

How come? We can only guess that best friend status is such an intimate, special kind of relationship that you can't imagine its ever happening unless you were a good listener. If you weren't, you and he or she wouldn't be best friends to begin with.

Going down the list, people who take this test usually think that their bosses would rate them higher than they rated themselves. Now part of that is probably wishful thinking. And part of it is true. We do tend to listen to our bosses better . . . whether out of respect or fear or whatever.

The grades for colleague and job subordinate work out to be just about the same as the listener rated himself . . . that 55 figure again.

But when you get to spouse . . . husband or wife . . . something really dramatic happens. The score here is significantly lower than the 55 average that previous profile-takers gave themselves. And what's interesting

APTITUDE

is that the figure goes steadily downhill. While newlyweds tend to rate their spouse at the same high level as their best friend, as the marriage goes on . . . and on . . . the rating falls. So, in a household where the couple has been married 50 years, there could be a lot of talk—but maybe nobody really listening.

Quiz #3

The average score is 62 . . . 7 points higher than the 55 that the average test-taker gave himself in Quiz #1. Which suggests that when listening is broken down into specific areas of competence, we rate ourselves better than we do when listening is considered only as a generality.

Of course, the best way to discover how well you listen is to ask the people to whom you listen most frequently: your spouse, boss, best friend, etc. They'll give you an earful.

?

TEN KEYS TO EFFECTIVE LISTENING

These keys are a positive guideline to better listening. In fact, they're at the heart of developing better listening habits that could last a lifetime.

Key	The bad listener	The good listener
1. Find areas of interest	Tunes out dry subjects	Opportunitizes; asks "What's in it for me?"
2. Judge content, not delivery	Tunes out if delivery is poor	Judges content, skips over delivery errors
3. Hold your fire	Tends to enter into argument	Doesn't judge until comprehension complete
4. Listen for ideas	Listens for facts	Listens for central themes
5. Be flexible	Takes intensive notes using only one system	Takes fewer notes. Uses 4 to 5 different systems, depending on speaker
6. Work at listening	Shows no energy output. Attention is faked	Works hard, exhibits active body state
7. Resist distractions	Distracted easily	Fights or avoids distractions, tolerates bad habits, knows how to concentrate
8. Exercise your mind	Resists difficult expository material; seeks only light, recreational material	Uses heavier material as exercise for the mind
9. Keep your mind open	Reacts to emotional words	Interprets color words; does not get hung up on them
10. Capitalize on fact thought is faster than speech	Tends to daydream with slow speakers	Challenges, anticipates, mentally summarizes, weighs the evidence, listens between the lines to tone of voice

Courtesy of the Sperry Corporation.

La Piel Perfecta

Fee Schedule
1272 Winston Plaza at Melrose Park Clinic
Melrose Park, IL. 60160
Ph # (708) 615-7546

Laser Hair Removal:

Small areas such as upper lip of chin or sideburns	$150.00 Initial	$100.00 Thereafter
Beard	$325.00	$200.00
Neck	$225.00	$175.00
Chest	$450.00	$300.00
Lower abdomen	$175.00	$100.00
Abdomen/Shoulders	$300.00	$200.00
Back	$500.00	$400.00
Underarms	$225.00	$175.00
Lower Arms		
Bikini Line		
Bikini Brazilian		
Thighs	$375.00	$250.00
Lower Legs	$350.00	$225.00
Entire Legs	$650.00	$450.00

Laser Vein Removal:

Facial	$150.00 Minimum	$250.00 Multiple areas
Legs	$300.00 for 1/2 hour treatment	$500.00 for 1 hour treatment

Laser Wrinkle Removal:

Photo rejuvenation $150.00 (includes microdermabrasion $1200.00 Micro Laser Peel $900.00 up to 40 microns deep   (15 to 20 days down time)

Botox:

The most common areas to treat facial wrinkles with botox are: The frown lines, forehead, crow's feet and smoker's lines. The price for a single area is $250.00, two areas $400.00 and $100.00 for any additional areas.

Collagen:

The most common areas to treat wrinkles with collagen are the laugh and smoker's lines. Skin test is free of charge. Thereafter, $350.00 for each c.c. of collagen.

$450.00   Hylaform
$1000.00   Bioform

Endermologie:

Cellulite Massage Therapy is to be performed twice or once a week for the consecutive five to eight weeks.

16 sessions for $960.00
10 sessions for $700.00

Plastic surgery consultation

Appointments: Ph # (708) 615-SKIN

La Piel Perfecta

Fee Schedule
1272 Winston Plaza at Melrose Park Clinic
Melrose Park, IL. 60160
Ph # (708) 615-7546

Messotherapy (fat reduction):
$200 per session. Requires 4 to 6 treatments.

Titan (skin tightening):
$1200 face and neck.

Tatoo Removal:
Small	$50.00
Medium	$100.00
Large	$150.00
Super large	$300.00 per 1/2 hour

Appointments: Ph # (708) 615-SKIN

????????????
PERSONALITY
????????????

Your Lifestyle Profile

The Lifestyle Profile was developed by the Department of Health and Welfare of Canada. The test will tell you whether your present lifestyle has a positive or negative effect on your health. The answers to the questions include many helpful tips on how you can improve your lifestyle if it is indeed having a negative effect on your health.

Indicate by circling or checking only the signs that apply to you. The plus (+) and minus (−) signs next to some numbers indicate more than (+) and less than (−).

Exercise

Amount of physical effort expended during the workday: mostly

Heavy physical, walking, housework ○   Desk work ▽

Participation in physical activities—(skiing, golf, swimming, etc.—lawn mowing, gardening, etc.)?

Daily ○   Weekly ▽   Seldom □

Participation in a vigorous exercise program?

3 times weekly ○   Weekly ▽   Seldom □

Average miles walked or jogged per day?

1 + ○   − 1 ▽   None □

Flights of stairs climbed per day?

10 + ○   − 10 ▽   □

Nutrition

Are you overweight?

No ○   5 to 19 lbs. ▽   20 + lbs. □

Do you eat a wide variety of foods—something from each of the following five food groups: (1) meat, fish, poultry, dried legumes, eggs, or nuts; (2) milk or milk products; (3) bread or cereals; (4) fruits; (5) vegetables?

Each day ○   3 times weekly ▽   □

Alcohol

Average number of bottles (12 oz.) of beer per week?

0 to 7 ○   8 to 15 ▽   16 + □

Average number of hard liquor (1½ oz.) drinks per week?

0 to 7 ○   8 to 15 ▽   16 + □

PERSONALITY

Average number of glasses (5 oz.) of wine or cider per week

0 to 7	8 to 15	16 +
○	▽	□

Total number of drinks per week, including beer, liquor, and wine?

0 to 7	8 to 15	16 +
○	▽	□

Subtotals

Drugs

Do you take drugs illegally?

No	Yes
○	□

Do you consume alcoholic beverages together with certain drugs (tranquilizers, barbiturates, antihistamines, or illegal drugs)?

No	Yes
○	□

Do you use pain killers improperly or excessively?

No	Yes
○	□

Tobacco

Cigarettes smoked per day?

None	− 10	10 +
○	▽	□

Cigars smoked per day?

None	− 5	5 +
○	▽	□

Pipe tobacco pouches per week?

None	− 2	2 +
○	▽	□

Personal Health

Do you experience periods of depression?

Seldom	Occasionally	Frequently
○	▽	□

Does anxiety interfere with your daily activities?

No	Occasionally	Frequently
○	▽	□

Do you get enough satisfying sleep?

Yes	No
○	▽

Are you aware of the causes and dangers of VD?

Yes	No
○	▽

Breast self-examination? (Women only)

Monthly	Occasionally
○	▽

Subtotals

Road and Water Safety

Mileage per year as driver or passenger?

− 10,000	10,000 +
○	▽

Do you often exceed the speed limit?

No	by 10 mph +	by 20 mph +
○	▽	□

Do you wear a seatbelt?

Always	Occasionally	Never
○	▽	□

Do you drive a motorcycle, moped or snowmobile?

No	Yes
○	▽

If yes to the above, do you always wear a regulation safety helmet?

Yes	No
○	□

Do you ever drive under the influence of alcohol?

Never	Occasionally
○	□

Do you drive when your ability may be affected by drugs?

Never	Occasionally
○	□

YOUR LIFESTYLE PROFILE

Are you aware of water safety rules?

Yes ◯   No ▽

If you participate in water sports or boating, do you wear a life jacket? (If not applicable, do not score.)

Yes ◯   No ▽

General

Average time watching TV per day (in hours)?

0 to 1 ◯   1 to 4 ▽   4 + ▢

Are you familiar with first-aid procedures?

Yes ◯   No ▽

Do you ever smoke in bed?

No ◯   Occasionally ▽   Yes ▢

Do you always make use of clothing and equipment provided for your safety at work? (If not applicable, do not score.)

Yes ◯   Occasionally ▽   No ▢

Subtotals

SCORING SECTION

Count the total number of ◯ ▽ ▢.
1 point for each ◯ ; 3 points for each ▽ ; 5 points for each ▢.

Your Lifestyle Profile will indicate where lifestyle changes should be made, but only if you answer the questions as objectively as possible.

Excellent: 34 to 45: You have a commendable lifestyle based on sensible habits and lively awareness of personal health.

Good: 46 to 55: You have a sound grasp of basic health principles. With a minimum of change you can develop an excellent lifestyle pattern.

Risky: 56 to 65: You are taking unnecessary risks with your health. Several of your lifestyle habits are based on unwise personal choices which should be changed if potential health problems are to be avoided.

Hazardous: 66 and over: Either you have little personal awareness of good health habits or you are choosing to ignore them. This is a danger zone—but with a conscientious effort to improve basic living patterns even hazardous lifestyles can be modified and potential health problems overcome.

Reprinted from the *Journal of American Insurance,* Winter 1979-80.

?

????????????????????
Can You Control Your Jealousy?
??????????????????????

Are you overly watchful? Suspicious? Resentful? Envious? These are characteristics of a jealous person. While most psychologists agree that jealousy is instinctive, they also realize that if this natural reaction becomes persistent or obsessive, you may have a problem.

Is your jealousy normal or excessive? Are you alienating a loved one with your jealousy? The following test will help you assess your own jealousy level.

?

PART 1: WHAT DO YOU KNOW ABOUT JEALOUSY?

1. Psychologists agree that sexual jealousy is a sign of neurotic insecurity.
   _____ True.   _____ False.

2. Women are more jealous than men.
   _____ True.   _____ False.

3. A new parent of either sex may be jealous of the other parent's relationship with the baby.
   _____ True.   _____ False.

4. Jealousy is usually a sign of low self-esteem.
   _____ True.   _____ False.

5. Jealousy isn't all bad.
   _____ True.   _____ False.

6. Men and women react differently to jealousy.
   _____ True.   _____ False.

7. Jealousy often has some basis in reality.
   _____ True.   _____ False.

8. Jealousy has its roots in the relationship of mother and child.
   _____ True.   _____ False.

9. Jealousy is irrational.
   _____ True.   _____ False.

10. An emotionally healthy person is one who has eliminated all jealousy from his or her life.
    _____ True.   _____ False.

?

PART 2: ARE YOU A JEALOUS PERSON?

Would you be jealous if . . .

1. your best friend had begun to date someone seriously and never seemed to have time for you anymore?
   a. Yes.
   b. No.
   c. Maybe.

2. your wife/husband showed too much interest in a member of the opposite sex at a party?
   a. Yes.
   b. No.
   c. Maybe.

CAN YOU CONTROL YOUR JEALOUSY?

3. you put in a lot of work on an important project at work, but someone else got the credit for it?
    a. Yes.
    b. No.
    c. Maybe.

4. a close colleague received the promotion you had set your sights on?
    a. Yes.
    b. No.
    c. Maybe.

5. your lover expressed a desire to date other people?
    a. Yes.
    b. No.
    c. Maybe.

6. your spouse suggested "swinging" with another couple?
    a. Yes.
    b. No.
    c. Maybe.

7. a friend told you she had seen your lover out with someone else?
    a. Yes.
    b. No.
    c. Maybe.

8. your spouse called to say that he or she would be working late with an attractive colleague?
    a. Yes.
    b. No.
    c. Maybe.

9. your spouse admitted to going to bed with someone else but insisted that it had just been a one-night stand?
    a. Yes.
    b. No.
    c. Maybe.

10. you discovered that your lover had also been having an affair with someone else?
    a. Yes.
    b. No.
    c. Maybe.

Answers: Part 1

1. False. Psychologists do *not* agree on this matter, but most believe that a certain amount of jealousy is probably inevitable in intimate relationships.
2. False. Both sexes are equally susceptible to jealousy.
3. True. Although traditionally it is the father who is jealous, the mother may also jealously guard her position as the most important person in her child's life.
4. True. If you have no confidence in yourself, you can't understand what your spouse or lover sees in you. So you are easy prey to fears that he or she will leave you.
5. True. A certain amount of jealousy may be healthy for a relationship because it sustains interest and keeps the relationship exciting.
6. True. Men tend to react with anger and possessiveness; women tend to react with depression and self-reproach.
7. True. Jealous suspicions may be completely unfounded, but often they are precipitated or aggravated by neglect.
8. True. The mother-child bond sets the pattern for all other relationships throughout life.
9. True. Of course it is, but so are all relationships, both friendships and romances. Human beings, since they are not computers or machines, cannot be expected to conduct their lives with complete rationality.
10. False. Eliminating jealousy is probably an impossible, if not an undesirable, ideal.

?

Evaluation: Part 2

Give yourself ten points for each question to which you answered "yes"; give yourself five points for each question to which you answered "maybe."

If your total number of points was between 75 and 100, you are more jealous than the average person. Try to understand the reasons for your jealousy; it may be that you have deep-seated feelings of insecurity and are afraid of being deserted. Usually, a person who is this jealous believes that he or she is unworthy of love and is unsure of his or her ability to keep a lover interested or satisfied. A score between 50 and 75 shows that your level of jealousy is about average. If you are

PERSONALITY

concerned about your jealousy, you may want to analyze the types of situations that are making you jealous; perhaps they could be dealt with in a more open and less upsetting way. But a certain amount of jealousy is normal, and very few people can expect to be completly free of jealousy. If your score was below 50, you are much less jealous than the average person, and you probably have a very healthy self-image.

?

The Friendship Test
A New Way to Rate Your Friends

BY SUZANNE LEVINE

This fascinating test, developed with the help of three experts, lets you see just how each of your friends measures up and if the friendship is worth keeping.

Have you and your husband ever come home from an evening with your "dearest" friends, fed up to here with her name dropping, his practical jokes, or their boring stories? Has your best friend ever turned a luncheon date into a cross-examination by probing into your private matters? Has a good friend ever let you do all the arranging for a get-together and then failed to show up? With friends like these, who needs enemies, right?

Unfortunately, some friendships aren't what you hope they'll be. When this happens, whose fault—yours or theirs?

Chances are it isn't anyone's fault, because friendship isn't a one-sided affair; friendship doesn't happen to people, it happens *between* people.

Charles Perroncel, pastoral counselor at the Institutes of Religion and Health in New York City, says that friendship is a matter of negotiation. "One of the main problems of friendship," says Perroncel, "is to know how close a relationship is possible or desirable with a certain person. People thrive on an assortment of relationships—casual relations, intimate relationships, love relationships, etc.—and we must be able to negotiate the right relationship with the right person. But before we can decide where others fit in relation to ourselves, we must know what we are all about. We also have to know what we want. I say 'want' instead of 'need' because adults don't strictly need anything from each other; we can take care of ourselves. We want associations with other people, understandings, companionships. A person who feels that he or she *needs* something from another adult cannot negotiate a relationship as an equal. The need puts the person in a weaker position so that he or she can only wheedle into a relationship instead of stepping right up to it."

William Brockman, Perroncel's colleague at the Institutes, points out that your choice of friends tells an awful lot about you. "Everyone tends to act out myths about himself in dealings with other people," Brockman says. "A man or woman who feels unworthy and unreliable will often seek out friends with the same qualities."

"A great friendship," says Brockman, "is one that is based on the assumption: 'I'm okay and you're okay.' Friendship is as simple and as complex as that."

How do *your* friends measure up? The quiz below is designed to help you find out. It will help you evaluate what you are getting out of your relationships with people you count on as close friends. The questions were developed with the help of Perroncel, Brockman, and Carl Goldman, a professional group therapist, who finds it helpful in getting to know a new patient to ask, "Tell us about your friends."

Answer all the questions quickly and truthfully, keeping one friend in mind as you take the test. You can take the test over again for *each* friend you want to rate. When you have answered the questions, score and evaluate your friendships as instructed at the end.

PERSONALITY

SECTION 1

1. If your friend (hereafter called F) were planning a surprise party for you, F would
   A. be able to make up a guest list of all the people you really like.
   B. probably invite at least one person you secretly dislike.
   C. have no idea whom to invite.

2. If F were going to use your home while you were away, which preparation would be most important to you?
   A. Locking your desk.
   B. Getting the house cleaned.
   C. Replacing the torn shower curtain.

3. You and F have disagreements
   A. occasionally.
   B. often.
   C. never.

4. F has an idea of your income that is
   A. just about on the nose.
   B. way high.
   C. way low.

5. If F asked you to sell charity tickets and you didn't want to, you would
   A. say no.
   B. take a few, secretly buy half yourself and return the rest.
   C. take them, but return them later, saying you couldn't find buyers.

6. If you felt in retrospect that you might have hurt F's feelings you would
   A. call up to straighten it out.
   B. assume F would bring it up if you had.
   C. feel awful and try to make it up next time.

7. If you call F to ask a favor, you
   A. ask the favor first, then chat.
   B. chat first, then ask.
   C. never get around to asking.

8. You and F visit best
   A. over a meal.
   B. doing things together.
   C. by phone.

9. If you had a tentative date with F and felt like staying home to finish a good book, you would
   A. call it off, telling F the truth.
   B. call it off with a made-up excuse.
   C. go anyway.

10. If F heard a piece of gossip about you, F would probably
    A. alert you to what was being said.
    B. try to discourage the gossiper from repeating it.
    C. pass it on.

SECTION 2

11. If F bought you a million-dollar lottery ticket and you won, you would expect F to
    A. secretly want a share.
    B. ask for a share.
    C. be genuinely happy for you.

12. If you were giving an important party, you would
    A. want to invite F.
    B. feel you had to invite F.
    C. not invite F and hope the word didn't get out.

13. In your friendship, F is your
    A. confidante.
    B. cheerer-upper.
    C. doer-with-er.

14. If F saw your child shoplifting, F would
    A. tell you about it.
    B. confront your child.
    C. say nothing.

15. If you didn't like a friend of F's, you would
    A. say so and suggest that F not invite you together.
    B. try to turn F off this person.
    C. think less of F.

16. If F recommends a movie, your evaluation of it is usually
    A. as enthusiastic.
    B. cooler.
    C. negative.

THE FRIENDSHIP TEST

17. If F were an expert bridge player and you wanted to learn, you would
    A. ask F to teach you.
    B. read a book about it before you asked.
    C. sign up for a course.

18. When you and F are making plans, your ideas prevail
    A. about half the time.
    B. rarely.
    C. most of the time.

19. In making a mental list of F's main interests and yours, you would find that
    A. certain strong interests overlap.
    B. just about all overlap.
    C. you have very few interests in common.

20. If someone were meeting you and F for the first time, which of you would make the greater impression?
    A. It would depend on the circumstances.
    B. Most likely F.
    C. Most likely you.

SECTION 3

21. If something illegal in your past were uncovered, F would
    A. be concerned but loyal.
    B. probably cool the relationship.
    C. drop you fast.

22. If F were giving an important party, F would
    A. want to invite you.
    B. feel obliged to invite you.
    C. not invite you and hope you wouldn't find out.

23. If F said something that hurt you, you would
    A. blow up on the spot.
    B. stew about it and bring it up a few days later.
    C. keep quiet but nurse a grudge.

24. If you worked hard to win a jingle contest and won, you would tell F
    A. that you worked very hard for it.
    B. that it just came to you.
    C. that the judging must have been a matter of chance.

25. If you and F had a lunch date and F called to suggest including someone you didn't know, you would feel
    A. optimistic about the new acquaintance.
    B. insulted.
    C. relieved.

26. If someone told you that despite appearances, F was disloyal to you, you would
    A. deal first with the friend who told you.
    B. deal first with F.
    C. assume it was true and say nothing.

27. If you gave F a stock tip and the stock went down, F would
    A. figure it was all in the game.
    B. want to make sure you had some of the stock.
    C. hold it against you.

28. How ill do you have to be to feel justified in calling off an appointment with F?
    A. Under the weather.
    B. Catching a cold.
    C. Running a fever.

29. If F gave you a gift that turned out to be defective, you would
    A. tell F and work out who would take it back.
    B. take it back yourself.
    C. keep it.

30. If you overheard F describing you to someone who had never met you, the description would sound
    A. pretty much the way you would describe yourself.
    B. like a total stranger.
    C. unflattering.

Score each section of the quiz (1, 2, 3) separately. Allow 1 point for each A answer, 2 points for each B answer and 3 points for each C answer. Total up the points for each section and check the figures against the scoring below.

SECTION 1 is geared to reveal how close you really feel to a friend, how open and trusting the relationship is.

Under 15 Points: You've got a nice give-and-take friendship. You feel confident enough of the relationship to relax in it.

PERSONALITY

Between 15 and 27: This isn't really an intimate friendship. You might feel better if you accepted it as just a satisfying acquaintanceship and didn't press for anything deeper.

Over 27: You're barely scratching the surface. You hardly know this friend, and it undoubtedly works both ways. Best to renegotiate this one and keep in touch in groups rather than one-to-one.

SECTION 2 will explain and clarify the above conclusions. It tests how well you respect and trust a friend and how realistic your appraisal is.

Under 15: A healthy sense of mutual respect makes this friendship important and valuable to you.

Between 15 and 27: You don't pay much attention to the relationship. When you do, you are probably more annoyed or disconcerted than enlightened by this friend's company.

Over 27: You're hanging around with a "creep," or at least that's the way it strikes you. Needless to say, you could do better in choosing a close friend.

SECTION 3 is the clincher. It gives an insight into how good you feel about yourself in this relationship.

Under 15: You're probably thriving on an "I'm okay; you're okay" outlook about this friend.

Between 15 and 27: You probably feel that you didn't really choose this friendship. It just sort of happened—and you are playing a role that may be comfortable, but it's a role nonetheless. And as such, it makes you feel like a bit of a phony. That's no way to run a friendship.

Over 27: This relationship is doing more harm than good. Any attempt to force intimacy is a waste of your time and an indignity to yourself.

© 1974 LHJ Publishing, Inc. Reprinted with permission of *Ladies' Home Journal.*

?

How Tolerant Are You?

Tolerance is something we all like to think we have. . . . It is not just a matter of flexibility, nor simply permissiveness, nor is it the bottling up of feelings that we would otherwise have vigorously expressed. It is clearly tied up with empathy—the capacity to put ourselves into another person's shoes and see the world from their viewpoint. In a strange way it is also our capacity to see how other people view us. Aggressive or apparently ill-mannered behavior on the part of another individual may reflect his or her misjudgment of your personality and your actions, and recognizing this misjudgment in others is one of the greatest measures of tolerance.

In our complex, overpopulated world, the faults of others are often amplified because of the sheer proximity between people—not only in a physical but also psychological sense. Tolerance, therefore, is an essential quality for peaceful and harmonious living in a society that admits, within the law, so many different ways of thinking and behaving. . . . While it is easy to detect intolerance in others, it is not so easy to pin it down in ourselves. This test, if answered honestly and accurately, will give you some pointers.

?

Mark your answers on a separate sheet.

1. When a friend does something you very much disapprove of, do you
    a. break off the friendship?
    b. tell him how you feel, but keep in touch?
    c. tell yourself it is none of your business, and behave toward him as you always did?

2. Is it hard for you to forgive someone who has seriously hurt you?
    a. Yes.
    b. No.
    c. It is not hard to *forgive*, but you don't forget.

3. Do you think that
    a. censorship is vitally necessary to preserve moral standards?
    b. a small degree of censorship may be necessary, to protect children for instance?
    c. all censorship is wrong?

4. Are most of your friends
    a. people very much like you?
    b. very different from you and from each other?
    c. like you in some important respects, but different in others?

5. You are trying to work and concentrate, but the noise of children playing outside distracts you. Would you
    a. feel glad that they are having a good time?
    b. feel furious with them?
    c. feel annoyed, but acknowledge to yourself that kids do make a noise?

6. If you were traveling abroad and found that conditions were much less hygienic than you are used to, would you
    a. adapt quite easily?
    b. laugh at your own discomfort?
    c. think what a filthy country it is?

PERSONALITY

7. Which virtue do you think is most important?
   a. Kindness
   b. Honesty
   c. Obedience

8. Do you discuss critically one friend with others?
   a. Often
   b. Rarely
   c. Sometimes

9. If someone you dislike has a piece of good luck, would you
   a. feel angry and envious?
   b. wish it had been you, but not really mind?
   c. think "Good for him"?

10. When you have a strong belief, do you
    a. try very hard to make others see things in the same way as you?
    b. put forward your point of view, but stop short of argument or persuasion?
    c. keep it to yourself, unless directly asked?

11. A friend is suffering from depression. Everything in his life seems to be fine, but he complains to you that he always feels depressed. Would you
    a. listen sympathetically?
    b. tell him to pull himself together?
    c. take him out to cheer him up?

12. Would you employ someone who had had a severe nervous breakdown?
    a. No.
    b. Yes, provided there was medical evidence of complete recovery.
    c. Yes, if he were suitable in other ways for the work.

13. "Morality is relative." Do you
    a. strongly agree?
    b. agree up to a point?
    c. strongly disagree?

14. When you meet someone who strongly disagrees with your views, do you
    a. argue and lose your temper?
    b. enjoy a good argument and keep your cool?
    c. avoid argument?

15. Do you ever read a periodical that supports political views very different from yours?
    a. Never.
    b. Sometimes, if you come across it.
    c. Yes, you make a special effort to read it.

16. Which statement do you most agree with?
    a. If crime were more severely punished, there would be less of it.
    b. A better society would reduce the need for crime.
    c. I wish I knew the answer to the problem of crime.

17. Do you think
    a. that some rules are necessary for social living, but the fewer the better?
    b. that people must have rules because they need to be controlled?
    c. that rules are tyrannical?

18. If you are a religious believer, do you think
    a. that your religion is the only right one?
    b. that all religions have something to offer their believers?
    c. that nonbelievers are wicked people?

19. If you are not a religious believer, do you think
    a. that only stupid people are religious?
    b. that religion is a dangerous and evil force?
    c. that religion seems to do good for some people?

20. Do you react to old people with
    a. patience and good humor?
    b. annoyance?
    c. sometimes a, sometimes b?

21. Do you think the Women's Liberation movement is
    a. run by a bunch of lesbians?
    b. an important, if overstated, social movement?
    c. a joke?

22. Would you marry someone of a different race?
    a. Yes.
    b. No.
    c. Not without thinking carefully about the various problems involved.

HOW TOLERANT ARE YOU?

23. If your brother told you that he was a homosexual, would you
    a. send him to a psychiatrist?
    b. accept him, and his lover?
    c. feel shocked and reject him?

24. When young people question authority, do you
    a. feel uneasy?
    b. think that it is a good thing?
    c. feel angry?

25. Which statement do you agree with?
    a. Marriage is a bad institution.
    b. Marriage is sacred and must be upheld.
    c. Marriage is often difficult, but seems to meet the needs of many people.

26. Do you think you are right—in matters of belief rather than fact—
    a. often?
    b. rarely?

27. If you stay in a household that is run differently from yours in matters of tidiness and regularity of meals, do you
    a. fit in quite happily?
    b. feel constantly irritated by the chaos or the rigid orderliness of the place?
    c. find it fairly easy for a while, but not for too long?

28. Do other people's personal habits annoy you?
    a. Often.
    b. Not at all.
    c. Only if they are extreme, or you are edgy.

29. Which statement do you most agree with?
    a. We should not judge other people's actions, because no one can ever fully understand the motives of another.
    b. People are responsible for their actions and have to take the consequences.
    c. Even if it is tough on some people, actions have to be judged.

?

SCORES

(Total your scores to find your analysis below.)

1.	a. 4	b. 2	c. 0	16.	a. 4	b. 2	c. 0
2.	a. 0	b. 0	c. 2	17.	a. 0	b. 4	c. 4
3.	a. 4	b. 0	c. 4	18.	a. 4	b. 0	c. 4
4.	a. 4	b. 0	c. 2	19.	a. 4	b. 4	c. 0
5.	a. 0	b. 4	c. 2	20.	a. 0	b. 4	c. 2
6.	a. 0	b. 0	c. 4	21.	a. 4	b. 0	c. 4
7.	a. 0	b. 2	c. 4	22.	a. 0	b. 4	c. 2
8.	a. 4	b. 0	c. 2	23.	a. 2	b. 0	c. 4
9.	a. 4	b. 2	c. 0	24.	a. 2	b. 0	c. 4
10.	a. 4	b. 2	c. 0	25.	a. 4	b. 4	c. 0
11.	a. 0	b. 4	c. 2	26.	a. 4	b. 0	
12.	a. 4	b. 2	c. 0	27.	a. 0	b. 4	c. 2
13.	a. 0	b. 2	c. 4	28.	a. 4	b. 0	c. 2
14.	a. 4	b. 0	c. 2	29.	a. 0	b. 4	c. 2
15.	a. 4	b. 2	c. 0				

EVALUATION

For a quick and very broad view of your level of tolerance compared to your family and friends, refer to the "Tolerance Thermometer." Use the space to the right of it to mark the names and scores of everyone who takes the test: you may find that the results will surprise you!

For a more detailed discussion of your individual level of tolerance, read the section of the following analysis that relates to your score.

Below 30: If your score lies in this range you are a particularly tolerant person. You are exceedingly aware of others' problems and difficulties and you have a natural capacity for accepting them even when they offend you. You will be a good friend and popular with others. You may find that other people abuse this sympathetic good nature because they have nothing to fear from recriminations. Even then, you do not get really cross with them.

31 to 60: You are a tolerant person and people will recognize you as one. If your score is above 50, however, you are probably tolerant and broad-minded in some areas only. Actually it is easy to be tolerant if one does not hold very firm beliefs about anything. Look through the questions again and note where you picked up high rather than low scores. Were these questions where personal comfort was directly concerned or where convictions or very strong ideological beliefs were touched upon?

PERSONALITY

61 to 89: You are not as tolerant as many people and if your score is higher than 80 you are basically an intolerant type of person. This will lead to clashes and short-term friendships. It will also mean that little things trouble you far more than they should and that you may waste emotional energy on what is really rather insignificant. It is very likely that you count yourself as someone with high principles, one tending to stick to important things rather than trivia. If you can get a wider experience of life and greater genuine contact with people, however, your tolerance temperature would come down and in the end you would feel happier for it.

Over 90: This high score indicates that you are a very intolerant person. If your score is over a hundred then you are also bossy, over-opinionated, and over-quick to take offense. The only kind of friends you are likely to retain are those interested in your money or generosity. If you really have scored this high, ask yourself *why* you are so unable to accept the faults in others. What are the aspects of other people that offend you most? Could it be that you are really punishing yourself for faults you see in yourself?

Excerpted with permission from *Understanding Yourself*, by Christopher Evans, © 1977, A & W Publishers, Inc. and Phoebus Publishing Company.

??

TOLERANCE THERMOMETER

Check your tolerance temperature. The higher your "temperature" on the thermometer, the more intolerant you are—and the closer to boiling point!

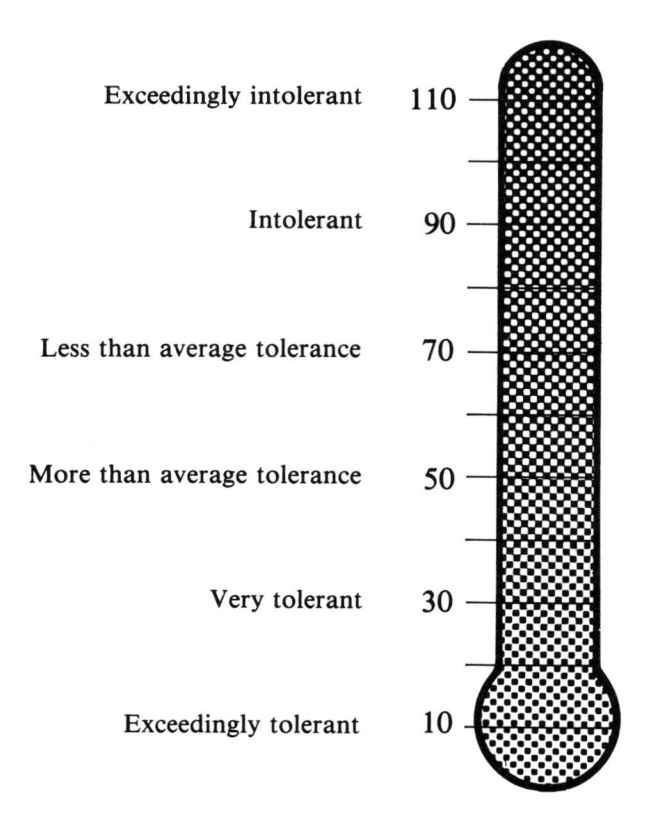

Exceedingly intolerant	110
Intolerant	90
Less than average tolerance	70
More than average tolerance	50
Very tolerant	30
Exceedingly tolerant	10

The Honesty Test

You probably think of yourself as honest. After all, you would never lie, steal, or cheat—would you?

Do you always tell the truth, or do you sometimes take the easy way out? Are you occasionally guilty of "little white lies"? Do you tell yourself that everybody does it?

Can you truthfully say that you have never taken anything that doesn't belong to you? Are you honest about not stealing from individuals, but not so scrupulous when it comes to "ripping off" large corporations or the government? Have you ever falsified an insurance claim or a tax return?

Perhaps you're not as honest as you thought you were. This test will show you just how honest you really are.

?

1. In a supermarket parking lot, you accidentally back into another car and dent the rear fender. No one has seen you. What do you do?
    a. Leave a note with your name, address, and telephone number.
    b. Drive away.
    c. Not sure.

2. Suppose someone else dents *your* car. Do you
    a. try to persuade the auto shop to pad its estimate so you'll get more money from the insurance company?
    b. instruct the repair shop to give a true estimate?
    c. Not sure.

3. In a department store, you buy a nineteen-dollar item with a twenty-dollar bill, and by mistake the clerk gives you a five-dollar bill as your change. Do you
    a. return it?
    b. keep it?
    c. Not sure.

4. Your monthly charge-account statement has arrived, and you see that your bill is $500 too low. You realize that the store has not charged you for a $500 chair you bought. Do you
    a. notify the store?
    b. say nothing?
    c. Not sure.

5. Suppose you find a wallet with several thousand dollars in it. Do you
    a. say nothing?
    b. report it to the police?
    c. Not sure.

6. You order a book through the mail, but after a month it hasn't arrived, so you write to the company and it agrees to send you another. The next day you receive the first book, and soon afterward the second one arrives. Now you have two books. Do you
    a. return one?
    b. keep them both or give one to a friend?
    c. Don't know.

PERSONALITY

7. Suppose your house burns down and you have to file a report with your insurance company. Do you
    a. report only what was actually in the house?
    b. include in the report a diamond ring that wasn't in the house because it had been lost a few months earlier?
    c. Don't know.

8. You are building a porch for your summer home. When the construction is almost finished, you learn that the porch violates a local zoning law. One of your neighbors, however, reports that the building inspector has been amenable to bribery in the past. Do you
    a. offer the building inspector a bribe?
    b. take down the porch?
    c. Don't know.

9. You are looking for a new job because you were fired from your last one. Do you
    a. tell the truth about why you left?
    b. pretend you're still working?
    c. hedge a little and try to present yourself in the best possible light?

10. A business colleague asks you to cover for her. She is taking the afternoon off, but she wants you to say she's at a meeting if anyone calls. Do you
    a. agree to go along?
    b. tell her you refuse?
    c. agree, but if anyone calls say only that she's not at her desk?

11. Suppose a friend asks you to give him a reference for a job that you don't think he can handle. Do you
    a. agree to give a favorable reference?
    b. tell your friend you won't do it?
    c. try to give a noncommittal reference that avoids mentioning his faults?

12. You are applying for a job for which a master's degree is a prerequisite. Although you have only a bachelor's, you're sure you can do the job. What do you do?
    a. List a master's degree on your resume.
    b. List only the degree you actually have.
    c. Not sure.

13. If you are a student, would you consider buying a term paper from one of the "term-paper factories"?
    a. Yes.
    b. No.
    c. Maybe.

14. When you were in school, did you ever cheat on exams?
    a. Yes.
    b. No.

15. Have you ever stolen a towel or anything else from a hotel or motel?
    a. Yes.
    b. No.

16. Have you ever taken home anything from the office—pens, pencils, stationery, etc.?
    a. Yes.
    b. No.

17. If you felt like taking a day off from work, would you call in sick even if you weren't?
    a. Yes.
    b. No.
    c. Maybe.

18. Suppose you are a salesperson with an expense account. When you take a client to lunch, do you
    a. report only what you spent?
    b. report a larger amount and pocket the difference?
    c. Don't know.

19. You are paid for some free-lance work that is not reported to the IRS. Do you include this income on your tax return?
    a. Yes.
    b. No.
    c. Maybe.

20. When you file your income tax return, do you
    a. claim only the deductions you're entitled to?
    b. exaggerate your deductions, even making up some expenses that you didn't really incur?
    c. only exaggerate a little, if you're sure you won't get caught?

THE HONESTY TEST

ANSWERS

Find the number of points next to the letter of each answer that you gave. Then add all the points to determine your total score.

1. a-5; b-0; c-2
2. a-0; b-5; c-2
3. a-5; b-0; c-2
4. a-5; b-0; c-2
5. a-0; b-5; c-2
6. a-5; b-0; c-2
7. a-5; b-0; c-2
8. a-0; b-5; c-2
9. a-5; b-0; c-2
10. a-0; b-5; c-2
11. a-0; b-5; c-2
12. a-5; b-0; c-2
13. a-0; b-5; c-2
14. a-0; b-5
15. a-0; b-5
16. a-0; b-5
17. a-0; b-5; c-2
18. a-5; b-0; c-2
19. a-5; b-0; c-2
20. a-5; b-0; c-2

EVALUATION

For those who attained a near perfect or perfect score, 90 to 100, you are scrupulously honest—so much so, in fact, that you may find it difficult to live in this imperfect world. With a score of 75 to 87 you are honest enough, at least for everyday purposes. Who cares if you tell a "little white lie" now and then? Doesn't everybody? The rest of you, with scores below 72, need to be careful or lying may become a way of life. Don't be disheartened, however, if your score was lower than you expected: you have plenty of company. Most people find it difficult or impossible to resist temptation *all* the time, and a perfect score of 100 on this test is a rarity. As Hamlet tells Polonius, "To be honest, as this world goes, is to be one man picked out of ten thousand."

?

How Assertive Are You?

Are you assertive? Do you feel confident of your ability to get what you want most of the time, or do you feel like a victim? Do you stand up for your rights, or do you let people push you around? Are you responsible for the circumstances of your life, or do you feel as though things are out of control? If you feel powerless, if you lack self-confidence or self-respect, if you are unable to express your feelings honestly, to others or even to yourself, perhaps you need to be more assertive.

?

1. Your next-door neighbors are playing their stereo late at night. You
    a. do nothing, even though it interferes with your sleep.
    b. angrily berate them for their lack of consideration, threatening to call the police.
    c. explain that you're trying to sleep and ask if they would mind turning the volume down.

2. A man (or woman) in whom you're not interested keeps calling you. Finally you say,
    a. "Er . . . well . . . not tonight; I have to wash my hair."
    b. "Get off my back, you leech! Don't call me; I'll call you!"
    c. "I'm sorry, but I don't want to go out with you, and I think you should stop calling me."

3. In a restaurant, you are served a tough, overcooked steak. You
    a. fume silently, complaining to your dinner partner.
    b. call the waitress over and loudly demand to see the manager.
    c. politely but firmly insist that the waitress bring you another steak.

4. An insurance salesman comes to your door. You
    a. let him in, even though you're not interested in buying insurance.
    b. slam the door in his face.
    c. say, "No, thank you, I'm not interested."

5. A friend drops in while you're in the middle of cleaning your house. You say,
    a. "Oh, hi . . . come in."
    b. "How can I get anything done with you here? Why don't you call first?"
    c. "I'm glad to see you, but I really don't have time to visit right now. Maybe some other time."

6. You buy something in a store, and as you are leaving you discover that you have been shortchanged. You
    a. think about it for a moment, then decide it isn't worth going back for a few cents.
    b. go back and loudly accuse the cashier of incompetence and/or stealing.
    c. go back to the cashier and explain that you were shortchanged, displaying the change you did get, which is still in your hand.

HOW ASSERTIVE ARE YOU?

7. Your spouse comes home for dinner several hours late. You
    a. quietly start preparing a second dinner.
    b. scream, yell, or cry that he is an inconsiderate jerk and can get his own dinner.
    c. calmly explain that you are disappointed and that his dinner is in the refrigerator.

8. Your supervisor unexpectedly asks you to work late on a night when you have an important date. You
    a. agree to work late.
    b. angrily refuse, criticizing the boss's poor scheduling practices.
    c. calmly refuse to work late and explain why.

9. Someone lights a cigarette and blows smoke in your direction. You
    a. suffer in silence.
    b. say, "Put that disgusting cigarette out! Don't you know they cause cancer?"
    c. say, "I'd really appreciate it if you wouldn't smoke here."

10. One of your employees has been coming in late to work. You
    a. grumble to the other employees but say nothing to the person who is late.
    b. loudly and angrily tell the employee that he or she will be fired unless he or she shapes up.
    c. ask the employee whether he or she has some particular reason for being late to work. If not, you say that you expect him or her to be on time from now on.

11. You notice a group of people at a party and decide you would like to approach them. You
    a. stand next to the group but don't say anything, hoping someone will notice you.
    b. interrupt the person who is speaking, saying that you disagree and state your viewpoint.
    c. wait until the speaker is finished and then introduce yourself.

12. Aunt Agatha, one of your least favorite relatives, has announced her intention to inflict herself upon you for a three-week visit. You say,
    a. "Why, of course; we'd love to have you."
    b. "No, we can't possibly entertain you this month; we have too many important things to do."
    c. "We'd love to have you come for the weekend, but not for a three-week stay; a shorter visit would be better for everyone."

13. Someone criticizes your hairstyle. You
    a. worry about it and finally change to another style.
    b. defensively rebuke the critic and refuse to change.
    c. ignore the criticism, realizing that you can't please everybody.

14. Someone asks you what you consider to be personal questions. You
    a. answer all the questions, later feeling embarrassed and manipulated.
    b. tell the person angrily, "It's none of your damn business."
    c. say that the questioner is prying and that you don't intend to discuss the matter.

15. You purchase an article of clothing in a store, but after you get it home you decide that you aren't satisfied with it. You
    a. don't return the garment.
    b. go back to the store and call the salesperson a crook for selling you defective merchandise.
    c. return the garment and quietly but firmly insist on a refund.

16. Someone cuts ahead of you while you are standing in line. You
    a. say nothing but fume inwardly.
    b. shout "Hey! What do you think you are doing?"
    c. tell the person to go to the end of the line; you don't allow people to cut in front of you.

PERSONALITY

17. A friend who has owed you money for years has never offered to repay you. You
    a. say nothing, wishing he would send you the money.
    b. drop some broad hints about people who don't meet their obligations.
    c. tell your friend that you want the money back immediately.

18. A salesperson calls you on the phone and tries to sell you something you don't want. You
    a. allow yourself to be drawn into a long conversation and finally agree to buy the product.
    b. hang up without saying anything.
    c. simply say, "No, I'm not interested," and hang up.

19. You eat dinner at a restaurant and you feel that you have been given poor service. You
    a. say nothing and leave the usual tip.
    b. don't leave a tip and complain loudly to the other patrons as you walk out.
    c. don't leave a tip and tell the management why.

20. You are asked to be the organizer for an office party, but you don't want to do it. You
    a. do it anyway.
    b. do it, but complain loudly so that everyone will know how miserable you are.
    c. quietly refuse without feeling guilty.

SCORING

Count the number of *a, b,* and *c* responses you gave. If you chose the *a* answers to most of the questions, you are *nonassertive*. You probably tend to deny yourself, to sacrifice your needs to those of others a good deal of the time. You hesitate to express your own opinions or feelings, have low self-esteem, and consider the wishes of others to be more important than your own. You fear trying new things and don't really get much enjoyment out of life. If you chose the *b* answers to most of the questions, you are *aggressive*. You respond to provocation with anger; you are likely to interrupt or to speak loudly and abusively. You tend to overreact. By your actions you seem to be saying that you value yourself above others, but this may be only a defense to hide your fear that you really aren't important. Aggression is often confused with assertion, but it differs from assertion in that it is compulsive and uncontrolled; the aggressive person is just as victimized as the nonassertive person. If you chose a majority of *c* answers, you are *assertive*. You insist on your own rights without infringing on the rights of others; you state your feelings and wishes honestly and directly without being rude or abusive; your self-esteem is high, but you have as much respect for others as you have for yourself.

?

????????????????????????????????
What Does Your Handwriting Reveal about You?
??????????????????????????????

Your signature is incredible. In our paper economy it's extremely valuable because it's so unique that only once in about 68 trillion chances could there be another person who writes exactly as you do. That's what makes handwriting phenomenal.

If you lost the use of your hands and had to learn to write with the pen in your mouth or toes, the same writing characteristics would appear in that writing that did in your handwriting. Studies such as those conducted by Dr. Werner Wolff and included in his book *Diagrams of the Unconscious* give evidence that many factors of your writing remain consistent throughout your lifetime. The brain impulses produce the consistent characteristics, and very often handwriting is called *brainwriting* as a result.

You write your signature more often than anything else. The probability is that you've played around with it, tried to make it appear impressive or distinctive, or tried to make it look like something other than the combination of letters that make up your name. Since your signature is so well practiced, it can slip off your pen or pencil easily and quickly. It's actually a confirmed habit.

Your signature is also your parade. Its letters march by for anyone to view them. Knowing you're on display, you may not step along in your normal way. You may want to strut your stuff by prancing like a baton twirler, goose-stepping like a soldier, or sliding along like an ice skater, depending on the impression you want to make.

How you handle your signature can be most revealing. In itself, it's significant; but to be fairly evaluated, it must be compared to your regular writing.

Although the following handwriting test is oversimplified to allow you, a non-graphologist, to make determinations about your writing, it will give you important clues about yourself.

On a piece of transparent paper, write the following:

This is the way I sign my name:_____
(Your Signature)

Place the paper on which you wrote the sentence and your name over the following lines and rest the imaginary baseline of your sentence on the heaviest line. Then answer the questions that follow.

PERSONALITY

1. Small letters without upper or lower loops (a, e, c, i, m, n, o, r, s, u, v, w) are
    a. within the first space.
    b. no taller than two spaces.
    c. taller than three spaces.
    d. different sizes.

2. Compared to your signature capitals and the capital that begins the sentence, the height of your personal pronoun "I" is
    a. smaller.
    b. about the same size.
    c. taller.
    d. different in style.

3. When the paper is held up against the light, the writing appears
    a. faint; hard to read.
    b. light in color, but easy to read.
    c. strongly colored or dense.
    d. sometimes light; sometimes dark.

4. The letters appear to form
    a. scallops at letter bottoms.
    b. saw-teeth.
    c. arches at letter tops.
    d. wiggles.

5. The letters appear to slant
    a. to the left.
    b. to the right.
    c. up and down.
    d. in different directions.

82

WHAT DOES YOUR HANDWRITING REVEAL ABOUT YOU?

6. The oval parts of the letters a, d, g, o, q are
    a. narrow and/or retraced.
    b. as wide as they are tall.
    c. very wide or full.
    d. various widths.

7. The letter parts that seem to predominate are
    a. lower loops of f, g, j, p, q, y, z.
    b. between upper and lower loops.
    c. upper loops of f, h, k, l, b.
    d. None predominate.

8. All upper and/or lower loops seem to appear
    a. long and lean.
    b. in good shape; average.
    c. wide and full.
    d. sometimes narrow; sometimes wide.

9. Compared to your writing generally, the height of the small letters and the height of the capitals in your signature generally are
    a. shorter.

    b. the same.

    c. taller.

    d. totally different.

PERSONALITY

TEST EVALUATION

Self-Regard. No. 1 and No. 2 are the mainstay of your self-concept. In No. 1 the small letters indicate the relative size of your ego. No. 2 tells you how a one-letter word, the personal pronoun "I," reflects the way you feel about yourself inwardly. The two should be taken in combination.

1.
   a. Unassuming; modest.
   b. Good self-assurance.
   c. Strong self-assurance.
   d. Inconsistent feelings; insecure.

2.
   a. Humble; introvertive.
   b. Secure about self-concept.
   c. Overdeveloped self-concept.
   d. Extraordinary self-concept.

Innate Temperament. No. 3 indicates the kind of pressure you exert in life—it's usually inherent but your environment can cause an impact in this area. Pressure is a measure of your available energy. The manner in which you meet life's challenges is indicated in No. 4 by your preference for curves or straight lines..

3.
   a. Use of nervous energy.
   b. Good sustaining energy.
   c. Strong energy.
   d. Changeable energies.

4.
   a. Flexible; friendly.
   b. Unyielding; argumentative.
   c. Proper; reserved.
   d. Unpredictable.

Relationship to Others. The slant of your writing can be a strong indicator of your responsiveness to others as shown in No. 5. The ovals in No. 6 are indicative of your capacity for give-and-take in life situations.

5.
   a. Defiant; aloof.
   b. Compliant; expressive.
   c. Self-reliant; evaluative.
   d. Depends on the situation.

6.
   a. Inhibited, ungiving.
   b. Outgoing; does what's expected.
   c. Extrovertive; generous.
   d. Vacillates.

Motivation. The upper and lower loops of No. 7 are clues to what spur you on while those in No. 8 show where the action is.

7.
   a. Money, possessions and/or sex.
   b. Day-to-day concerns.
   c. Intellectual pursuits.
   d. Balanced interests.

8.
   a. Thinking and operating restricted.
   b. Good operational functioning.
   c. Strong imaginative powers.
   d. Thinking and operations depend on urges and mood of the moment.

Genuine vs. Facade. When your signature is like the rest of your writing, you're A-OK; otherwise, you're puttin' on.

9.
   a. Assumes an air of humbleness and humility.
   b. Sincere and genuine.
   c. Wears armor of bravado; wants to impress.
   d. Hides what he/she is.

Note: The combinations of the above qualities give an astronomical number of possible character variations.

Courtesy of the American Association of Handwriting Analysts, a nonprofit organization.

??

??????????????????????????
How Do Your Manners Measure Up?
??????????????????????????

In the days of Emily Post, manners were cut-and-dry; there were specific rules about what to do in a given social situation and what to wear while you were doing it.

Today's world is different. Manners are more casual, less formal. Certain trends of the sixties and seventies, such as the counter culture, the glamorization of youth, and the women's movement, have had a profound effect on social customs. Indeed, many previously accepted customs are now considered anachronistic and affected. Few people today have time to be concerned with the finer points of "gracious living"—which fork to use with which course, or how to word a formal invitation. But there are some things that never go out of style, and there will always be a need for good manners. The following questions will test your knowledge of etiquette à la Emily Post.

?

1. Traditionally, one introduces
    a. a younger person to an older person and a man to a woman.
    b. an older person to a younger person and a woman to a man.
    c. in alphabetical order if possible.

2. If someone mispronounces a word, it's best to
    a. correct him or her softly but firmly.
    b. wait a few minutes and then use the word yourself, pronouncing it correctly.
    c. avoid using the word, by paraphrasing if you have to.
    d. pronounce the word wrong too.

3. If someone compliments your dress or suit, you should say,
    a. "What, this old thing? I've had it for years."
    b. "Do you really like it? I don't."
    c. "No, yours is much more attractive."
    d. "Thank you."

4. The correct way to answer a home telephone is
    a. "Smith residence."
    b. "Mr. Smith speaking."
    c. "John Smith speaking."
    d. "Hello."

5. The best way to ask a woman (or a man) for a date is
    a. "What are you doing Saturday night?"
    b. "Have you seen *A Chorus Line*?"
    c. "I have two tickets to *A Chorus Line* on Saturday night. Would you like to go with me?"
    d. "What do *you* want to do?"

6. When visiting a sick person in the hospital,
    a. take a gift of candy, cake, or fruit.
    b. sit on the edge of the patient's bed so that an air of informality prevails.
    c. ask the patient all about his or her illness.
    d. stay for only a short time, and don't do anything that will tax or upset your friend.

PERSONALITY

7. If a lone woman in an elevator full of men is standing in the back of the elevator,
    a. the men should make every effort to let her off the elevator first.
    b. the men should simply get off the elevator first.
    c. before deciding what to do, the men should ask the woman if she's a "women's libber."
    d. the woman should call the men "male chauvinist pigs" if they hesitate.

8. If you find yourself in a private home where no ashtrays are provided, you should
    a. refrain from smoking.
    b. use the wastebasket.
    c. lay your lighted cigarette on the coffee table.
    d. ask, "Do you mind if I smoke?"

9. Your host asks whether you'd prefer Scotch or Bourbon. You reply,
    a. "Whatever you're having."
    b. "Whichever is easier."
    c. "Bourbon" or "Scotch."
    d. "Rye."

10. A good house guest
    a. offers to take his or her hosts out to a restaurant.
    b. eats whatever is served.
    c. quietly refuses anything he or she cannot eat, without making a fuss.
    d. gives a long, apologetic explanation of his or her allergies or dislikes.

11. A good weekend host
    a. lets his guests know of any special plans, so that they can bring the appropriate clothing or equipment.
    b. asks guests when they would like to eat, sleep, bathe, etc., and changes the family's plans accordingly.
    c. gives guests a choice of activities such as swimming, tennis, or golf, and keeps asking them, even after they've decided, just in case they might have changed their minds.
    d. considers the weekend a failure if the guests would rather just relax and talk or read.

12. Which is the correct method for using a knife and fork?
    a. American style—hold the fork in your left hand, the knife in your right (if you are right-handed) and switch hands after you cut your food so that you are eating with your right hand.
    b. European style—keep the fork in your left hand and eat with that hand.
    c. Either way is correct, but European is probably smoother and more graceful.
    d. Cut all your food at once at the beginning of the meal.

13. If you are sending an invitation to a married couple in which the woman has retained her maiden name, you should
    a. address separate invitations.
    b. address them as Mr. & Mrs. . . . using his last name.
    c. send one invitation addressed to Mr. . . . and Ms. . . . , which should be written on one line.

14. A butler is addressed
    a. by his first name.
    b. by his last name.
    c. as "butler."
    d. as "sir."

15. Approximately how long should the cocktail time last before dinner is served?
    a. For two hours.
    b. For as long as everyone is having a good time.
    c. Up to one hour maximum.

16. If a former alcoholic is at your party, you should
    a. introduce him/her to everyone as a reformed alcoholic.
    b. treat him/her as you treat your other guests, asking what he/she would like for a predinner drink.
    c. offer him/her fruit juice or soda.

HOW DO YOUR MANNERS MEASURE UP?

ANSWERS

1. a	7. b	13. c
2. c	8. a	14. b
3. d	9. c	15. c
4. d	10. c	16. b
5. c	11. a	
6. d	12. c	

EVALUATION

You are a proper host or guest if you scored from 14 to 16; you know what is right and wrong, at least when it comes to etiquette. A score from 11 to 13 shows that you know what is expected but might not behave in the traditional, conservative style; and though you need to learn a little more about the finer points of gracious living, you would certainly know how to handle yourself at a party or in your own home. If you scored below 11 you could stand a little improvement. Even though today's manners are more casual, it can't hurt to know good manners because they never go out of style.

?

Your Weather Sensitivity Risk-Factor Profile

Forecasting the weather is now routine. We expect accurate weather reports every night on the news and in the daily papers. But the science of meteorology has been taken one step further, with a new field of study called Human Biometeorology. This new science is capable of forecasting people's comfort, health, moods, and behavior—as factors influenced by the weather! The potential is unlimited. The following weather sensitivity test will show how the weather affects you and how this information can lead to a better understanding of the human condition.

Give yourself the indicated points if you answer "yes" to a question. Answer all questions.

Trait	Points
Physique	
Are you lean, slender, or lanky?	3
Are you muscular, or of average build?	0
Are you broad, stocky, or stout?	1
Temperament	
Do you tend to be amiable, extroverted, or jolly?	1
Are you often emotionally changeable, excitable?	3
Do you tend to be easily led, or acquiescent?	3
Are you often irritable, or moody?	1
Do you tend to be easily depressed or pessimistic?	2
Are you often shy, inhibited, or private?	3
Do you tend to be nervous?	4
Socioeconomic Status	
Are you a professional, executive, or upper class?	3
Are you a middle management or a white collar worker?	0
Are you a blue collar, a clerical, or a factory laborer?	3
Age	
Are you 10 to 19 years old?	3
Are you 20 to 29 years old?	2
Are you 30 to 39 years old?	1
Are you 40 to 49 years old?	2
Are you 50 to 59 years old?	3
Are you older?	4
Sex	
Are you female?	3

From *Weathering: How the Atmosphere Conditions Your Body, Your Mind, Your Moods—And Your Health* by Stephen Rosen. Copyright © 1979 by Stephen Rosen. Reprinted by permission of the publisher, M. Evans and Company, Inc., New York, New York 10017.

EVALUATION

Add up the points you have checked to find out your weather-sensitivity score:

A score of 0 to 5 points indicates that you are relatively weather-resistant, or generally indifferent to the weather—except for the seasonally-dependent illnesses, or normal weather-related diseases, and the daily, monthly, or yearly weather changes.

From 6 to 10 points suggests that you are weather-receptive, and frequently aware of your reactions to weather changes.

Between 11 to 15 points, you are weather-sympathetic, and never indifferent to weather conditions.

If your score is 16 to 20 points, you are weather-susceptible, or always in touch with the weather and the symptoms it induces in you.

From 21 to 25 points, you are weather-responsive, and every passing front is felt in your body, your moods, and your behavior; they mirror the atmospheric conditions.

Above 25 points indicates weather-keenness, the ultimate sensitivity to weather in which severe pain or pleasure tends to accompany each weather situation. exceptional cases, it may reach extraordinary feelings about the weather, experienced by those rare individuals (often geniuses) who have a special "feel" for the weather, or weather-intimacy.

??????????????????????????
Are You Disorganized?
??????????????????????????

We all know people whose desks are piled high with papers but who say, "I know where everything is." Conversely, there are people who are compulsively neat, whose homes and offices are immaculate, but who can't find things when they need them.

Disorganization is a psychological problem. And the consequences can be serious. Your job and personal life can suffer if there are too many times when you just can't find what you need. To find out if disorganization is a problem for you, take this test; your answers will tell if you need to clean up your act.

?

1. Is your desk at work or at home piled high with papers?
   _____ Yes.   _____ No.

2. Do you have trouble finding a particular article of clothing in your closet?
   _____ Yes.   _____ No.

3. Do you feel that you *could* be organized if you only had more space?
   _____ Yes.   _____ No.

4. Do you have piles of newspapers and magazines at home that you don't have time to read?
   _____ Yes.   _____ No.

5. Are there papers on your desk that have been there for at least a week?
   _____ Yes.   _____ No.

6. Do you ever find something at the bottom of a pile that you didn't know was there?
   _____ Yes.   _____ No.

7. Do you sometimes spend fifteen minutes or more looking for a letter or document that you need?
   _____ Yes.   _____ No.

8. Have you ever forgotten where a letter was filed and been unable to find it?
   _____ Yes.   _____ No.

9. Do you ever lose your glasses or keys?
   _____ Yes.   _____ No.

10. Do you ever put down your handbag or briefcase and later forget where you left it?
    _____ Yes.   _____ No.

11. Is straightening up something that you put off until there is an even more disagreeable task to be done?
    _____ Yes.   _____ No.

12. Do you ever forget appointments?
    _____ Yes.   _____ No.

13. Have you ever been unable to find something for several months?
    _____ Yes.   _____ No.

14. Do you put off doing particular jobs and then have to rush to get them done at the last minute?
    _____ Yes.   _____ No.

PERSONALITY

15. At the end of the day do you find that you've failed to complete most of the things you'd planned to do?
    _____ Yes.   _____ No.

16. When you were a child, did your parents have to nag you to get you to clean up your room?
    _____ Yes.   _____ No.

17. Do you find yourself going through the same papers over and over, unable to decide what to do with them?
    _____ Yes.   _____ No.

18. Are there books on your shelves that you haven't looked at for years?
    _____ Yes.   _____ No.

19. Are there clothes in your closet that you haven't worn in the last year or two?
    _____ Yes.   _____ No.

20. Are you saving things that you've never used simply because they might come in handy someday?
    _____ Yes.   _____ No.

EVALUATION

If you answered yes to as many as four questions, don't worry. You're still pretty well organized. If you had between four and ten yes answers you could stand a little improvement, but your life isn't being controlled by disorganization. More than ten yes answers and your life is being managed by paperwork and possessions.

If you've got it, but can't find it, how can you use it? To start organizing yourself, relax and take one thing at a time.

At work, set aside a particular time each day to go through your paperwork. Try to deal with as much of it as possible. What you can't deal with immediately, assign a priority—that way you can deal with such matters the next day. And, when you file papers, be sure to put the papers in a folder category where you will remember to look for them.

Your belongings at home can be organized in the same manner. Go through your closets and drawers and decide what you want to do with each article. If you don't need the article, don't hang on to it, it will only clutter up your life. You can apply the same principles to your bills when it's time to pay them. Keep all your financial records in the same place and deal with all bills at a specified time each week.

If nothing else, getting organized will put you back in control of your life.

?

????????
GENERAL
?????????

??????????????????????
Should You Return to School?
??????????????????????

Should you go back to school? Will furthering your education lead to a promising career? What are the immediate rewards when you graduate?

Before you answer any of these questions, ask yourself, "Why do I want to go back to school?" Do you want to do so to get ahead at your job, or are you fulfilling an inner need for academic achievement?

More and more adults are finishing their educations, updating job skills, and pursuing hobbies. But your life will get pretty hectic when you return to school. To see if you will be able to handle new demand on your free time, take this test and see if completing your education is practical.

?

1. The returning student should choose a major that is as specialized as possible.
   ____ True. ____ False.

2. Going back to college may require a lot of effort, but once you get your degree you are sure to find a job.
   ____ True. ____ False.

3. It is more difficult for an older applicant to get into college than for a high school senior.
   ____ True. ____ False.

4. You can learn about specific colleges from their catalogs, which are available in most libraries or from the colleges themselves.
   ____ True. ____ False.

5. A good way to get your feet wet is to try a few noncredit courses first.
   ____ True. ____ False.

6. Student loans and scholarships are only for younger students.
   ____ True. ____ False.

7. The GED is a high school equivalency test.
   ____ True. ____ False.

8. Correspondence courses are an easy way to get a college degree.
   ____ True. ____ False.

9. You can receive college credits for watching television.
   ____ True. ____ False.

10. Most community colleges have open admissions.
    ____ True. ____ False.

11. After attending a community college for two years you can transfer to a four-year institution and complete your bachelor's degree.
    ____ True. ____ False.

12. You may receive up to one year of college credit by taking the CLEP examinations.
    ____ True. ____ False.

GENERAL

13. One of the things that worries returning students most is social interaction with younger students.
    _____ True.   _____ False.

14. An older student may attend classes with the youngsters but should avoid participating in the same extracurricular activities.
    _____ True.   _____ False.

15. Mothers who go back to school tend to suffer guilt feelings.
    _____ True.   _____ False.

16. It is easy to neglect your spouse when you are busy with schoolwork.
    _____ True.   _____ False.

17. It is particularly important for an adult, who usually has family responsibilities, to make up a strict study schedule and adhere to it strictly.
    _____ True.   _____ False.

18. Returning students can learn almost as quickly as younger students, but their memories are not as good.
    _____ True.   _____ False.

19. The best time to study is in the evening.
    _____ True.   _____ False.

20. If you know your subject you will do well on exams, so it's a waste of time to study or prepare for tests.
    _____ True.   _____ False.

❓ ANSWERS

1. False. If you have a specific career you will want to select an appropriate major, but don't neglect your general education. It's also a good idea to have training in another career that you can use as a backup in case you can't find employment in the field that is your first choice.
2. False. You can never be absolutely certain of finding a job. Also, the demand for different careers fluctuates greatly.
3. False. Admissions officers know that older applicants tend to be better motivated, and they have been known to bend the rules for a well-qualified older applicant.
4. True. If your library doesn't have the college catalogs you need, you can write to the admissions offices of the colleges. There is also a book called the *College Handbook* that gives information about major colleges.
5. True. Noncredit courses will give you a sense of what it's like to be in college.
6. False. Scholarships, grants, and loans are available to all students who qualify, regardless of age. And they're not just for people with low incomes; many are available to people in the middle-income brackets. Adults often ignore such resources; they shouldn't.
7. True. If you don't have your high school diploma, you can take the GED (General Educational Development) tests, with or without taking some high school courses first to prepare for it. Most American colleges and universities accept the high school equivalency certificate you will get for passing the GED as the equivalent of a high school diploma.
8. False. Most colleges and universities will accept only a limited number of correspondence school credits. It is virtually impossible to get a degree this way.
9. True. Some colleges and universities offer credit for watching certain educational TV programs.
10. True. Most community or two-year colleges have open admissions, which means that virtually anyone who wants to can enroll.
11. True. Be sure to check the requirements of the four-year college you wish to attend, however, to make sure that you will be meeting the requirements for your major field.
12. True. The CLEP (College-Level Examination Program) offers college credits for the knowledge you already have.
13. True. Adults in business suits and dresses may feel out of place among nineteen-year-olds in jeans and work shirts. In time, however, you will learn to speak their language, and they will probably value your point of view.
14. False. Extracurricular activities make college much more fulfilling than it would otherwise be, and there is no reason to deprive yourself of them.

15. True. You must guard against the feeling of guilt that your children are being neglected. You will have to give up something, so leave out some of the unimportant household chores that you used to do, but make time for important things so that you'll be there when your children really need you.
16. True. Spouses tend to be less demanding than children, so you may find that you are spending less time with your spouse without realizing it.
17. True. When you're a young undergraduate with no other responsibilities you can spend all day studying or put things off until the last minute, but the older student often can't afford to do this.
18. False. Younger and older students can learn equally quickly, and their memories are approximately equal.
19. False. The best time to study is whenever *you* find studying most effective. Many students, especially those with families, find that studying early in the morning is best because they are more alert and there are fewer distractions.
20. False. It is true that you should study regularly all semester long; the most efficient studying is that which is done often and for short periods of time (no more than an hour at once). You should go over your notes immediately after class, if possible, and summarize what you've learned. However, it is especially important for returning students to be well versed in test-taking techniques. If you haven't taken a test in a long time, get one of the many books available on studying and test-taking and practice the methods it recommends.

EVALUATION

If your score was between 18 and 20, you are ready to go back to school. No matter how difficult you find the course work, there will be few surprises in store for you because you have realistic expectations. Be sure that your family is kept informed of your plans, and discipline yourself to eliminate the unimportant things in your life and to schedule the important things so that you have enough time for them.

A score between 15 and 17 shows you still may have a successful academic career. The important concept here is planning. Analyze on paper your reasons for wanting to go back to college. If these reasons include specific career goals, try to determine the best way to meet those goals. Perhaps you can choose a major that will make you employable in several different, though related, fields. If so, this will improve your chances of finding a good job after you have your degree.

If your score was below 15, you may have some research to do before you are ready to go back to school. Analyze your academic and career goals, as suggested above. Then investigate the educational possibilities. Deciding why you want to go to college and what you expect to get out of it will help you choose a college and a major subject. High school seniors receive much guidance in these choices, and you can give yourself the same guidance through library research, talking with other returning students, and self-analysis.

The National Cooking Institute Cooking Test

?????????????????????????
?????????????????????????

The National Cooking Institute was established in 1977. The following test, written by the faculty of the Institute, is designed to see if you are a kitchen gourmet. Though this test won't help you become a better cook, it will show you what the basics of culinary artistry are, and show you what you need to know to become a gourmet cook.

?

1. The individual considered to be the founder of haute cuisine is
   a. Bocuse.
   b. Carême.
   c. Point.
   d. Escoffier.

2. In baking, the amount of gluten in the flour determines, to a large degree, the
   a. degree of proof that can be given.
   b. temperature at which the product is baked.
   c. amount of color in the crust.
   d. toughness of the baked product.

3. A glacé made from reducing brown beef or veal stock is called
   a. glacé de viande.
   b. glacé de volaille.
   c. demi glacé.
   d. none of these.

4. The three major classifications of cheese are
   a. ripened, aged, cured.
   b. soft, hard, processed.
   c. semi-soft, semi-hard, ripened.
   d. soft, semi-soft, hard.

5. The chef responsible for cuisine minceur is
   a. Escoffier.
   b. Bocuse.
   c. Guérard.
   d. Troisgros brothers.

6. The definition of chaud-froid is
   a. prepared cold, served cold.
   b. prepared hot, served hot.
   c. prepared hot, served cold.
   d. none of the above.

7. In the milling of wheat flours, the best flours come from the first sifting and are called
   a. patent.
   b. clears.
   c. white.
   d. straight.

8. Brunoise means
   a. brown slowly.
   b. small dice ⅛" x ⅛".
   c. chopped fine.
   d. none of the above.

9. The thickening of starch when in solution is referred to as
   a. structure.
   b. gelatinization.
   c. conduction.
   d. coagulation.

THE NATIONAL COOKING INSTITUTE COOKING TEST

10. A shirred egg is
    a. cooked in cream.
    b. baked.
    c. poached.
    d. cooked in the shell—boiling water poured over, covered tightly, and allowed to sit for 7 minutes.

11. The protein in flour is called
    a. patent.
    b. millings.
    c. gluten.
    d. clears.

12. An example of a temporary emulsion is
    a. mayonnaise.
    b. hollandaise sauce.
    c. honey-fruit dressing.
    d. roquefort dressing.

13. La nouvelle cuisine refers to
    a. fresh vegetable only.
    b. fresh vegetables only, plenty of fat.
    c. following the principles of classical cookery but using only fresh ingredients and cutting the carbohydrates in half.
    d. fresh ingredients only, zero amount of fat.

14. A rough-cut vegetable combination of onion, celery, and carrots usually used in conjunction with braising is called
    a. mirepoix.
    b. sachet d'épices.
    c. bouquet garni.
    d. none of the above.

15. The purpose of punching a yeast-raised dough is to
    a. kill yeast activity.
    b. prevent crust formation.
    c. control yeast activity and condition the dough evenly.
    d. smell the gas being released.

16. The size of an egg is correlated with
    a. the quality of the egg.
    b. the age of the chicken.
    c. the diet of the chicken.
    d. none of the above.

17. Items covered with a sauce, and sprinkled with crumbs or cheese and then browned are called
    a. duxelle.
    b. provencale.
    c. au gratin.
    d. au bisque.

18. The four factors that indicate maturity in melons are
    a. size, use, grade, color.
    b. aroma, age, hardness, weight.
    c. sweetness, aroma, color, softening.
    d. weight, outer texture, variety, decay.

19. The condition of "weeping" when baking custard pies is caused by
    a. poor formula used.
    b. over baking.
    c. under baking.
    d. too much starch.

20. Prepared mustard is classified as a
    a. spice.
    b. condiment.
    c. relish.
    d. seasoning.

21. The color of the finest milk-fed veal is
    a. red.
    b. pink.
    c. light red.
    d. dark red.

22. The basic temperature for deep frying is
    a. 250°-300°.
    b. 290-325°.
    c. 350-375°.
    d. 400-425°.

23. Natural juices served with a prime rib are called
    a. pan gravy.
    b. jus lié.
    c. au jus.
    d. consommé.

24. In order to develop the gluten in a dough, yeast doughs should be:
    a. cool.
    b. well mixed.
    c. warm.
    d. fermented.

25. An example of a permanent emulsion is:
    a. French dressing.
    b. Italian dressing.
    c. mayonnaise.
    d. hollandaise sauce.

?

KEY

1. b	10. b	19. b
2. d	11. c	20. b
3. a	12. b	21. b
4. d	13. c	22. c
5. c	14. a	23. c
6. c	15. c	24. b
7. a	16. b	25. c
8. b	17. c	
9. b	18. c	

EVALUATION

25 to 21 You are an exacting, perfectionist, at-home kitchen gourmet. The next step is to open your own restaurant.

20 to 16 With your strong background in food preparation, you should be able to prepare small intimate dinners as well as large company feasts. It is clear that you have studied food preparation, and with a little more experience you could be a true kitchen gourmet.

15 to 11 At least your family likes your meals. Knowing how to cook for those you love is a fine accomplishment but there is so much more to know in the culinary arts field. Take some time and learn the finer kitchen secrets; you could surprise your family and yourself.

10 to 6 Thank goodness for TV dinners and instant soup. Knowing how to boil water and the like is nothing to be proud of, especially since learning how to prepare good food is a simple matter of study and practice.

5 to 0 Stay out of the kitchen if you know what is good for you. If you want to watch, fine, but keep your hands off the food until you learn some of the basics of food preparation.

Courtesy of the National Cooking Institute, Denver, Colorado.

?

???????????????????????????
How Smart a Traveler Are You?
??????????????????????????

Whether you're taking a trip to a foreign country for business or pleasure, you'll find your travels more enjoyable with a little advance preparation. Unless you've been there before and know your way around, it's wise to read something about the places you intend to visit. Guidebooks, including less expensive paperbacks, cover every part of the world and are available in most bookstores. Foreign government tourist bureaus distribute free brochures and other literature covering their history and principal attractions. (Your travel agent should have their addresses.)

You should also be alert to the possible pitfalls that confront the traveler outside the United States. Below are questions dealing with money exchange, medical assistance, legal status of United States citizens journeying abroad, and other matters with which the practical traveler should be familiar.

?

1. You are carrying medicines containing narcotic drugs. How do you avoid problems with foreign customs officials?
2. If you need emergency medical or dental assistance while abroad, to whom should you turn for help?
3. Since the dollar's value often fluctuates widely, where can one obtain the best exchange rates?
4. What kind of medical facilities are available aboard ships?
5. What is my best course of action should I be arrested for any reason while outside the United States?
6. If you're a naturalized American citizen, is there any danger of being detained in the country of your birth?
7. Is an American driver's license universally valid?
8. Since some countries, including several Arab nations, bar entry to persons with an Israeli stamp on their passports, should you tear out a page with such a stamp?
9. Visas are required by many countries and allow a specific length of stay. What should you do if you want to stay longer?
10. If you're taking a foreign camera abroad, how do you avoid being asked to pay duty on it when returning home?
11. Telephoning home while traveling abroad can be expensive. What's the best way to hold down the cost?
12. Do you need to make seat or sleeping car reservations on European trains, and how far in advance should they be made?
13. Can you obtain redress if injured in a taxi while abroad?
14. If a foreign airline loses your luggage, what are your rights for compensation?
15. What's the best way to receive mail during foreign trips? Do our consulates do this for tourists?
16. May a foreign hotel demand your passport and hold it overnight? Can you legally refuse to turn it over?
17. What sort of information on foreign travel can you obtain from the U.S. Government?
18. Where can one still hunt big game on an African safari?
19. Does one need a passport, visas, or shots for a cruise?

GENERAL

20. Can the captain of a ship perform a marriage ceremony?
21. If you suddenly find yourself stranded or out of money while abroad, who can help you?
22. Is credit card insurance adequate for the average traveler?
23. Though you're within the duty allowance, can you be charged for bringing in certain items from abroad?

?

ANSWERS

1. You should carry a doctor's certificate attesting that the drugs are for your personal use. If possible, leave all such medicines in their original containers.
2. All American embassies and consulates will provide a list of local doctors and dentists. Large hotels also can help. Emergency medical assistance is available from International SOS Assistance Inc., 1420 Walnut Street, Philadelphia, PA 19102, and from Assist Card International, 745 Fifth Avenue, New York, NY 10022, for a moderate fee. The International Association for Medical Assistance to Travelers, a non-profit organization, will provide names of doctors abroad in return for a donation.
3. Usually, the best rates are offered by banks and travel agencies, including the airport currency counters. Often you receive a little more than at the hotels and shops. Don't deal in the black market. You risk arrest, or at the least being cheated.
4. International law requires all passenger ships to carry a doctor. The elaborateness of the medical facilities depends mostly on the size of the ship, but many vessels have full operating rooms and a few even have a dentist on board. Freighters, which carry only a few passengers, are exempt.
5. If you're in a dispute abroad that could lead to legal or police action, you should contact one of our consular offices. While our foreign service officials cannot serve as attorneys or give legal advice, they can provide lists of local attorneys and help you find legal representation. While they will do whatever they can to protect your legitimate interests, they can't get you out of jail. They'll visit you and also contact your friends and relatives.
6. The State Department says a foreign nation, particularly some in the Middle East and Eastern Europe, could detain you if you were born there, if one of your parents or your spouse is still a citizen of that country, or if the laws of that country specify that its nationals can never give up their allegiance. In some instances, this could mean you could be required to fulfill military and other obligations. If you're in any of the above categories, it would be wise to check with the consular officials of such countries before you leave.
7. Some countries do not accept a United States driver's permit, but nearly all recognize the international driver's license obtainable through your local automobile club.
8. All U.S. passports have numbered pages and any mutilation could cause you problems not only at foreign destinations but also when you return home. Some nations refuse admission to persons whose passport indicates a visit to a country with which it has no diplomatic relations. Some African countries, for example, won't allow anyone to enter if a passport indicates a previous stop in South Africa. Algeria and Libya will bar anyone with an Israeli entry stamp. Accordingly, you should apply for a second passport, which may be used only for travel to such areas.
9. Normally, visas are good for three months except in the Soviet Union, Poland, some Arab countries, and other areas either where stays are limited or where specific dates are prescribed. Since requests for visa extension involve a certain amount of red tape, you should apply to the local immigration authorities at least three weeks to a month before your visa expires.
10. Prior to departure, you should obtain a form from a United States Customs office certifying that the camera was your property before departure.
11. Many hotels, especially those in Europe, add a small service fee to the basic telephone charges entered on a client's bill. Other hotels actually double or triple the cost of the call. A few hotels and hotel chains have voluntarily joined Teleplan, committing themselves to a reasonable surcharge and to compliance with a posted rate schedule. If your hotel doesn't do this, and you should find out before placing the

call, it's better to phone home collect since charges are much lower. Other options would be to obtain a credit card before you leave (Find out first if it will be accepted in the countries you're visiting.) since surcharges generally are reasonable. It is also cheaper to call from the United States, so whenever possible have calls made to you in Europe rather than calling home. Also, many foreign phone companies have centers at airports and local post offices where you can make calls and pay only for the cost of the call.

12. On long distance trips reservations should be made, particularly during the busy season. Reservations for sleeping car accommodations are absolutely necessary. In some TransEurope Express (TEE) trains, which are all first class, advance reservations for meals can also be made for service at your seat.

13. The problem is that since the taxi company is not subject to United States laws you must hire a foreign attorney, which is usually difficult and expensive. Reputable tour and sightseeing companies normally carry some form of insurance to cover accidents involving their local services. It always is wise to carry personal comprehensive insurance as an added precaution.

14. The rules regarding lost baggage aboard a foreign airline have been defined by the Warsaw Convention, which declares that the maximum of $9.07 a pound or $20 a kilo will be paid for lost articles of baggage. In addition, foreign airlines utilize tariffs that do not appear on the airline ticket and that further limit their liability. There have been court decisions, however, which direct foreign carriers to make known their liability limitations in bold readable print, and, if they fail to do so, the aggrieved consumer may sue for the actual value of the articles lost. In any litigation, you should always be able to prove the value of your baggage contents. Baggage insurance is advisable.

15. United States embassies and legations don't serve as drops for private mail. American Express offices provide this service, as do some banks. Post offices in most countries will hold mail for arrivals. Correspondence should be addressed to General Delivery (Poste Restante). Hotels you'll be using along the way will also keep your mail until you check in. Be sure to indicate "Hold for Arrival."

16. When you register at some foreign hotels you may be required to fill out a police information card and also to leave your passport overnight for checking by the authorities. These are normal procedures under local law.

17. There's a wealth of literature available free or for a nominal charge. For free copies of *Customs Hints* write U.S. Customs, P.O. Box 7118, Washington, DC 20044. Free copies of the booklet *Visa Requirements of Foreign Governments* are available from any local passport facility. Free copies of travel information covering various Eastern European countries, the Soviet Union, Scandinavia, Italy, Morocco, Greece, and the Middle East are available from the Office of Passport Services, Department of State, Washington, DC 20524. *Background Notes on the Countries of the World* is a series of pamphlets of interest to travelers and is available for seventy cents from the Superintendent of Documents, U.S. Government Printing Office, Washington, DC 20524.

18. Many African countries, including Kenya, have banned big game hunting to insure animal conservation. A few countries have limited kill allowances. Contact the tourist office of the country you intend to visit.

19. In general, cruise passengers stopping in a port only for a few hours need little or no identification beyond the ship's boarding pass. In the Caribbean, only Cuba requires a passport. In Europe, a passport is required but visas usually are not. On the other hand, if the cruise calls at the People's Republic of China, a visa is definitely required even if you don't intend to get off the ship. Check with the ship line at least three weeks before departure for the most up-to-date information on visa and immunization requirements.

    One thing you'll definitely need is proof of citizenship or residency to reenter the United States. A passport, of course, is best, but voter registration cards, birth certificates, or alien registration cards are also acceptable.

20. A popular myth notwithstanding, it is either illegal or against cruise line policy in most cases for a ship's captain to perform a marriage ceremony in international waters. Usually a

member of the clergy is aboard a cruise ship, but it is best to check this before sailing, as well as other possible legal requirements such as marriage license and blood tests.

21. The American consul will give you a hand in contacting your family, friends, employer, or your bank. If you've lost your money, your credit cards, or your traveler's checks, contact the police and the appropriate issuing authority. While they will help with the arrangements in the case of groups stranded because of accidents, malperformance by tour operators, etc., don't count on United States officials to lend you money or pay for your trip home.

22. The free insurance provided by such cards as Diner's Club and American Express is helpful but falls considerably short of giving you sufficient protection. Diner's Club cardholders have $50,000 flight insurance. For six dollars a month, however, this can be increased to $200,000 for accidents on passenger conveyance and by another $50,000 for other accidents. This covers husband, wife, and children.

    American Express provides $25,000 free insurance for accidents on land, sea, and air carriers. Husband, wife, and children under twenty-three are included. For three dollars extra when you buy your ticket American Express gives you additional $250,000 coverage. Check with your employer on coverage when you're traveling on business. Also consult your insurance agent for other inexpensive and comprehensive travel policies available.

23. Items bought in quantities over and above the normal limit from duty-free shops and other stores abroad can be taxed. Under trademark laws, the American owner of a registered trademark or trade name is protected against the unauthorized importation by others of foreign merchandise bearing the trademark or trade name. There are restrictions, for example, on the importation of certain well known cameras made in Germany and Japan, and on perfumes made in France.

A twenty-four page customs brochure lists hundreds of trade names, giving specific information as to the conditions and restrictions governing their importation into the United States. Articles falling under these rules include lenses, cameras, binoculars and optical goods, tape recorders, radios, and musical instruments, jewelry and precious metalware, perfumes, colognes, and toiletries. A free copy of *Trademark Information for Travelers* is available from Public Information Division, U.S. Customs Services, 1301 Constitution Avenue, NW, Washington, DC 20229.

EVALUATION

A perfect score on this test makes you more than ready for a trip abroad. Knowing how to react to possible problems and how to cope with all situations will make your trip, whether business or vacation, a pleasure. Those with a correct score of 75 percent show their colors as seasoned travelers who know that a trip abroad needs preparation—and, that the only way to prepare is to get all the information before you leave. If you missed more than half, you have a lot to learn before your next trip. Remember: to make any trip a success, you've got to get ready before you go.

Courtesy of Eric Friedheim, editor and publisher of *The Travel Agent*, the travel industry news magazine.

How Good a Driver Are You?

Every time you get behind the wheel of your car, you have a responsibility—to yourself, to your passengers, and to the other drivers on the road. Everyone has to take a driving test to get a license, of course, but how long has it been since you passed yours? Do you think you could still pass it?

The ultimate test of whether you are a good driver is not whether you can pass a written test, but how alert you are and how well you respond to emergencies in actual driving. Knowing the rules of the road is a good way to start.

1. In most states, you may park within _____ feet of a stop sign.
    a. 15
    b. 25
    c. 35

2. How much space should you allow between your car and the car ahead of you?
    a. As much space as you think you need to stop.
    b. One car length for each 10 MPH of speed.
    c. More than one car length for each 10 MPH of speed, especially in hazardous conditions or low visibility.

3. A solid yellow line on your side of a two-lane road means that
    a. you may not pass.
    b. it is safe to pass if there are no cars in the other lane.
    c. you are on a one-way street.

4. A stop sign is
    a. red and eight-sided.
    b. red and six sided.
    c. yellow and eight-sided.

5. If you have a blowout, you should
    a. brake immediately.
    b. pump the brakes.
    c. hold the steering wheel firmly, take your foot off the accelerator, and steer onto the shoulder only when the car has almost stopped.

6. If two cars approach from opposite directions on a narrow road that isn't wide enough for both of them
    a. the car going north should back up and let the car going south pass.
    b. the car going uphill should back up and let the car going downhill pass.
    c. both cars should squeeze right as far as possible and pass with caution.

7. When you park on a hill facing downhill, you should
    a. turn your front wheels away from the curb.
    b. turn your front wheels toward the curb.
    c. turn your rear wheels away from the curb.

8. When driving in a fog, you will probably be able to see best with your
    a. high beams.
    b. low beams.
    c. parking lights.

GENERAL

9. If your car skids, you should
    a. turn your wheels in the direction of the skid.
    b. turn your wheels in the opposite direction from the skid.
    c. brake quickly and firmly.

10. A yellow diamond-shaped sign warns of
    a. a railroad crossing
    b. a school crossing.
    c. a variety of possible driving hazards.

11. A YIELD sign is
    a. red.
    b. yellow.
    c. green.

12. Modern cars have brakes
    a. usually on the front wheels.
    b. usually on the rear wheels.
    c. on all four wheels.

13. In most states, you may not park within ____ feet of a fire hydrant.
    a. 10
    b. 20
    c. 30

14. When you back up, you should
    a. use your side mirror.
    b. use your rear-view mirror.
    c. look through the rear window.

15. What is the best way to tell whether there is a car in your blind spot?
    a. Look over your shoulder.
    b. Check both rear-view and side mirrors.
    c. Have an extra side mirror installed on the passenger side.

16. When two vehicles approach an intersection at the same time
    a. the driver on the right has the right-of-way.
    b. the driver on the left has the right-of-way.
    c. nobody "has" the right-of-way; however, the driver on the left is expected to yield to the driver on the right.

17. At 50 MPH, how many feet will you need to stop?
    a. 250.
    b. 350.
    c. 450.

18. If your brakes fail, you should
    a. turn off the engine.
    b. use the emergency brake or shift into reverse.
    c. pump the brake pedal several times; if necessary, shift to low gear and look for a place to stop.

19. If another car pulls out in front of you and you are about to hit it, you should
    a. slam on the brakes.
    b. quickly steer around it, passing on the left.
    c. step on the brake pedal hard, then let up and continue pumping the brake; if you have to, steer onto the shoulder, but do not brake while you are turning.

20. A flashing red light at an intersection means
    a. stop
    b. yield
    c. caution.

21. Which of the following is true of seat belts?
    a. If you are in a collision, they may do more harm than good by trapping you in your car.
    b. They can save your life by keeping you from being thrown out of your car or into the steering column.
    c. They're nice to have if they're offered as standard equipment, but don't spend money on them if they're optional.

22. If you weigh about 150 pounds, how many drinks will it take to affect your driving?
    a. One.
    b. Two.
    c. Three.

23. Your gas mileage is probably best at
    a. 20 MPH.
    b. 50 MPH.
    c. 70 MPH.

HOW GOOD A DRIVER ARE YOU?

24. It is safest to
    a. drive faster than the other cars on the road.
    b. drive slower than other traffic.
    c. drive at the same speed as other traffic.

25. You can increase your gas mileage if you
    a. drive at a steady speed, using the brake as little as possible.
    b. approach each stop light at full speed, stop quickly, and take off again quickly when the light changes in order to spend as little time idling as possible.
    c. always drive as slowly as possible.

ANSWERS

1. b	10. c	19. c
2. c	11. a	20. a
3. a	12. c	21. b
4. a	13. a	22. a
5. c	14. c	23. b
6. c	15. a	24. c
7. b	16. c	25. a
8. b	17. a	
9. a	18. c	

EVALUATION

For convenience, enjoyment, and the feeling of freedom that comes from being able to go anywhere at any time, cars are hard to beat. So long as we are going to own cars, we need to know how to operate them efficiently and safely.

21 to 25 A. You can be justifiably proud of your knowledge of driving rules, and if you practice what you know, your skills will be No. 1.

17 to 20 B. Whether you like it or not the automobile is here to stay, and your average score shows that you should learn a little more about written driving laws. Though departments of transportation require both written and practical tests for a license, knowing the rules will make driving all that much easier.

16 and below C. Your below average score shows that you might be better off on public transportation—at least until you learn the law of the land. Keep your car, but keep it parked until you know better.

Approved by Warren Rumsfield, North American Professional Driver Education Association (NAPDEA).

?

Testing Your Traffic Safety Knowledge

The National Safety Council is involved in all facets of traffic safety. Through research and educational programs they hope to reduce the number and severity of accidents. The following test is one of their self-evaluating tests, designed to help each and every one of us learn more about traffic safety.

Virtually everyone is a participant in the traffic milieu daily. We usually like to know all about those things that immediately surround us. Let's check your knowledge of traffic safety.

1. Most accidents happen within (a) 25, (b) 75, (c) 150, (d) 200 miles from the homes of the drivers involved.
2. In the United States, a traffic fatality occurs on the average of (a) ten per day, (b) one every ten minutes, (c) ten per hour, (d) one every hour.
3. The most favorable accident rates are found on (a) city streets, (b) two-lane rural roads, (c) limited-access interstate highways, (d) state-trunk highways.
4. Approximately 19 percent of all traffic fatalities are (a) pedestrians, (b) motorcyclists, (c) car passengers, (d) bicyclists.
5. A traffic sign that is round in shape means (a) stop, (b) railroad crossing, (c) no U-turn, (d) pedestrian crossing.
6. When following another vehicle on the highway, you should maintain a distance of one car length for every (a) 10, (b) 15, (c) 20, (d) 25 miles of speed.
7. When meeting or overtaking a stopped school bus with red lights flashing, you must (a) blow your horn before passing, (b) stop and then proceed cautiously, (c) flash your headlights, (d) stop and remain stopped until bus moves.
8. Seat belts should be used by (a) the driver only, (b) the driver and all passengers, including children, (c) only those riding in the front seat, (d) all riders except children under four years old.
9. At night, you should switch your headlights to low beam when following another vehicle within (a) 600, (b) 450, (c) 300, (d) 150 feet.
10. If a driver had a blood-alcohol concentration of 0.13 percent, he would be (a) impaired but fit to drive, (b) almost sober, (c) legally drunk and unfit to drive, (d) virtually comatose.
11. The chance of death or serious injury in an accident at 70 MPH is (a) 4, (b) 2, (c) 3, (d) 0 times greater than at 50 MPH.
12. The first thing to do if your car catches fire is to (a) stop and get out, (b) speed up and get to a service station, (c) pull off the road and turn off the ignition, (d) check your insurance policy.
13. The best escape route from a submerged auto is (a) by opening a door, (b) rolling down a window, (c) breaking the windshield, (d) through the trunk.
14. If you are the first to come upon an accident scene, you should (a) warn oncoming traffic, (b) send someone to notify the police, (c) make certain the wrecked cars' ignitions are turned off, (d) all of the above.

TESTING YOUR TRAFFIC SAFETY KNOWLEDGE

ANSWERS

1. a
2. b
3. c
4. a
5. b
6. a
7. d
8. d (Children under four years old, or under forty pounds, should be seated in an approved child restraint.)
9. c
10. c
11. a
12. c
13. b
14. d

EVALUATION

Score 1 point for each correct answer. A score of 11 to 14 should keep you alive and well for a long time. A score of 7 to 10 indicates that you should keep your eyes open at all times. A score of 6 or below doesn't leave much hope for you.

Courtesy of the National Safety Council.

?

??????????????????
How Well Do You Know Your Car?
??????????????????

Over 80 percent of American households own at least one car. In 1978, the average car owner spent over $350 for repair, maintenance, tires, oil, and accessories. And though the automobile repair industry continues to be the cause of many consumer complaints, many Americans just don't know how to take care of their cars.

If you panic when something goes wrong with your car, it is time you learned how to take care of it. Knowing routine maintenance will help you better care for your car and alert you when repairs are necessary; being aware of problems will help you give the mechanic an idea of the problem.

Americans are so dependent on their cars, they *have* to know how to take care of them. Your answers to the following test will show what you know now and how much more you should learn to make your driving a little easier.

?

1. If your engine won't turn over but the horn and headlights work, the problem is probably with
    a. the battery.
    b. the starter.
    c. the electrolyte.

2. When "jump-starting" a car
    a. connect the positive post of the dead battery to the positive post of the booster battery and the negative post of the dead battery to the negative post of the booster battery.
    b. connect the positive post of the dead battery to the negative post of the booster battery and the negative post of the dead battery to the positive post of the booster battery.
    c. connect the positive post of the dead battery to the positive post of the booster battery and the negative post of the booster battery to the engine block of the stalled car.

3. Corroded battery terminals should be cleaned with
    a. vaseline.
    b. soap and water.
    c. baking soda

4. When working on a battery, you should remove all jewelry or watches because
    a. you might get an electric shock.
    b. the metal may become hot and burn you.
    c. you might drop something metallic into the battery.

5. If your ammeter shows a condition of discharge, the problem is most likely to be with the
    a. battery.
    b. alternator.
    c. starter.

6. Some cars have as many as _____ kinds of fluid that need to be checked.
    a. five.
    b. seven
    c. eleven

HOW WELL DO YOU KNOW YOUR CAR?

7. If you're caught in traffic during the summer, the best thing to do is to
   a. turn on the air conditioner and roll up the windows.
   b. turn on the heater.
   c. roll down the windows and turn off the air conditioner.

8. Engine knocks or pings are a sign of
   a. water in the gas tank.
   b. incorrect spark timing.
   c. bad valve lifter.

9. A compression gauge measures
   a. oil pressure in the crankcase.
   b. air pressure in the tires.
   c. vapor pressure in the cylinders.

10. Vibration of the steering wheel or looseness in steering may be a sign of
    a. improper alignment.
    b. overinflation.
    c. underinflation.

11. Tires that are worn at the center indicate
    a. overinflation.
    b. underinflation.
    c. improper alignment.

12. Tires that are worn only on the inside indicate
    a. overinflation.
    b. underinflation.
    c. improper alignment.

13. An engine that lacks power and gets poor gas mileage may have
    a. worn valves or piston rings.
    b. broken valve lifters.
    c. a faulty starter

14. If your car pulls to one side, steers erratically, or shimmies, it may need
    a. new shock absorbers.
    b. new springs.
    c. new ball joints.

15. Which of the following statements is true?
    a. Rear brakes last longer than front brakes.
    b. Front brakes last longer than rear brakes.
    c. All four brakes will last about the same length of time.

16. If your car pulls to one side when you stop, you should replace
    a. the brake shoes on that side of the car.
    b. the brake shoes on the other side of the car.
    c. the brake shoes on both sides of the car.

17. Which of the following statements is true?
    a. Drum brakes are less likely than disc brakes to "fade" (failing to hold after being used for a long time, as on a hill).
    b. Drum brakes are more likely than disc brakes to fade.
    c. Drum and disc brakes are equally likely to fade.

18. If your engine mounts give way, it is possible that
    a. the engine will fall out of the car.
    b. the fan will damage the radiator.
    c. the fuel line will be severed.

19. If you hear a clunking from underneath the car when accelerating, you probably need to replace
    a. the rear axle assembly.
    b. the universal joints.
    c. the driveshaft.

20. Which of the following is true?
    a. You can easily add transmission fluid to a car with a manual transmission, but an automatic usually has to be taken to a service station.
    b. You can easily add transmission fluid to a car with an automatic transmission, but a car with a manual transmission usually has to be taken to a service station.
    c. You can add your own transmission fluid with either type of car.

?

ANSWERS

1. b. If the horn and headlights work, the battery must be all right, so the problem is more likely to be with the starter.
2. c. For safety, the final cable should be grounded to the engine block. Also, be sure that the caps of both batteries are tightly closed, and cover them with a damp cloth, if available, to dissipate any gas that may escape.

GENERAL

(Many newer batteries have hidden vent caps that make the cloth unnecessary.) Batteries contain an acid that produces an explosive gas, so keep sparks, flames, and cigarettes away from them.

3. c. Clean batteries with baking soda.
4. b. A battery can turn a piece of metal red-hot almost instantly.
5. b. The fact that the battery is discharging shows that it is being used to provide all of the electrical power needed, which may mean that the alternator is not supplying electrical energy to recharge the battery. Another possibility is a bad connection, or a broken drive belt.
6. c. The fluids are engine oil, fuel, radiator coolant, battery electrolyte, transmission fluid, power steering fluid, rear axle lubricant, air conditioning refrigerant, windshield washer solvent, and shock absorber fluid.
7. b. Running the heater makes the engine coolant circulate faster. Running your air conditioner in stalled traffic will overheat your engine. You should turn off the air conditioner and race the engine occasionally to turn the fan faster and cool the engine.
8. b. Knocking or pinging usually indicates bad spark timing.
9. c. A compression gauge measures how effectively the air-fuel mixture is being compressed in the combustion chamber.
10. a. Such steering problems may be an indication of incorrect alignment or tire balance.
11. a. If tires are overinflated, they wear more at the center.
12. c. If tires are worn unevenly (on either side), front end alignment is probably needed.
13. a. Loss of engine power may also be caused by problems with points, spark plugs, condenser, rotor, distributor cap, or coil; PCV valves or hoses; improper spark timing or improper spark gap. Poor gas mileage may be caused by an automatic choke or carburetor that needs adjustment, a dirty air cleaner or PCV valve, high fuel pump pressure, or even a sticking needle valve.
14. c. New ball joints may be needed. These symptoms are similar to those caused by improper front end alignment.
15. a. Rear brakes last about twice as long as front brakes.
16. c. Although the brake shoes on the side toward which the car is pulling are still holding, you should replace both sides now so that the car will brake evenly.
17. b. Drum brakes are more susceptible than disc brakes to fading.
18. b. Two of the possible effects are sudden stalling and damage to the fan and radiator. However, late model cars, which have "safety mounts" that lock together when their rubber parts give way, usually don't have these problems.
19. b. A clunking from underneath the car may come from worn universal joints.
20. b. With an automatic transmission, you simply pour the transmission fluid into the dipstick opening. With a manual transmission, the car must be placed on a lift, and the procedure is fairly complicated.

EVALUATION

Less than 2 incorrect answers shows that you are at home in and around your car; you always keep your car in top running condition, and you often do simple maintenance, such as an oil change or perhaps even a tuneup. With 5 to 7 incorrect answers, you aren't completely at sea; you have some idea of how your car works, but major repairs probably mystify you. If you answered 5 or more incorrectly you should, for your economic benefit as well as your safety, know more about how your car works and what is likely to go wrong with it.

?

???????????????????????
Can You Survive in the Outdoors?
???????????????????????

In today's modern, urbanized world, many of us have lost touch with nature and the wilderness. There are no more frontiers, and the last of our open spaces, in this country at least, are rapidly being settled.

For some of us, the only daily contact with the outdoors is getting in and out of a car, subway, bus, or train on the way to and from work. But there are still weekends, vacations, hiking, hunting, fishing, and trips to the beach. And whether you're in a heavily populated area or alone in the wilderness, you should know how to survive in the great outdoors; survival techniques may be called into play when you least expect it.

?

1. If you are lost in the woods without a compass, you can tell direction by looking at your watch.
   _____ True.   _____ False.

2. You can't find your bearings at night, because the sun is down.
   _____ True.   _____ False.

3. To avoid being struck by lightning, the best thing to do is to stand under a tree.
   _____ True.   _____ False.

4. Poisonous snakes can be recognized by their lance-shaped, triangular heads.
   _____ True.   _____ False.

5. Three of anything—three sounds, or three articles arranged in a row—is a universally recognized distress signal.
   _____ True.   _____ False.

6. If, while hiking in the woods, you come upon a large bear, the best thing to do is to yell and wave your arms to frighten it away.
   _____ True.   _____ False.

7. You will rarely find snakes out in the open in the daytime.
   _____ True.   _____ False.

8. If you are lost, you can find your way by following a stream.
   _____ True.   _____ False.

9. You have a better chance of finding food near a body of water.
   _____ True.   _____ False.

10. Since some plants are poisonous, it's best never to eat plants when you're in the wilderness.
    _____ True.   _____ False.

11. One should never eat insects because they carry disease.
    _____ True.   _____ False.

12. If you are lost in the desert, your thirst will tell you when and how much to drink.
    _____ True.   _____ False.

GENERAL

13. Salt water may not taste very good, but you can drink it if you have no other water.
    _____ True.   _____ False.

14. You can become sunburned or dehydrated even in the winter.
    _____ True.   _____ False.

15. It is possible to die of the cold at temperatures in the forties.
    _____ True.   _____ False.

16. If you think you may be frostbitten, you should rub snow on the affected part.
    _____ True.   _____ False.

17. Some snakes and spiders are poisonous, but there are no poisonous lizards in the United States.
    _____ True.   _____ False.

18. The symptoms of a bite from a poisonous spider are sometimes mistaken for indigestion or appendicitis.
    _____ True.   _____ False.

19. If you are bitten by a poisonous snake and severe symptoms develop, the best method of treatment is still the time-honored one of making a cut in the skin over each fang mark and sucking out the poison.
    _____ True.   _____ False.

20. If you are swimming in the ocean and you see a shark, you should splash the water to frighten it away.
    _____ True.   _____ False.

?

ANSWERS

1. True. If you point the hour hand toward the sun (keeping the face horizontal) south will be halfway between the sun and twelve o'clock. This method cannot be used near the poles or the equator.

2. False. In the Northern Hemisphere, you can locate the North Star by sighting along the two stars on the lowest side of the Big Dipper. The North Star can also be found by drawing an imaginary line from the center star of the constellation Cassiopeia (made up of five stars) and the innermost of the two stars on the handle of the Big Dipper; the North Star will be about midway between them. In the Southern Hemisphere, you can find south by sighting along the long axis of the Southern Cross.

3. False. To avoid being struck by lightning you should stay away from the highest point in the area. Try to find a low valley or a cave, but don't stand next to a tree, especially if it's the only tree in a field or meadow. Don't stand out in the open so that *you* are the highest point in the area, and remember not to touch anything metallic.

4. False. There is no single distinguishing characteristic of a poisonous snake. The poisonous snakes found in the United States are the rattlesnake, the copperhead, the water moccasin (or cottonmouth), and the coral snake. Most are fairly timid and will strike only when disturbed.

5. True. Three gunshots or whistle blasts or a trail of three stones on the ground may lead rescuers to you. Presumably this is a variation of the traditional SOS signal—three dots, three dashes, three dots.

6. False. Acting agressively may provoke the bear to attack you. If it hasn't noticed you, make it aware of your presence by rustling some branches or talking. If the bear still comes toward you, try to make a slow retreat; climb a tree if you have to. If the bear does attack, play dead. Curl up with your knees to your chest and try to cover your face and neck. Very few encounters with wild bears get to the attack stage, however.

7. False. Because snakes are cold-blooded, they cannot maintain a steady temperature; a snake's body temperature varies with its surroundings. Therefore, snakes will come out and bask in the sun on a cool day; on a hot day, they will stay hidden under a bush or a rock.

8. True. Following a stream is usually a good bet. As soon as you realize you are lost, you should stop, sit down, relax, and try to remember landmarks that you have passed. Then climb a tree or a hill and look for some of these landmarks; see if you can figure out where you are. The most important thing to remember is not

CAN YOU SURVIVE IN THE OUTDOORS?

to panic; you probably are not very far from civilization.

9. True. Fish are difficult to catch with makeshift equipment (or even with good fishing equipment), but frogs, snails, crabs, clams, shrimp, crayfish, salamanders, turtles, and insects are easier to snare.

10. False. Plants are a good source of food if you know which ones to avoid. There are 300,000 species of plants in the world, of which 120,000 are edible. Learn to recognize poison ivy, poison oak, and poison sumac. If you're really desperate and you're in doubt as to whether a particular plant is edible, try a small amount and wait several hours. Then try a little more, and wait for at least five or six hours. If there are no ill effects, the plant is probably okay. This method should only be used when there are no other food sources available.

11. False. Insects are a good source of protein. However, some of them *do* contain disease-causing parasites, so cook all insects before you eat them.

12. False. Your thirst is not an accurate indicator of how much to drink; you can become dehydrated if you drink only when you are thirsty. You can survive a loss of up to 10 percent of body weight by dehydration without permanent harm, provided you restore the lost weight by drinking water as soon as possible.

13. False. Never drink salt water. Because its salt concentration is so high, body fluids must be drawn off to eliminate it. This will eventually cause the kidneys to cease functioning.

14. True. Snow reflects sunlight even on cloudy days, and you can become dehydrated at any time if you don't drink enough water; the average adult needs about two quarts a day.

15. True. The effects of cold are multiplied by wind chill, especially when one is in the rain or is wearing wet clothing.

16. False. Never apply snow to a frostbitten area. Try to warm the affected part by immersing it in warm water or holding a warm hand on it, but do not rub the part.

17. False. The gila monster and the beaded lizard, both found in the American Southwest as well as in Central America and Mexico, are poisonous, but they are not very dangerous because they are sluggish and slow-moving.

18. True. Acute abdominal cramps are one of the symptoms of the bite of a poisonous spider.

19. True. Commercial snakebite kits are sold for this purpose, or you can use a pocket knife and suck out the poison with your mouth. You should also apply pressure (but not a tourniquet) on the limb at a point two to four inches closer to the heart than the bite. If possible, immobilize the affected part; moving it will spread the poison. For more information on what to do in the event of a snakebite, contact your local chapter of the American Red Cross.

20. False. Swim slowly away; don't splash or use frantic swimming movements. If the shark comes close to you, you may be able to frighten it away by lunging at it or hitting or kicking it on the nose. Do this only as a last resort, however. Sharks rarely attack unprovoked, but they can be attracted by a commotion or by blood in the water.

?

EVALUATION

18 to 20: *Woodsperson.* Whether you're stranded in the woods, marooned on an island, or stuck in a snowstorm, you would know what to do. Your knowledge of outdoor lore and first aid techniques makes you a self-sufficient individual.

14 to 17: *Scout.* You won't be stranded for long, but you won't be able to cope all that well either. Coupled with your common sense, your knowledge will keep you safe and out of trouble, but it can't hurt to learn a little more.

Below 14: *Tenderfoot.* You have no choice but to keep those tenderfeet out of trouble by staying close to people and civilization. That is, until you are ready to learn a little more about survival in the great outdoors.

?

??????????????
PERSONAL RELATIONSHIPS
??????????????

??????????????????????
Are You Marriage Material?
??????????????????????

Nine out of every ten Americans marry at least once. One out of every two marriages ends in divorce.

Marriage is a social, economic, emotional, and legal commitment. There are no guarantees that a marriage will work, but there are ways to discover if you are ready to be married. There are practical matters to discuss, finances to arrange, and emotions to sort out.

?

1. You should think of yourself first in your marriage.
   _____ True. _____ False.

2. Marriages between people of different religions or different races have higher divorce rates.
   _____ True. _____ False.

3. Love is the single most important factor in a marriage.
   _____ True. _____ False.

4. Money should be used for the needs of both people, not just for those of one person.
   _____ True. _____ False.

5. You should tolerate, not change, your spouse's habits.
   _____ True. _____ False.

6. Sex is the cause of most marital trouble.
   _____ True. _____ False.

7. If you change yourself sufficiently, you will automatically have a happy marriage.
   _____ True. _____ False.

8. Keeping your anger inside will do more harm than good.
   _____ True. _____ False.

9. There should be no need to seek outside help; a couple should be able to solve their own problems.
   _____ True. _____ False.

10. Having children always helps a marriage.
    _____ True. _____ False.

11. The higher paid earner should make all the money decisions.
    _____ True. _____ False.

12. Being married is always better than being single.
    _____ True. _____ False.

13. Going out sometimes with friends but without your spouse will help your marriage.
    _____ True. _____ False.

14. The longer a marriage lasts the happier it is.
    _____ True. _____ False.

15. If one person wants a child but the other doesn't, the couple should have a baby anyway.
    _____ True. _____ False.

16. If your partner is having a sexual problem, you should discuss it together openly and honestly.
    _____ True. _____ False.

PERSONAL RELATIONSHIPS

17. A hug or a kiss is the best way to settle a marital quarrel.
    _____ True.   _____ False.

18. Being happy is all it takes to make a marriage work.
    _____ True.   _____ False.

19. In marriage, one person should make all the decisions.
    _____ True.   _____ False.

20. A little jealousy is healthy in a marriage.
    _____ True.   _____ False.

???

SCORING

1. True.	8. False.	15. False.
2. False.	9. False.	16. True.
3. False.	10. False.	17. False.
4. True.	11. False.	18. False.
5. True.	12. False.	19. False.
6. False.	13. True.	20. True.
7. False.	14. False.	

EVALUATION

20 to 18: You are more than ready to get married. Knowing how to take care of your mate and yourself will help ensure your happiness. Marriage is the beginning, and starting off on the right foot can make it a worthwhile venture.

17 to 12: You probably want to get married, but you may not be ready. You must develop skills, insight, and confidence to make your marriage a success. Think about exactly what you want and make sure of what you need before you sign the papers.

11 or below: Getting married should not be in your near future. You should take a look at yourself and what you expect from marriage; you should also re-evaluate your present relationship and decide if you are getting what you want and need. It takes a lot of give and take to make a marriage work, and you aren't ready to give all that is necessary. Pass up the marriage until you can straighten out your needs and desires, because getting married might seem easy, but getting divorced isn't.

?

Singles Lifestyle: Can It Work for You?

In our couple-oriented society, it is generally assumed that anyone who isn't half a couple wants to be, or at least ought to be. Single people are subjected to pressure from friends and family who assume that their unmarried status is temporary and undesirable; single people are made the objects of social and economic discrimination.

If you're single and want to stay that way, or if you're contemplating becoming single, this test will help clarify your feelings.

?

1. Every so often I put off cleaning my house or apartment and let the dishes and laundry pile up.
   _____ True.   _____ False.

2. I don't like friends to drop in without calling first.
   _____ True.   _____ False.

3. Sometimes I just have to be alone to unwind.
   _____ True.   _____ False.

4. I often go out unexpectedly with business associates for drinks or dinner after work.
   _____ True.   _____ False.

5. I don't like eating meals alone.
   _____ True.   _____ False.

6. My schedule is irregular; I eat and sleep at odd hours.
   _____ True.   _____ False.

7. There are times when people—any people—drive me crazy.
   _____ True.   _____ False.

8. The idea of taking a vacation alone bores or frightens me.
   _____ True.   _____ False.

9. I have a satisfying sex life, but there are many times when I'm just not in the mood.
   _____ True.   _____ False.

10. It depresses me to come home to an empty apartment.
    _____ True.   _____ False.

11. I am embarrassed to be seen in public alone.
    _____ True.   _____ False.

12. I value my privacy.
    _____ True.   _____ False.

13. I feel lonely on holidays and weekends.
    _____ True.   _____ False.

14. I like being able to date different people.
    _____ True.   _____ False.

15. When I'm sick I like having someone take care of me.
    _____ True.   _____ False.

16. I feel self-conscious going to a restaurant alone.
    _____ True.   _____ False.

PERSONAL RELATIONSHIPS

17. I enjoy doing favors for people.
    _____ True.   _____ False.

18. I enjoy going to the movies or the theater alone.
    _____ True.   _____ False.

19. When I come home at night I'd like to be able to talk to someone about my day.
    _____ True.   _____ False.

20. I enjoy traveling alone.
    _____ True.   _____ False.

21. I find it hard to meet people.
    _____ True.   _____ False.

22. I'm afraid of growing old alone.
    _____ True.   _____ False.

23. My love affairs rarely last more than a year or two.
    _____ True.   _____ False.

24. My job requires that I spend a lot of time traveling.
    _____ True.   _____ False.

25. I like to go places on the spur of the moment and would probably resent having to tell someone where I'm going or adjust my plans to someone else's schedule.
    _____ True.   _____ False.

???

ANSWERS

Following are the answers usually given by people who are happier living alone. The number of answers you gave that coincide with these is your score.

1. True.
2. True.
3. True.
4. True.
5. False.
6. True.
7. True.
8. False.
9. True.
10. False.
11. False.
12. True.
13. False.
14. True.
15. False.
16. False.
17. False.
18. True.
19. False.
20. True.
21. False.
22. False.
23. True.
24. True.
25. True.

EVALUATION

If your score was between 19 and 25, your single status obviously agrees with you. You are a fearless, intrepid adventurer, and the most important thing to you is your freedom—freedom to go anywhere and do anything, freedom to explore new relationships, both love affairs and friendships. If you ever marry, it will be to someone who shares your needs for independence and privacy. A score between 12 and 18 shows that you are a middle-of-the-roader who needs people but doesn't want them around all the time. You value spontaneity and have the courage to try new things without worrying about what people will think. Your social contacts are many and varied, ranging from love affairs to platonic relationships to same-sex friendships. For you, marriage would be a partnership between equals, with each partner free to go his or her own way. If your score was below 12, you would rather be married than single. You need the security that a long-term relationship will bring, and your personal growth will be furthered by a deep emotional commitment to one person. Because you have this need, you must guard against the tendency to "come on too strong," to expect each new relationship to be the love of your life. Instead, learn to take things as they come and to value each relationship for what it has to offer.

?

How Romantic Are You?

Are you preoccupied with thoughts of romance? Are you in love or wishing you were in love? Do you daydream about amorous adventures? If you answered yes to any of these questions, then you are a full-fledged romantic. If you want to see just how romantic you really are, take this test.

1. If you won a million dollars in a lottery, you would
   a. put it in the bank.
   b. retain an investment counselor.
   c. splurge on an expensive vacation.

2. On a Sunday afternoon you would prefer to
   a. go for a walk in the park.
   b. read the *Times Book Review.*
   c. paint your kitchen cabinets.

3. On a typical date you would prefer to
   a. have an intimate dinner for two at your apartment.
   b. go to the theater.
   c. go to a disco.

4. Your preferred style of dress is
   a. flamboyantly original.
   b. tailored and businesslike.
   c. fashionably up-to-date.

5. The decor of your house or apartment is
   a. starkly functional.
   b. eclectic and nostalgic; you keep things for their sentimental value.
   c. meticulously coordinated.

6. Your favorite type of meal would be
   a. dinner at the Four Seasons.
   b. Thanksgiving dinner with your family.
   c. a picnic in the country with one special person.

7. Your favorite drink is
   a. a martini.
   b. champagne.
   c. scotch and water.

8. Your spouse or lover comes home with two tickets for a weekend in the Bahamas. You say,
   a. "I'd love to go."
   b. "Don't be ridiculous; we can't afford it."
   c. "But I planned to clean the house this weekend."

9. You think wishing wells are
   a. fun; you always toss a coin in and make a wish.
   b. a rip-off; you wouldn't waste your money on them.
   c. nice, but only for silly, impractical people.

10. After a love afair is over, you
    a. recover quickly.
    b. feel miserable and take a long time to get back to normal.
    c. start dating someone else immediately to forget.

PERSONAL RELATIONSHIPS

11. You prefer to sleep in (or would want your partner to sleep in)
    a. a flowing negligee.
    b. pajamas.
    c. nothing.

12. Have you ever written a poem?
    a. Yes, once.
    b. Yes, several.
    c. No, never.

13. If you were a singer, you would be
    a. Barbra Streisand.
    b. Bette Midler.
    c. Edith Piaf.

14. Your favorite composer is
    a. Bach.
    b. Mozart.
    c. Brahms.

15. Your favorite opera is
    a. *Don Giovanni.*
    b. *Pagliacci.*
    c. *Tristan und Isolde.*

16. In your fantasies, the career you choose for yourself is that of
    a. a doctor.
    b. a lawyer.
    c. an artist.

17. In your dreams, you are
    a. rich and famous.
    b. an inventor who solves all the world's problems.
    c. an adventurer in a different place and time.

18. If you had to live in another century, you would choose
    a. the eighteenth century.
    b. the twenty-first century.
    c. the Stone Age.

19. Your favorite novel is
    a. *Fear of Flying.*
    b. *Portnoy's Complaint.*
    c. *Anna Karenina.*

20. Your favorite movie is
    a. *Gone with the Wind.*
    b. *Last Tango in Paris.*
    c. *Animal Crackers.*

?

ANSWERS

1. c	8. a	15. c
2. a	9. a	16. c
3. a	10. b	17. c
4. a	11. a	18. a
5. b	12. b	19. c
6. c	13. c	20. a
7. b	14. c	

?

EVALUATION

20 to 18 In the sky. You are hopelessly, incurably romantic. With your visions of love, beauty, and adventure you'll keep your head in the clouds and your feet off the ground.

17 to 14 On earth. You are a sensible, practical person with occasional flights of romanticism. There's nothing wrong with a little bit of reality tucked in between your daydreams and imaginings.

13 or below Down under. You have both feet firmly planted on the ground. You are a no-nonsense person who deals on a logical, rational level when confronted with emotional situations. Your head and heart are steady and unromantic.

?

Are You Thinking about Parenthood?

Founded in 1972, the National Alliance for Optional Parenthood is a nonprofit organization whose goals are: 1) to increase marital options, 2) to promote personally effective and responsible decisions about whether to have a child (or another child) or to be childfree, and 3) to make the childfree choice socially accepted and respected by society, government, and institutions.

There may be a time in your life when you think you might want to become a parent. But the decision to have a child, or another child, to adopt a child, or to be childfree should be a conscious decision. Questions should arise like: "Do I have the skills for parenthood?"; "Do I want a child?"; and "Do I understand the time, expense, and sacrifice involved in childrearing?" The following exercise, prepared by the National Alliance for Optional Parenthood, will help you consider some of the attitudes and motives you might now be taking for granted. Take a few minutes to help yourself sort out your feelings about parenthood/childfree options.

Directions: On the scale of 1 to 8, circle the number to the left of each question that best suits your attitude; 8 is for a truly important reason, and 1 is for a reason that hardly influences you.

REASONS FOR HAVING CHILDREN

Unimportant   Important

1 2 3 4 5 6 7 8 I don't want to cope with people wondering why I didn't have children.

1 2 3 4 5 6 7 8 I want to experience the sheer entertainment that children can provide.

1 2 3 4 5 6 7 8 I want to have someone with characteristics I believe are important.

1 2 3 4 5 6 7 8 I want someone to stand by me when I'm old.

1 2 3 4 5 6 7 8 I want to make my parents happy.

1 2 3 4 5 6 7 8 I want to be needed.

1 2 3 4 5 6 7 8 Raising a child will give me a feeling of accomplishment.

1 2 3 4 5 6 7 8 I want the warmth and closeness of a family.

1 2 3 4 5 6 7 8 I want someone to carry on the family business.

1 2 3 4 5 6 7 8 I want the satisfaction of giving myself to someone else.

1 2 3 4 5 6 7 8 I want to add interest to my home life.

1 2 3 4 5 6 7 8 I feel that life just wouldn't be complete without having a child.

PERSONAL RELATIONSHIPS

REASONS FOR REMAINING CHILDFREE

1 2 3 4 5 6 7 8 My spouse and I will have a more satisfactory relationship without children.

1 2 3 4 5 6 7 8 I want to concentrate on my own growth and development.

1 2 3 4 5 6 7 8 My partner wants to remain childfree.

1 2 3 4 5 6 7 8 I want to be free from the responsibility of child rearing.

1 2 3 4 5 6 7 8 I want to travel freely.

1 2 3 4 5 6 7 8 I want to continue to enjoy my leisure time.

1 2 3 4 5 6 7 8 I want to put my full energy into my career.

1 2 3 4 5 6 7 8 I want to devote more time and energy to society's problems.

1 2 3 4 5 6 7 8 I want to be able to use my income for things I want to do.

1 2 3 4 5 6 7 8 I want to do my part to control population growth.

1 2 3 4 5 6 7 8 I'd prefer to use my talents in other ways.

1 2 3 4 5 6 7 8 I want to maintain my privacy.

???

EVALUATION

Your answers to this exercise will not be right or wrong. This is not a scientific test, and there is no score. This exercise is designed to help you sort out *some* of your motives and attitudes about childfree and parenthood options, including childbearing, childrearing and lifestyle. The results of this exercise will be your own feelings about some of the issues involved in parenthood and childfree options. There is no score that can tell you whether you should have a child or be childfree. Making a lifestyle decision requires a great deal of attention and thought, more than an exercise score alone could ever indicate.

The most important thing to remember is that this exercise *will not* tell you whether you should have a child, or whether you will be a good or happy parent; this test *will* make you aware of your own feelings about parenthood to help you in making a decision about your future. Choosing to be childfree or a parent is not a question of one set of skills being better than the other, or one way of life being right and the other wrong. It is a question of choosing what you feel you want. There are many more individualized questions that you should ask yourself, but these twenty-four questions are a good place to start. Reviewing your own answers could help you sort out your own feelings, emotions, and motives.

Whatever your answers, remember that having a child involves effort, responsibility, sacrifice, and expense, as well as joy and happiness. If you are unsure of what to do, take all the time you need. Talk to friends, parents, childfree adults, counselors, and your partner. Just make sure your decision is an informed and conscious one.

Courtesy of National Alliance for Optional Parenthood, Washington, D.C.

How Do You Rate as a Single Parent?

As the 1980s begin, nearly 20 percent of all families in the United States are single parent families. The divorce rate has more than doubled during the previous fifteen years and there are over one million divorces each year. Families headed by women who have never been married increased by 71 percent from 1970 to 1977, and it is estimated that 100,000 unmarried women over twenty-five had children in 1977. It is projected that one out of two children born in the late '70s will spend some time during childhood or adolescence living with a single parent. And single parenthood has become a permanent life-style for a large number of mothers and fathers.

Like any other parent, single parents must cope with a variety of parenting problems. Single parents, however, are likely to experience even more stress since they must not only parent *alone* but must also adjust to the circumstances that made them single parents. The issues single parents must deal with have been addressed in a variety of books by numerous experts—professionals in the mental health field as well as single parents themselves. Many of these books, and the collective experience of over three-quarters of a million single parents who have been or continue to be members of Parents Without Partners, Inc. during the twenty-three years since the beginning of the organization, form a significant body of knowledge about single parenting. This knowledge is reflected in this test concerned with your understanding of those single parent roles, attitudes, and expectations that influence your effectiveness as a single parent.

The following test addresses the special situations of single parents more than specific parenting skills. Part 1 includes questions of a general nature about single parents, children, and societal attitudes. Part 2 deals with separated, divorced, and single parents. There are several questions about widowed single parents and never-married parents in Parts 3 and 4. Not all questions have just one good answer.

PART 1: SINGLE PARENTS AND THEIR CHILDREN

1. For the most part, society developed a more positive attitude toward single parents during the 1970s.
   ____ True. ____ False.

2. Now that you are a single parent, you must be both mother and father to your children.
   ____ True. ____ False.

3. As a single parent, you must
   a. concentrate on meeting your children's needs.
   b. encourage cooperation by children in meeting household responsibilities.
   c. work harder to keep the house clean, cook, garden, make household repairs, chauffeur children, and earn money as well.
   d. develop an authoritarian attitude so your children will turn out right.

4. Children living in a single parent home
   - (a.) suffer permanently from the lack of a (usually) male role model.
   - b. don't do as well in school as children from two-parent homes.
   - c. need sympathy and help.
   - d. tend to have lower self-esteem than children who live with two parents.

5. The widow across the street has invited you to attend a meeting of a local group for single parents with her. You
   - a. make the excuse of another engagement.
   - b. tell her you have to bake cookies for the PTA.
   - c. frankly admit that you are fearful about meeting new people.
   - d. ask her about the kinds of activities the group has.

6. Most single parents want to remarry as soon as possible to find a father/mother for the children.
   _____ True.   _X_ False.

7. It is a sign of weakness to seek professional counseling.
   _____ True.   _X_ False.

8. If you begin to date, you must
   - a. make sure the children meet him/her right away.
   - b. plan family activities with your children for your dates.
   - (c.) introduce your date to your children after a good relationship has developed between the two of you.
   - d. drop the date immediately if the children are critical.

PART 2: SEPARATED/DIVORCED SINGLE PARENTS

9. Ideally, both parents together should tell their children about their separation.
   _X_ True.   _____ False.

10. In telling the children about the separation, parents should
    - a. wait until the departing parent leaves.
    - b. reassure them about provisions for their security.
    - c. ask a trusted friend or relative to talk with the children.
    - d. tell honestly about the reasons for the separation without imposing unnecessary details.

11. Since honesty is the best policy, it is advisable to let the children know just how awfully the absent parent behaved.
    _____ True.   _____ False.

12. Since school personnel tend to feel that academic and behavioral problems are the result of children coming from a "broken home," you should not tell the teacher about family problems.
    _____ True.   _____ False.

13. When an ex-husband does not send child support payments regularly, the mother should
    - a. let it be known that she can't buy things the children want because "Daddy hasn't sent us money."
    - b. enlist family members to find ways they can manage until the problem is resolved.
    - c. ask her parents to help with essentials, if they are able.
    - d. turn to social services or get legal assistance to help her family.

14. When children ask, "Why doesn't daddy/mommy visit us?" a good answer is
    - a. "I've been wondering about that myself."
    - b. "You really miss daddy/mommy, don't you?"
    - c. "Don't mention that evil man/woman!"
    - d. "Daddy/mommy loves you very much, but he/she is busy with his/her own life."

15. Father has a woman friend who spends a lot of time with him. Mother should forbid visits with the children when the woman friend is there.
    _____ True.   _____ False.

HOW DO YOU RATE AS A SINGLE PARENT?

16. It has been demonstrated that fathers who have custody of their children do not do as well as mothers. Therefore, custody is usually given to mothers.
    _____ True.   _____ False.

17. When your date arrives, your children ask him/her, "Are you going to marry mom/dad?" The best response is to
    a. try to hide your embarrassment and change the subject.
    b. answer, yourself, with "When I decide to get married you'll be the first to know."
    c. hope your date ignores the question.
    d. listen carefully to the date's response.

18. Mother has set a curfew time for fifteen-year-old Cindy. Cindy threatens to call her father if the curfew is enforced and threatens to go live with him. Mother should
    a. pack Cindy's bags.
    b. call her former husband and ask for his support.
    c. leave the room and refuse to discuss it.
    d. find a time to discuss the issue after everyone has cooled off.

19. The absent parent has not kept up with child support payments. The other parent should
    a. refuse to let the children visit him/her.
    b. take him/her to court.
    c. separate issues of support and visiting and attempt to work out the nonpayment problem.
    d. enlist the children to influence him/her to get payments current.

20. As a visiting parent, you feel really depressed after you've spent a weekend with your children. Your best course is to stop the visits; it will be better for all concerned.
    _____ True.   _____ False.

21. When you visit with your children, the best thing to do to show that you still love them is to buy them things you know the other parent can't afford.
    _____ True.   _____ False.

22. Mother/Father has been dating someone for several months. The relationship has become special. It is now time to
    a. end it if there is no promise of marriage.
    b. involve him/her more with the children.
    c. invite him/her to move in.
    d. warn the children to expect a new father/mother soon.

23. There are so many divorces; it must be fairly easy to raise a child alone.
    _____ True.   _____ False.

24. Divorce is
    a. an opportunity for personal growth.
    b. a sign of failure in the marital relationship.
    c. evidence of personal inadequacy.
    d. a disaster for all concerned.

25. Joint custody means
    a. both parents have responsibility for major decisions about the children.
    b. children live half the year with mother and the other half with father.
    c. children will benefit if the joint custody arrangements are followed.
    d. parents who fight with each other may have troubles with joint custody.

26. One problem with joint custody, or coparenting, is that former spouses may continue their dependency on each other instead of developing separate lives or making a "clean break."
    _____ True.   _____ False.

PART 3: WIDOWED SINGLE PARENTS

27. It is important to remember a spouse/parent who has died as a perfect person.
    _____ True.   _____ False.

28. When your spouse has died, you should tell the children that
    a. he/she has gone to live with God.
    b. he/she is having a long sleep now.
    c. he/she would want you to be brave and not cry.
    d. he/she is dead and will never come back.

PERSONAL RELATIONSHIPS

29. Becoming involved with others and seeking to involve yourself in activities will help you and your children adjust to the loss of a loved one.
    _____ True.   _____ False.

30. A sensible course for a widowed single parent is to
    a. allow yourself and the children time for grieving.
    b. permit the children to attend the funeral.
    c. admit that you don't know all the answers about death.
    d. find ways to cope through art, physical activity, or creative self-expression.

31. As a widow/widower, you must now live for your children.
    _____ True.   _____ False.

32. Widowed single parents have little in common with divorced single parents.
    _____ True.   _____ False.

33. Statements such as, "Father/Mother would have wanted/not wanted you to do this," is one way to carry on the influence of the dead parent over the children.
    _____ True.   _____ False.

PART 4: NEVER-MARRIED SINGLE PARENTS

34. Societal attitudes have relaxed in censuring pregnancy out of wedlock.
    _____ True.   _____ False.

35. Reasons for the increased number of unmarried parents include
    a. allowing single persons to adopt children.
    b. increased sexual activity among adolescents.
    c. a failure to use contraceptive techniques.
    d. women are becoming more self-sufficient.

36. Never-married parents
    a. have less inner turmoil than divorced parents.
    b. generally are able to find creative child care and living arrangements.
    c. must balance social lives with parental responsibilities.
    d. should not tell the child about his/her father.

37. Many never-married mothers are overprotective of their child(ren).
    _____ True.   _____ False.

???

ANSWERS AND DISCUSSION

1. *True.* The beliefs of the social anthropologists of the 1960s, who asserted that a two-parent family was the only healthy form, has given way to the realization that there are many other healthy family forms. Increasingly, churches have responded to the needs of single-parent families. They have instituted support and social groups and sponsored special seminars for single parents. Tax laws have recognized the head of household category and allowed child care expense credit for working parents. Displaced homemaker programs, shelters for battered wives, and educational and welfare programs have responded to single parent needs. Women's credit rights have been established. State and federal legal systems have addressed the problem of child custody and support, as well as divorce law reform. At the workplace, flextime benefits single parents (and households in which both parents work).

2. *False.* It is self-evident that you can only be one person—one parent. A mother may assume some "traditional" father roles, such as pitching baseballs to her son, fixing faucets, and changing the oil in the automobile. A father may shop, cook, wash clothes, and clean house—roles formerly performed by his wife. But it is more a question of choice and survival than attempting to fill both parental roles—roles that are less rigidly defined in modern times. Fathers can be nurturing and mothers can be self-sufficient to a greater degree than previously thought.

HOW DO YOU RATE AS A SINGLE PARENT?

3. *b* is the best answer here. Yes, you must meet your children's needs, but yours are important, too. A happier person is a better parent. You may need to work hard, but careful planning and enlisting everyone's help may prevent an energy crisis. Mother's priorities may change from waxing floors and baking goodies to working full-time. Fathers may focus on less work and career and more on making time to spend with children. An authoritarian parent does not guarantee "perfect" children, and extreme strictness may cause children to rebel. It is likely that a single-parent home will be more democratic than two-parent homes. All family members share household tasks and even make decisions together about matters that affect everyone. Developing responsibility and pride from contributing to the family are valuable in training children. Many children from single parent homes consider themselves more responsible and "mature" than their peers living with both parents.

4. This is a trick question. None of these definitely apply. Some research has indicated that boys from "fatherless" homes score lower on masculine-feminine trait tests, but conclusive statements about whether this is good or bad are not possible. The facts about the causes of homosexuality are complicated and related more to relationships of sons to both father and mother and not to single-parent living by itself. Big Brothers, Scouts, or male relatives may be alternatives to the missing male role model. While some children don't do as well in school as two-parent children, it is not solely due to living with a single parent. Other factors, such as economic or social problems, may be at the root of school or behavior problems. Single parent children do need support, encouragement and assistance, but *not* sympathy. Feeling sorry for them will not be helpful since it may cause the children to feel sorry for themselves. Children who are pitied may develop the attitude that "the world owes them a living" for all they have suffered and that they don't have to take responsibility for their own lives . . . "others will 'do it' for them." Recent research showed that the amount of conflict in the home perceived by children is the determining factor of low self-esteem, not family structure. The more conflict and fighting, the lower the self-esteem, whether single or two-parent household.

5. *c.* This is a good opportunity to discuss some of your feelings with a fellow single parent. Attending adult group meetings will give you an opportunity to make new friends and to develop interests of your own. Your getting out may even be encouraged by your children, especially older ones. Being the only focus of a parent's life places undue stress on children. Remember, a happier person is a better parent. You need some time for yourself and adult relationships, and going to activities with a friend is a good way to begin socializing.

6. *True*—but this is a trick question. Many single parents do remarry (the remarriage rate is higher for men than for women). And many single parents with young children, a stressful situation under the best of circumstances, feel that they may be depriving children of a full family experience. They also sense that having another person to share the responsibilities of parenting will help reduce their anxieties. Even though the feeling, "I must find a mother/father for the children" is common, it is a poor reason to seek a mate. Often a marriage "for the sake of the children" is contracted in haste, without full consideration of the long-term effects or the stepparenting problem that must be dealt with. Giving yourself time to become secure as an independent individual will diminish your need to marry to find a parent for the children.

7. *False.* Single parents may undergo very powerful stresses and intense emotional turmoil. It is more a sign of strength to admit that life is difficult and that assistance in sorting out feelings or exploring options may be valuable. Many single parents undergo (usually) short-term counseling during their most stressful periods. Friends can be empathetic, but a professional with mental health training can increase understanding and abilities to manage daily tasks and plan sensibly and realistically for the future.

8. *c.* Especially when children are young, it is better to introduce them to dates only as the dates become important in your life. A constant parade of different men or women may be confusing, especially at first. Family outings with dates should be informal. Don't wait too long for family outings, as your relationship with your date may be far more intense than the relationship of the children with your date—a possible source of problems. Children may be

critical of anyone and everyone, and you must decide whether you will allow them to dictate your choices or not. Beginning dating should be treated very casually to avoid situations that become too quickly intense and threatening, either to you or the children. Children gradually accept a parent's need and right to have special friends.

9. *True.* If this is possible, it gives the children a chance to ask both parents questions and to get assurances from both that their needs will be met. Even though couples can't live with each other, their responsibilities as parents do not end with divorce. It is best to prepare children in advance of the actual separation no matter how young the children are. Be prepared to sense unspoken fears, self-blame, and even anger—and deal with it. Talking with children about a separation when parents themselves may be extremely upset is difficult, but it must be done. A good book for parents (as well as children) is *The Boys and Girls Book about Divorce,* by Richard A. Gardner.

10. *b* and *d.* You may have to plan several sessions together over a period of time to answer questions and to make sure children understand family changes. In this way it is easier to reassure children that they will still have two parents who care for them. If this is not possible with both parents, sometimes a trusted friend or relative will be helpful. Most children have friends whose parents are divorced. You can use well-managed single-parent situations as an example. Even though children may sense that there are problems between their parents, it is important not to "spring" such an important change as a separation on them without preparation and reassurances about their security. This is especially true for younger children whose entire world depends on their parents. Do not make the mistake of thinking that "they are too young to understand." In a recent California study of divorce and children, it was found that over 80 percent of young children had *not* been prepared. It took these children a much longer time to adjust. Even though school-age children and teens have interests and ties beyond the family, details about any changes should be carefully explained.

11. *False.* If you paint the absent parent black, the children (who after all are part of both parents) may react by over-idealizing or taking sides (openly or covertly) with the absent parent. They may also become confused and may feel diminished in worth. Good advice, however, is not to endow the absent parent with exceptionally positive characteristics if he/she has been behaving in an uncaring manner, ignoring children, mistreating the family, or coping unsuccessfully with alcoholism or emotional illness. A careful middle path is best, for a child needs to love both parents. Keep communication lines open with your children, and allow them to ask as many questions as they want. Be prepared to give explanations over and over again.

12. *False.* Here is another trick question. Single parents will be hearing the negative term "broken home" less and less as teachers and school administrators are gaining understanding through in-service workshops. Also, many teachers are now single parents. Many schools offer creative programs to students on loss or divorce, and junior and senior high schools may have peer counseling groups. Most teachers and counselors are willing to cooperate with parents and give extra support and understanding when children are suffering initial insecurities or fears due to the separation of the parents. While some school personnel in rural areas or small towns may be less aware of how to support children, in general the attitudes of educators are changing along with the other institutions of society. So, by all means, let your children's teachers in on the family changes that may affect school performance. Teachers and counselors may be your best allies since children spend a good part of the day in school. Be sure to inform schools about arrangements with the other parent, as schools may now arrange to have records sent to noncustodial parents if cooperative parenting is the plan between you and your former spouse.

13. *b, c,* and *d.* Spending time with the absent parent is healthy for children, regardless of how well financial obligations have been met. Putting children in the middle of parental hostilities, using them to "get even," or using money as a weapon cause confusion and resentment in children and are a leading cause of poor adjustment following divorce. Turning to family members, including parents, and attempting procedures of negotiation, mediation,

HOW DO YOU RATE AS A SINGLE PARENT?

or court intervention may be alternatives to solve the problem. Almost all states have child support enforcement offices to assist in court ordered payment collections.

14. *b.* Reflecting what you think children are feeling is a good opening to a discussion of the issue. You may be able to determine whether the child feels rejected or different from other children. You may learn about the intensity of sad or angry feelings. Older children may be able to contact or visit father at a later time (with adequate preparation or counseling if there is a mental illness or similar problem). Telling a child that "daddy loves you" when daddy does not write or visit or show loving behavior does a disservice. There are many painful events in life to adjust to, and having an uncaring father may be one of them. If you feel a child is very much upset, you might seek professional counseling for the child, the entire family, or yourself in finding ways to deal with the situation.

15. *False.* While this may happen if mother feels rejected, abandoned, or has very strong moral values, controlling visitation in this way does not foster good relationships between children and both parents. There are many things you cannot control about your child's life after he reaches school age. Unless unhealthy or dangerous activities are going on, it is best to leave the relationship between the child and the father (and his friends) to *them* and not interfere. Young children rarely make moral judgments without adult prompting and it might not be constructive to create tension in the child by forcing him to accept your judgment against a parent with whom he or she identifies. If the wounds of separation are still open, or children are having difficulty, mother might attempt to discuss the situation with the former husband. He may agree to introduce a girl friend to the children later.

16. This is another one to make you think. Many fathers have demonstrated very well that they can handle single parent responsibilities. Current research tends to substantiate that fathers can be competent, nurturing parents. "Traditional" views of judges and some mental health advisors—which fathers' rights groups define as prejudice—are the main reason custody in disputed cases is usually awarded to mothers. Many modern mothers may agree to have their children live with fathers. The *average* agreement negotiated between separating parents permits the children to live with mother and visit liberally with father. Many creative kinds of arrangements can be made for children.

17. *d.* This question is often asked by children. You can learn much about how your date reacts with children by the way he responds. Also *b.* The statement ("you will be the first to know") respects your children's right to be concerned about you and any more family changes and also respects your right to be the one to decide such things as whom and when you will marry. Don't punish yourself if you are caught off guard the first time and follow *a* or *c.*

18. *a* is a little extreme, but all the rest are useful solutions to resolve Cindy's power play. If mother has a good relationship on parenting issues with Cindy's father, he would be a strong ally to help defuse the problem. *c*—refusing to become involved in a power contest (in which no one can win) is also a useful technique. That must then be followed up by *d* so that the issue of who decides when Cindy comes home can be agreed upon. Cindy is more likely to follow an agreement if she has had a say in it. Children are adept at seeking power. Threatening to live with dad so they can get their way hit mom's sensitive spot. If mom wants to be the "favorite" parent, perhaps she'd better reevaluate that idea. Competition between divorced parents is not constructive and can only lead to more power plays like the one described.

19. *c*, first. Putting children in the middle (by *a* and *d*) of financial disagreements between parents is one ploy guaranteed to have negative effects on the children. Instituting legal proceedings may be a last resort, although many states have initiated creative ways to handle court-ordered support payments. A Federal Child Support Enforcement office has even been established to cope with the problem—a significant one for large numbers of single parents. As to keeping children from visiting, the decision must take into account health, mental state, and economic situation of the absent parent. Children, again, adjust better if they have free access to the other parent.

20. *False.* While many fathers/mothers do stop visiting because they feel pain, guilt, loss of

status as a full-time parent, or other negative feelings, others gradually develop a more natural parenting relationship by keeping in close touch, calling, and seeing children regularly. Part-time parenting *is* difficult and can never be the same as living with your children full-time. If the parent the children live with is cooperative (after all, he/she needs time away from the children), a loving relationship can be maintained and noncustodial parents can have considerable influence on their children. A California stury of divorce and children found that almost half of the fathers had a much closer relationship with their children after the divorce.

21. *False.* Many visiting parents try to be "Santa Claus"—buying expensive gifts, taking children to expensive shows and outings, to make up for guilt (or even to "show up" the other parent). This kind of behavior does not build healthy parent-child relationships. Children usually understand that love cannot be bought in this way. It might ease guilt temporarily (just as spanking a child temporarily relieves parental anger or fear), but it is nonconstructive in the long run. A more natural, doing-things-together plan of activities and simple outings, such as walking in the park or preparing a meal together, uses everyday events to make shared time meaningful and pleasant.

22. *b.* It is not honest to keep an important person in your life out of the children's lives. It is best to take the middle path between a constant parade of different dates through the home and never allowing children to know what you are doing when you are out two or three evenings a week. Many formerly marrieds are living together before remarriage. As this is a very new development, it cannot be said whether such living arrangements are helpful or not as a preparation for a more permanent commitment, and they may stimulate strong feelings about moral issues as well. But, nevertheless, many children have accepted such an arrangement when the two adults have a sound relationship and believe it is constructive for all concerned.

23. *False.* Titles of publications such as *Creative Divorce* and *Divorce: Chance of New Lifetime* belie the stress and pain experienced by the adults and children involved in divorce. Initial adjustment may involve a difficult reorganization of many lives. Even a negative relationship is a relationship, and when it is over, there is much anxiety. It is true that in time single parenting becomes easier as parents become whole persons instead of part of a couple. Many single parents feel that divorce—whether sought or not—has made them stronger people, but few would want to relive the first year after separation over again. And the fact remains that parenting alone and part-time parenting after divorce require strength and determination, and are far from easy.

24. *a* and *b*. Many values are expressed in this question. There may still be people who consider divorce a disaster caused by personal inadequacies of the marital partners. But times have changed since clergymen or counselors routinely told spouses with marital difficulties to "go home and try a little harder." A negative view does not contribute to constructive adjustments. According to the Morton Hunts in the book, *The Divorce Experience,* many divorced people have experienced personal growth and development after initial painful adjustments. As research verifies, children also adjust. Even though parental divorce is the single most traumatic event (in the eyes of children) they may experience, children gradually learn coping skills that may be helpful in later life. Staying together "for the sake of the children" is seldom a wise course when there is hostility or violence between parents. Divorce cna be an opportunity for growth as well as a cause of pain and disruption. That divorce occurs when the marriage relationship "dies" or fails is reflected in many laws citing "no-fault" or "irreconcilable differences" between partners.

25. All can be true, although children are less likely to be willing to change households every six months after they are in school. If parents live in the same neighborhood, this could work. Some arrangements may have the children moving every two or three days within the same neighborhood. Other parents rotate time in the house where the children live permanently. The basis for joint custody is the shared responsibility for major decisions, medical care, and support. California is the first state to require judges to consider joint custody as first preference. The belief that children fare better with free access to both parents is reflected in the California law, which also provides that, if joint custody is not possible,

priority should be given to the parent who is likely or willing to allow the freest access to the other parent. Judges, who see only the minority of divorcing couples that cannot negotiate an agreement out of court, take a skeptical view of joint custody. But more and more couples are negotiating (and renegotiating) joint custody arrangements each year and making them work.

26. This is neither true nor false, since both spouses remain parents of the same offspring as long as they both live and thus keep parenting ties with each other. A "friendly" divorce is a way of living that recognizes that the children should be cared for by the two people who care about them the most. Some mental health professionals believe that a child's self-esteem and identity will suffer unless he/she lives with only one divorced parent. "Co-parents" believe that children can feel good about themselves living in two homes—with either caring parent. Parents with those expectations are successful in maintaining joint custody arrangements. It has been suggested that informal joint custody in which every detail is not stipulated is better since circumstances do change. It is better to adjust to changes informally than to go to court again and again.

27. *False.* Overidealization or "enshrining" of the dead parent by the surviving family creates an image of a superhuman being. The living parent has limits, as do all humans, and can never live up to children's expectations or fantasies. It just isn't real, and such a belief about the dead parent may interfere with relationships of parent and children with real, imperfect, normal human beings.

28. *d.* If you tell children that their parent has "gone to live with God," you will probably have a church/synagogue dropout. If you tell children the parent is having a "long peaceful sleep," you may have an insomniac. Preventing children from crying or expressing grief over their loss bottles up strong feelings that must be expressed in some way. Death is final, and all family members must come to terms with that fact.

29. *True.* Widowed parents find that shared activities are helpful after intense mourning has been expressed.

30. All of these are sensible courses. There are many helpful books or support groups that widowed parents can use to assist them in roles for which they are unprepared. Workshops on the subject of death and dying have become widespread. A school counselor or teacher may also be helpful with the children, and many a classroom has discussed a fellow student's loss of a parent and has proved supportive and understanding.

31. *True*, of course. But, as an adult human being, you may have much of your life and many rich experiences ahead of you. Your needs are important too.

32. *False.* It is true that many a successful marriage is ended through death, but similar mourning experiences must be worked through by both widowed and divorced. Through group discussions it is known that anger, guilt, and sadness must be dealt with by both. Daily tasks of living and pressures of single parenting are similar, and most widowed parents find that they have more in common with the divorced because, with differences, both are parents.

33. *False.* Using this way to control children's behavior is emotional blackmail. It can be very disturbing to children, as there is no way they can check on the truth of their parent's interpretation.

34. *True.* Many American families have accepted unmarried pregnancies for some time. A probable indicator of more general societal acceptance is the increasing number of older (25 to 45) unmarried women who are having children—an increase of about 20 percent from 1974 to 1977.

35. All four may contribute to the rise in the number of unmarried parents. Women are having more children (as discussed in Item 34 above), and adults of both sexes may adopt children in many states. More women are also finding that they can be financially independent and are accepted in nontraditional life styles, although incomes of families headed by women are among the lowest of all categories in Census Bureau reports. It is no great secret that adolescents are becoming pregnant in increasing numbers, despite "availability" of contraceptive information.

36. *a, b, c.* It is fortunate that never-married mothers do not have to cope with the traumatic changes of divorce in addition to their sole responsibility for their children. Even though there may be a severed relationship with a man, there may have been little expectation of

PERSONAL RELATIONSHIPS

a continuing commitment. Since an unmarried mother has made the decision to keep her child, her main feelings may be heavy responsibility and aloneness. For this reason, many are motivated to share housing or child care with other single parents (or a family), thus developing an informal, supportive ''extended'' family. This also allows unmarried mothers an opportunity for a needed social life they could not otherwise enjoy. Most children will want to know about their father. It is best that the information come from the mother, and being told simply and with caring will usually prevent the child from blaming himself or feeling unwanted.

37. *True*. Many never-married parents put such energy and thought into raising their child that they may restrict the growing child's independence. Many single mothers agree that this may be so, even though they understand that such strong emotional investment in the child may not be helpful.

Copyright © by Parents Without Partners, Inc.

?

Test Yourself: How Good a Parent Are You?

By Leah Yarrow, Associate Editor of Parents

You've told yourself a hundred times you won't make the same mistakes your parents did. So what mistakes are you making? Maybe you're not making any. Here's your chance to lock horns with the experts.

Each day parents face situations that can try even the most stalwart souls. Although they deal with those situations as best they can, doubts always linger: did they do the right thing?

Now you can find out how well you're coping with those all-too-familiar moments by quizzing yourself. A panel of experts in child development, education, and psychology helped devise the following scenarios—and the answers. (For some scenarios only one right answer is provided, while for others there is a logical progression.) The multiple choices provided after each scenario represent only a few of the possible approaches.

1. Eight-year-old Jimmy arrives home from school looking downcast. He flings his books on the kitchen table and stares dejectedly at his glass of milk. Suddenly he looks up and says, "Mom, am I stupid? The teacher called me stupid when I missed a multiplication problem." His mother should
    a. chastise Jimmy for not having finished his homework the previous night. If he had, he would have known the answer.
    b. explain that calling someone a name doesn't mean the name is appropriate. Talk about name-calling (perhaps he's done it, too), how it makes others feel, and why people do it.
    c. schedule a conference with the teacher, who must have a problem if he calls children names.
    d. promise to help with Jimmy's homework, if he feels inadequate.

2. Mrs. Smith and her four-year-old daughter Nancy are doing the weekly grocery shopping. Nancy takes pride in helping her mother push the big cart, and she volunteers to find a carton of milk. When she returns, her mother is talking to a friend who is overweight. After staring at the woman Nancy says, "Mommy, why is that woman so fat?" Her mother should
    a. ignore Nancy's question, and hope her friend didn't hear.
    b. angrily tell Nancy that's not a nice thing to say, make her apologize, and send her to get another grocery item.
    c. quietly explain that everyone weighs different amounts, that some people eat more, and that some people have physical problems that make them heavy.
    d. tell Nancy the friend is not fat.

3. Jonathan, six months old, is an extremely sweet child who loves to get attention from his parents and grandparents. Unlike other babies, he never resists being held or played with. Today his aunt is visiting from out of town and his mother wants this first meeting with her son to be impressive. But when she picks Jonathan up to introduce him to his aunt he begins to whimper. His diapers aren't soiled and he was fed, so his mother pays no attention. As the aunt tries to take the baby he begins to scream and squirm. Embarrassed, his mother should
   a. tell Jonathan this is his aunt and he should behave nicely. Make him stay in his aunt's arms as long as possible so he gets used to her.
   b. take him back, reassure him that everything is okay, and put him back on the floor to play.
   c. isolate him in his room for a period of time, saying that if he can't act properly he can't be in the same room with anyone.

4. The Greens and their two-year-old son Jeremy have ben invited to a dinner celebration at their cousin's home. Before dinner Jeremy plays contentedly with his toys and goes to anyone who beckons him. At the dinner table he eats only a few bites and becomes irritable. By dessert time Jeremy is alternating between screaming and pounding on the floor. His parents have been unable to get him to sleep or to distract him. They should
   a. go home.
   b. take him to another room and tell him he must stay there until he can be quiet.
   c. threaten to spank him if he doesn't calm down.

5. Cynthia, twelve, knows she must be waiting at the corner for the school bus at 8:30 A.M. or she'll miss it, but she is chronically late. Some days she doesn't get out of bed on time; other days she dawdles in the bathroom or while getting dressed. Often her mother has to drive her to school so she'll get there on time and sometimes she still doesn't get there on time. Her mother has been threatening and cajoling her but nothing seems to have worked. She should
   a. offer her a reward (a movie, special treat) for being on time every day for a week.
   b. make her miss school every time she misses the bus.
   c. have her go to school at whatever stage of readiness she is at when the bus arrives (without breakfast or in her nightgown).
   d. have her go to bed an hour earlier than usual and buy her an alarm clock for which she is responsible.

6. The white, newly upholstered couch in the living room seems like an ideal drawing board to five-year-old Susan. So, she takes her mother's bright red lipstick and merrily begins drawing circles and squiggly lines on the couch. Her mother should
   a. slap the lipstick out of Susan's hand and scream, "Don't you ever draw on the furniture again," while promising a spanking later.
   b. take the lipstick firmly away and explain why she shouldn't have drawn on the couch. Have her watch every stage of the repair, from calling the store to the couch's being cleaned.
   c. take the lipstick and draw on Susan's favorite party dress saying, "Now, how do you like that?"
   d. have Susan participate in paying the cost of cleaning by contributing pennies from her piggy bank.

7. Fifteen-year-old Melinda was told in no uncertain terms to be home from her date by midnight. Melinda hasn't dated often and, because she is out with a seventeen-year-old boy, her parents are more concerned than usual. When she isn't home by 12:30 her parents are quite worried. When Melinda walkes in unharmed at 12:45 her parents should
   a. tell her she's grounded for a month for causing so much anxiety.
   b. tell her how relieved they are, explain how worried they were, and tell her that if she is delayed she must call them. Warn of future punishment if she doesn't comply.
   c. tell her they were so worried they called the police and that her boyfriend will be picked up. Later, tell her they didn't really call the police but next time they will.

TEST YOURSELF: HOW GOOD A PARENT ARE YOU?

8. Late one afternoon Michael's mother comes into his room to put the laundry away. As she leaves the room she notices a new red squirt gun on a corner of his desk. She doesn't think her nine-year-old son had any money that day because his allowance had been withheld as punishment. So his mother suspects the gun was stolen from a local store. She should
   a. go next door to where Michael is playing and confront him with the evidence in front of his friends.
   b. wait till his father comes home, then confront him and have his father punish him with a spanking. Afterward she should make Michael throw the gun away.
   c. confront Michael when he returns home and, after determining he didn't pay for the gun, make him go to the store and pay for it.

9. Three-year-old Maria has been unhappy since her sister was born two months ago. She becomes cranky easily and, rather than playing quietly as she used to, constantly interrupts her mother and clamors for attention. Today her mother left the room for a few seconds and when she returned she found Maria trying to dump the baby out of her cradle. She should
   a. immediately and firmly stop Maria. Without anger tell Maria she won't let her hurt the baby and that because Maria is so little her mother has to control her behavior for her.
   b. run in and push Maria roughly aside, pick up the baby and cuddle it. Tell Maria she's a bad girl.
   c. after making sure the baby is all right, spank Maria and tell her that she must never go near the baby again unless an adult is present.

10. After a refreshing shower, Mr. Jones stands in the tub dripping and reflecting on the previous evening. He is rudely brought back to the present, however, when the bathroom door bangs open and his six-year-old daughter Becky bursts in to ask a question. His daughter has never seen him naked before. Mr. Jones should
    a. quickly grab a towel, cover himself, and tell Becky to get out of the bathroom immediately.
    b. act as if nothing has happened. Let Becky watch while he dries himself and she asks the question.
    c. while reaching casually for a towel, tell Becky that he's finishing his shower and that he'll be out of the bathroom in a minute to answer her question.

11. Cora, four, is sitting on the floor watching television, the fingers of one hand twisting and untwisting bunches of hair. Her mother, during the past few months, has repeatedly told her to stop it because she'll damage her hair. This morning, when she sees Cora playing with her hair again, she is really annoyed. She should
    a. leave Cora alone and try to figure out why she is twisting her hair.
    b. switch off the television and tell her she can't watch it until she learns to stop twisting her hair.
    c. smear something gummy or sticky on her hands to remind her not to touch her hair.
    d. threaten to shave her head.

12. As five-year-old Lisa sits down at the dinner table her mother asks her if she has washed her hands. Although Lisa says, "Yes," as she reaches for a piece of bread her mother sees Lisa's hands are still covered with the modeling clay she had been playing with. This is not the first time Lisa has lied, although all the lies have been innocuous. Her mother should
    a. angrily say, "Why did you tell me you washed your hands when you obviously didn't? This lying has gone on long enough." Deprive Lisa of dinner as punishment.
    b. explain that she takes Lisa at her word. Try to make her see how awful it would be if she couldn't trust what her mother said to her.
    c. ignore her dirty hands and silently vow to check her hands before every meal.

13. When Mrs. Jones brought her infant son home from the hospital it was difficult to become adjusted to the 2 A.M. feedings. But today Mrs. Jones woke up at 2 A.M. and her seven-week-old son didn't. She went back to sleep, feeling sure he'd be up soon. When she awoke at 6 A.M. he was still asleep. Alarmed, Mrs. Jones should

a. immediately awaken the baby and fed him.
b. check to be sure the baby is all right without awakening him.
c. call the pediatrician.

14. The Simons's ten-year-old son Gregory had been begging to take piano lessons for almost a year when his parents finally agreed to sign him up for weekly lessons. The piano teacher's classes are given on a semester basis of approximately fifteen weeks, allowing vacation time in between. After eight lessons, Gregory announces to his parents that he is tired of the piano and doesn't want lessons anymore. His parents should
    a. let him quit immediately.
    b. make him finish the fifteen weeks.
    c. tell him that if he doesn't continue he'll have to quit his other activities, too.

15. Just before lunchtime, eight-year-old Carl walks in the back door of his house and slams it. Looking at his mother making sandwiches, he says, "I hate that Bobby. I'm going to kill him." Carl's face is very red and angry-looking. His mother should
    a. ask him why he is angry enough to kill someone.
    b. explain why killing is a terrible thing to do.
    c. send him to his room for saying such a terrible thing.

?

EVALUATION: THE EXPERTS' ANSWERS

1. *b.* Discussing how it feels to be called a name increases the child's ability to empathize and helps him understand how silly name-calling really is, according to Bettye Caldwell, director of the Center for Child Development and Education, University of Arkansas at Little Rock. Both *c* and *d* can be very positive actions following the discussion; *a* only leads to further hurt feelings and, potentially, to additional problems at school.
2. *c.* Children are naturally honest and will often say anything that comes to mind. They have not yet learned to judge the effects of certain comments. A simple explanation will suffice, but a child's questions should always be answered.
3. *b.* Between the ages of six months and one year children often experience "stranger anxiety," according to Dr. Maria Piers of the Erikson Institute for Early Childhood Education. They are acquiring the important ability to distinguish between family and strangers. Children of that age cannot be forced to accept strangers and must get used to them in an environment free from pressure.
4. *a.* When a child is out of control, he is asking to be led away and protected from his own inability to control himself, says Dr. Edward Zigler, a psychology professor at Yale. Children must be relieved of situations they can't handle.
5. *d.* It is possible that Cynthia is not getting out of bed on time because she simply hasn't had enough sleep. By setting an earlier bedtime, her parents will be able to discover whether this is the real problem. The alarm clock will also make her more aware of time and her control over waking and getting ready for school. *a* will only teach the child to expect a reward for completing any task. Both *b* and *c* are damaging to the child.
6. *b.* This is the best choice because it not only immediately puts a stop to the damage, but also provides a reasonable explanation for why the activity is not acceptable. Both *b* and *d* develop a child's awareness of the natural consequences of his behavior. *c* provides punishment that is out of scale to the "crime," and establishes the parent as a vengeful individual.
7. *b.* Teenagers often misunderstand curfews and see parents' anger when curfews are broken as the parents' attempt to control their children's lives and limit their independence. If teens understand that parents are simply concerned about their welfare and if they have discussed with their parents the curfews set, they will be more willing to oblige by being on time and calling when delayed.
8. *c.* Children must be made to realize the consequences of their actions and learn to rectify the situation, according to Dr. Marilyn M. Smith, executive director of the National Association for the Education of Young Children. Parents should not "cover up" a theft or act in a way

TEST YOURSELF: HOW GOOD A PARENT ARE YOU?

they don't want their children to imitate, as in *b*.

9. *a*. Children can be frightened by their own behavior and relieved by the parental control. Smith also recommends making sure the child gets enough time alone with the parents. A child who acts as Maria did is feeling extremely threatened by the presence of a new family member and must be reassured of her place in the family. Depriving the child of contact (as in *c*) will make her even more resentful and decrease the likelihood of adjustment.

10. *c*. Zigler cautions parents to treat the situation casually because the fact of the parent's nudity is not likely to be important to the child. After all, the child has come in because she has a question to ask, not to gape. Covering oneself immediately and banishing the child from the bathroom give the message that the body is dirty, that something awful is happening. At the same time, allowing the child to watch is probably more than she can handle.

11. *a*. A habit such as hair twisting or thumb-sucking indicates that the child has a need. It's not the behavior itself that needs correcting but the underlying reason for the behavior, says Piers. Many of these habits are developmental phenomena that disappear later, she adds.

12. *b*. Everyone, but particularly children ages two through five, often have the sense that their parents know when they're telling a lie. Zigler says it is therefore important to emphasize social contracts, making clear that the parent takes the child at his word and that the parent doesn't know when the child is not telling the truth.

13. *b*. Sleeping patterns in the first six to twelve weeks of life may be erratic and shouldn't be cause for immediate alarm, says Ruth Watson Lubic, general director of the Maternity Center Association. Babies must adjust to the difference between the home and the hospital. Parents should check to make sure the baby is breathing normally, but let him awaken naturally.

14. *b*. A ten-year-old has the ability to understand commitment and the importance of carrying something through. The notion of finishing what you start is an important part of teaching responsibility.

15. *a*. When a child is angry enough to threaten to kill someone, he needs catharsis, not a lecture, according to Zigler. The first thing to do is to find out why the child is angry; have him talk about it to let some of the emotion out of his system. If the threat is accompanied in a short time by regressive behavior (bed-wetting, for instance), professional help should be sought. But if the parent perceives the child is just making the threat to get a rise out of the parent, it should be ignored.

Copyright © Parents Magazine Enterprises. Reprinted from *Parents* by permission. From an article by Leah Yarrow in the March 1979 issue of *Parents*.

?

??????????????????
HEALTH/BEAUTY
??????????????????

??????????????????
What's Your Nutritional IQ?
??????????????????

Everyone knows that what we eat is important, but few of us know what nutrients our bodies need or what foods will be good sources of vitamins and other nutrients.

The concept of good nutrition is simple. Nutrition is the process by which food, composed of nutrients, is assimilated into the system through body chemicals and functions; in turn, the body reacts to the nutrients affecting your physical and psychological health. It is also easy to understand that different people need varying amounts of nutrients, but there are some basic tenets of good nutrition that apply to everyone. No matter how much it seems a cliché, attention to good nutrition is the only way to bulid a strong body and a sound mind. Your answers to the following test will determine if you know the basics of nutrition and will tell you how much more you could know, for your own good health.

?

1. Proteins are needed primarily for
    a. energy.
    b. building and maintaining body tissues.
    c. preventing disease.
    d. athletic training programs.

2. The most concentrated source of energy (the source that gives the greatest amount of energy per gram) is
    a. proteins.
    b. carbohydrates.
    c. fats.
    d. vitamins and minerals.

3. The world's population obtains 70 percent of its energy from
    a. proteins.
    b. carbohydrates.
    c. fats.
    d. vitamins and minerals.

4. Plants store energy for future use in the form of
    a. starch.
    b. sugar.
    c. amino acids.
    d. chlorophyll.

5. In the human body starch is changed to
    a. carbohydrates.
    b. DNA.
    c. glucose.
    d. sucrose.

6. Lactase is
    a. a deficiency of vitamin D.
    b. a deficiency of vitamin C.
    c. milk sugar.
    d. an enzyme that enables the body to digest lactose.

7. The U.S. per capita consumption of sugar is
    a. 100 pounds per year.
    b. 200 pounds per year.
    c. 400 pounds per year.
    d. 500 pounds per year.

HEALTH/BEAUTY

8. Each pound that you gain represents how many extra calories beyond what you need to maintain your weight?
   a. 1500.
   b. 2500.
   c. 3500.
   d. 5500.

9. Taking vitamin pills is
   a. not as good as getting natural vitamins from food.
   b. a good idea; the more the better.
   c. unnecessary if you eat a balanced diet.
   d. expensive.

10. Vitamin B_{12}, necessary for the normal development of red blood cells and the functioning of all cells, is found in
    a. leafy green vegetables.
    b. whole-grain cereals.
    c. meats, fish, shellfish, and milk.
    d. fruits and green and yellow vegetables.

11. Beriberi, a dysfunction of the nervous system, is caused by a deficiency of
    a. Vitamin B_1.
    b. Vitamin C.
    c. Vitamin A.
    d. Vitamin B_5.

12. A deficiency of niacin causes
    a. scurvy.
    b. pellagra.
    c. pernicious anemia.
    d. rickets.

13. Vitamin C
    a. has been proven to cure colds.
    b. can be stored in the body for indefinite periods of time.
    c. is needed only by growing children.
    d. is also known as ascorbic acid.

14. The best source of Vitamin D is
    a. fresh meat.
    b. leafy green vegetables.
    c. citrus fruits.
    d. milk and butter.

15. Vitamin E has been proven to
    a. be effective in treating heart disease.
    b. clear up skin blemishes.
    c. increase sexual potency.
    d. help certain anemias.

16. Vitamin K is essential for
    a. night vision.
    b. growth of red and white blood cells.
    c. functioning of the nervous system.
    d. clotting of the blood.

17. The most abundant mineral found in the body is
    a. calcium.
    b. phosphorus.
    c. sodium.
    d. potassium.

18. The FDA (Food and Drug Administration) excludes from its definition of food additives substances that
    a. are generally recognized as safe.
    b. have been proven to be completely free of harmful agents.
    c. have been selected by the Surgeon General.
    d. have been known to cause cancer in laboratory animals.

19. The letter *K* inside an *O* on the outside of a package of food indicates that the product
    a. is OK for human consumption.
    b. contains Vitamin K.
    c. complies with Jewish dietary laws.
    d. all of the above.

20. *Salmonella* poisoning is caused by
    a. poorly cooked pork.
    b. contaminated eggs or poultry.
    c. spoiled cream-filled pastries.
    d. improperly sealed home-canned meats or vegetables.

WHAT'S YOUR NUTRITIONAL IQ?

ANSWERS

1. b	8. c	15. d
2. c	9. c	16. d
3. b	10. c	17. a
4. a	11. a	18. a
5. c	12. b	19. c
6. d	13. d	20. b
7. a	14. d	

EVALUATION

A score of 19 or 20 is a sign of a nutritionally conscious person. Knowing what nutrients you need to keep yourself in good condition is what good nutrition is all about. If you know what to eat but don't pay attention to such knowledge you probably scored 17 or 18; you are only hurting yourself by not making sure your body gets the vitamins and nutrients it needs. If you scored a 15 or 16, you're probably in good health, but it wouldn't hurt to do a little studying to keep yourself fit. Anyone who attained a score lower than 15 could be nutritionaly "underweight." Knowing the principles of good nutrition and putting them into practice will only make your life that much healthier.

?

???????????????????????
Are You Naturally Healthy?
???????????????????????

The American Natural Hygiene Society, Inc., of Chicago, promotes a program for a healthy lifestyle based upon the scientific and common sense care of one's mind and body. The Society believes that living in harmony with "Nature's law" will reduce and possibly remove the causes of disease.

Health is the normal state of the body. You can maintain a healthy body simply by being sensitive to your body's natural signs and requirements. Common sense will make sure you get the most out of life. Yet so many of us don't pay attention to our body's signs or needs. Your answers to the following test will let you know if you are taking good care of yourself.

A scientific and common sense approach to the care of one's mind and body results in a program for living that can only be beneficial. If we recognize that health is the normal tendency of the body, it stands to reason that we can maintain a healthy body, to a great extent, by simply being sensitive to its natural requirements and avoiding the known causes of ill health. These causes are all the improper living practices that are so common: overworking, overeating, inadequate rest or exercising, emotional stress, and any other overindulgence. Natural health care provides sound guidelines for maintaining a sound body.

?

1. To help me wake up in the morning, I
    a. take a hot shower.
    b. have a cup of coffee.
    c. go jogging.
    d. get enough sleep so that I wake up feeling refreshed.

2. When I have a cold, I
    a. drink plenty of liquids.
    b. take a couple of aspirins.
    c. take an extra dosage of Vitamin C.
    d. go to bed and abstain from all food and liquids except water until the crisis is past.

3. The proper amount of water necessary per day is
    a. two to four glasses.
    b. none.
    c. as much as is demanded by thirst.
    d. six to eight glasses.

4. The best food for an infant is
    a. cow's milk.
    b. goat's milk.
    c. mother's milk.
    d. any milk since they are all equally good.

5. The basic cause of disease is
    a. toxemia—an excess of metabolic waste.
    b. pathological germs such as bacteria and viruses.
    c. unknown.
    d. psychosomatic.

6. The best time to eat is
    a. three meals a day at the same time every day.
    b. when hungry.
    c. several small meals throught the day.
    d. any time.

ARE YOU NATURALLY HEALTHY?

7. The best way to ensure enough vitamins is to
   a. take supplements.
   b. eat a natural diet, unprocessed and largely raw.
   c. not worry about it.
   d. take vitamin shots regularly.

8. When I feel tired, I
   a. have a cup of coffee, tea, or soft drink to perk me up.
   b. take only those stimulants prescribed by my doctor.
   c. rest or sleep.
   d. use mind over matter to convince myself that I'm not really tired.

9. Sun bathing should be done
   a. when the sun is strongest to get the maximum benefit.
   b. in moderation.
   c. as much as possible.
   d. never; it's not healthy.

10. The proper amount of protein needed by an adult is
    a. twenty to twenty-five grams per day.
    b. one hundred twenty grams per day.
    c. forty to sixty grams per day.
    d. sixty to one hundred grams per day.

11. To eliminate stress, I
    a. take a mild tranquilizer.
    b. drink camomile tea.
    c. think about something else.
    d. allow myself to feel the stressful feelings and "get them out of my system."

12. The best way of preventing disease is
    a. be immunized.
    b. mind over matter.
    c. taking vitamins and/or food supplements.
    d. living in harmony with nature.

13. Fasting is
    a. physiological rest.
    b. starvation.
    c. dangerous.
    d. abstention from all solid foods.

14. Exercise is best
    a. in moderation.
    b. done to exhaustion.
    c. avoided.
    d. done in the morning.

15. Symptoms such as coughing, sneezing, running nose, rashes, swollen glands, and diarrhea
    a. should be fought with medication immediately.
    b. are the body's way of eliminating unwanted substances.
    c. can be dangerous if left untreated.
    d. should be treated only with natural remedies.

16. When I have a fever I
    a. eat plenty of chicken soup.
    b. don't feel like eating so I don't.
    c. eat to keep my strength up.
    d. only drink juices, herbal teas, or honey and lemon.

17. To improve elimination I
    a. eat plenty of bran.
    b. take an herbal laxative.
    c. eat an abundance of raw fruits and vegetables.
    d. drink lots of water.

18. Chronic disease such as arthritis, heart disease, asthma, colitis, etc.
    a. start with the suppression of the symptoms of acute disease.
    b. are incurable.
    c. are hereditary.
    d. are inevitable with the aging process.

19. Refined sugar
    a. is a good source of energy.
    b. is all right in moderation.
    c. is a major cause of illness.
    d. is an acceptable food unless you are overweight.

20. My state of health is
    a. something I cannot control.
    b. best taken care of by professionals.
    c. not important enough to warrant too much of my attention.
    d. my responsibility.

HEALTH/BEAUTY

ANSWERS

1. *d.* Inadequate rest and sleep are major factors in poor health. During sleep, the nerve energy required to perform the body's proper function is restored. Lack of such nerve energy leaves our organs functioning at a lower level of efficiency and eventually may lead to their breakdown.
2. *d.* When the natural waste products of metabolism accumulate faster than the body can eliminate them, we experience the symptoms of a cold, flu, or other acute illnesses. When the body cannot eliminate its waste through normal channels it then increases its use of minor organs of elimination such as the mucous membranes, skin (such as in measles, chicken pox, etc.), etc.
3. *c.* Thrist is an instinctive mechanism of the body which tells us when we need water. Overdrinking, like overeating, is harmful.
4. *c.* Cow's milk was meant for baby cows; goat's milk for goats. The makeup of a mother's milk is ideally suited for her child and is the best food available.
5. *a.* The body can be compared to a fireplace. As its fuel (food) is consumed, ashes (waste) are produced. Unless the ashes (waste products) are removed, the fire cannot burn and will smother in its own ashes. If the (toxic) by-products of metabolism are not eliminated our cells also cannot function properly.
6. *b.* Hunger, like thirst, is a natural way the body has of telling us that it needs food. Food taken in the absence of hunger cannot be assimilated and overtaxes the digestive system needlessly.
7. *b.* Vitamins (and minerals) are abundant in raw foods. By eating a diet of fresh fruits, vegetables, nuts, and seeds, all the essential vitamins and minerals are available to us in their natural state.
8. *c.* The body tells us when we need to rest and sleep by making us feel tired. Sleep is a time of repair and rejuvenation. Stimulants, whether in the form of a drug or in the disguise of a drink such as coffee, tea, or soda pop, are harmful and poisonous to the system.
9. *b.* Sunlight is a necessary ingredient in the metabolism of food. But even a good thing can be overdone, thereby losing its good effects. Sun bathing should be done before 11 A.M. or after 2 P.M., not when the sun is strongest.
10. *a.* An excess of protein can lead to serious problems. Twenty to twenty-five grams (approximately 4 oz.) is all that most people can use in a day.
11. *d.* The body has natural mechanisms for eliminating stress. They are: crying (grief), laughing (mild fear and embarrassment), raging (anger), trembling (strong fear), and yawning (boredom). If we allow the natural healing process to occur, emotional distress should be reduced.
12. *d.* While a positive attitude and emotional poise are necessary, they alone are not sufficient. We cannot "will away" the effects of destructive habits. The best way to prevent disease is to eat a natural diet, get adequate rest and sleep, sunshine, pure water, clean air, exercise, and to maintain emotional poise.
13. *a.* Fasting is an opportunity for organs to rest, repair themselves, and eliminate any toxic substances that have accumulated. The energy that normally is used for digestion is rechanneled to those parts of the body where cleansing is needed.
14. *a.* All good things in moderation. Exercise is beneficial but if we exhaust ourselves we defeat our purpose.
15. *b.* These symptoms are beneficial and are part of the body's attempt at healing. Suppression will lead to another and probably more serious illness (crisis of elimination) later on.
16. *b.* When we have a fever we often lose our appetite. This is an indication that food is not wanted and cannot be used by the body. Food eaten in the absence of hunger is not well assimilated.
17. *c.* All laxatives are irritants. The body, in its effort to expel a laxative, sends everything else in the digestive tract along with it. The roughage found in raw fruits and vegetables has a natural laxative effect and tends to regulate elimination.
18. *a.* Advanced age should not be synonymous with disease. By allowing our bodies to throw off unwanted waste products (through the minor healing crises of colds, and other acute illnesses) and by eliminating destructive habits from our lifestyle, we build a natural immunity to disease.

ARE YOU NATURALLY HEALTHY?

19. *c.* If sugar were eaten in its natural state (the sugar cane plant) it would not be harmful. It is the processing that removes the vitamins and minerals from the sugar plant that makes it objectionable.

20. *d.* You are the only one who can build and maintain good health for yourself. You have the ability to be self-sufficient in the area of health care simply by supplying the necessary ingredients and letting your body do the rest.

??

EVALUATION

If you answered correctly 15 or more questions then you've got a healthy body and mind. As the saying goes, if you take care of the inside, the outside will take care of itself. A score between 10 and 14 shows that you enjoy good health, but could use a little more common sense in your daily diet and exercise program. If you scored below 10, don't lose hope, just shake off some of your old beliefs and try using a little natural health care. It's the only body you'll ever have, so you have to take care of it.

For further information on the subject of self-sufficient health care, contact the American Natural Hygiene Society, Inc., 1920 West Irving Road, Chicago, IL 60613; telephone (312) 929-7420, Department T.

Courtesy of American Natural Hygiene Society, Inc.

?

???????????????????????????
Are You Taking Care of Your Body?
???????????????????????????

We all like to look good. Who wouldn't like to draw admiring stares at the beach, be able to run a mile without huffing and puffing, or enjoy an illness-free life to a ripe old age? But in spite of our desires and our good intentions, sometimes we forget to treat our bodies as well as we know we should.

The following questions will help you decide if your diet, exercise, and other habits are all that they should be for a long and happy life. If some of your answers are Nos, don't be dismayed! It is an easy matter, in most cases, to go from an out-of-shape body to a body beautiful, though it may take a little time—and thought.

?

1. Are you within five pounds of the recommended weight for your height?
   _____ Yes. _____ No.

2. Do you eat three nutritionally balanced meals a day?
   _____ Yes. _____ No.

3. Do you keep your consumption of "junk foods" to a minimum?
   _____ Yes. _____ No.

4. Do you avoid candy, sweet desserts, and soft drinks?
   _____ Yes. _____ No.

5. Do you snack on fruits and vegetables instead?
   _____ Yes. _____ No.

6. Do you limit your intake of coffee, tea, and other stimulants?
   _____ Yes. _____ No.

7. Do you eat fish or chicken more often than beef?
   _____ Yes. _____ No.

8. Do you eat no more than two eggs per week?
   _____ Yes. _____ No.

9. Do you make it a point to eat breakfast every morning?
   _____ Yes. _____ No.

10. Do you walk at least two miles a day?
    _____ Yes. _____ No.

11. Do you participate in sports regularly and often?
    _____ Yes. _____ No.

12. Do you have hobbies and outside interests that enable you to relax and forget about work?
    _____ Yes. _____ No.

13. Do you get enough (but not too much—about seven or eight hours for the average adult) sleep every night?
    _____ Yes. _____ No.

14. Do you have regular medical examinations?
    _____ Yes. _____ No.

ARE YOU TAKING CARE OF YOUR BODY?

15. Are you a nonsmoker?
    _____ Yes.   _____ No.

16. Are you a nondrinker?
    _____ Yes.   _____ No.

17. Do you drive carefully and within the speed limit?
    _____ Yes.   _____ No.

18. Do you always wear a seat belt whether you are the driver or a passenger?
    _____ Yes.   _____ No.

19. Do you use prescription drugs only in accordance with your doctor's instructions?
    _____ Yes.   _____ No.

20. Do you use over-the-counter drugs sparingly, never exceeding the recommended dosage on the label?
    _____ Yes.   _____ No.

EVALUATION

If you answered seventeen or more questions in the affirmative, you're probably in very good shape, and chances are you'll stay that way as long as you continue to exercise and eat sensibly. It might be wise, however, to think about any questions you answered with a No. It's an old saying but it's true: Take care of your body and your body will take care of you.

A score of 14 to 17 "Yes" answers shows that, while you may be aware of the need for appropriate exercise and proper diet, you're not putting that knowledge into practice. When you finally do make up your mind to take off that extra weight and to get into good physical condition, don't get carried away! A crash diet can do far more harm than good, as can too-vigorous exercise. Set up a diet or exercise program in consultation with your doctor, and soon enough you will reach your desired goal.

Fourteen or fewer "Yes" answers could be an indication of trouble ahead. Remember: dieting alone won't take off those unwanted pounds, nor will a haphazard and irregular exercise program make you physically fit. A combination of the right diet and the right exercise is what you need, and with that combination as a continuing part of your total life you will look and feel great in less time than you might imagine possible.

?

??????????????????????????????
Can You Distinguish the Facts from the Myths in Diets?
??????????????????????????????

For the past twelve years Lean Line has dedicated itself to creating the realistic diet—a way to lose weight and still enjoy food. Lean Line now has offices in seven states, and they offer over 300 classes in as many cities for the diet-conscious.

The purpose of the Lean Line Test is to offer you an opportunity to change your attitude about dieting. The true-or-false questions are simple, but they will dispel any dieting myths to which you may subscribe.

?

1. A person on a weight reduction program should avoid eating in restaurants.
   _____ True.   _____ False.

2. In order to lose weight, you should cut out all bread and cereal products.
   _____ True.   _____ False.

3. Potatoes are no more fattening than most other vegetables.
   _____ True.   _____ False.

4. Unless you lose at least two pounds a week, you are not a successful dieter.
   _____ True.   _____ False.

5. Eating one food over and over again is the best way to diet.
   _____ True.   _____ False.

6. If you enjoy the food you're eating, then you probably won't lose weight.
   _____ True.   _____ False.

7. Eating quickly is a good way to "get the meal over with."
   _____ True.   _____ False.

8. It's a good idea to eat all meals and snacks in a particular place.
   _____ True.   _____ False.

9. Shopping with a list is a good idea.
   _____ True.   _____ False.

10. Your emotional state has nothing to do with your diet.
    _____ True.   _____ False.

11. When you crave something sweet, sucking on a lemon wedge will dispel the desire.
    _____ True.   _____ False.

12. It's a good idea to keep a written record of the food you eat.
    _____ True.   _____ False.

13. If you tend to retain water, stay away from foods high in salt content.
    _____ True.   _____ False.

14. Cream cheese, peanut butter, and ice cream are "forbidden foods" when dieting.
    _____ True.   _____ False.

15. When losing weight, a strenuous exercise program is essential.
    _____ True.   _____ False.

CAN YOU DISTINGUISH THE FACTS FROM THE MYTHS IN DIETS?

16. A vitamin deficiency can be a serious matter.
    _____ True.   _____ False.

17. If one eliminates fiber from the diet, weight loss will be accelerated.
    _____ True.   _____ False.

18. Water is an important factor in successful weight loss.
    _____ True.   _____ False.

19. When a person is overweight, there is usually one specific problem causing the condition.
    _____ True.   _____ False.

20. Maintaining a weight loss requires more than losing weight.
    _____ True.   _____ False.

?

ANSWERS

1. False. Although eating in a restaurant presents a unique set of circumstances for the dieter, avoidance is not the answer. In fact, if you order sensibly, it is sometimes easier to dine out than to eat at home, since you are not handling or preparing the food yourself.

    Our suggestion is to order foods without sauces or gravies and to be very specific when telling the waitress how you want your food prepared. Fish should be prepared dry (a little lemon juice and paprika adds a delightful touch). Meat and poultry are best served plain. When dieting, stay away from the gourmet section of the menu.

2. False. Successful weight loss depends on the use of a wide variety of foods in the proper quantities. Bread and cereal products are only dangerous if they are used to excess. Consuming these foods within the structure of a balanced program in reasonable amounts is necessary for good nutrition.

3. True. For years dieters have "shied away" from eating potatoes because of the erroneous belief that "potatoes are fattening." The truth of the matter is that the most "dangerous" part of the potato is the sour cream and butter we put on top of it. Eating a baked or boiled potato one or two times a week is perfectly okay. Green beans, cauliflower, broccoli, carrots, etc., may be used on other days.

4. False. If your body was a perfect machine, it would operate in such a way that you would lose exactly the same amount of weight each week. Since it is not, and we have to deal with many factors affecting the weekly weight loss, it is better to determine our success rate by looking at the monthly average rather than the week-by-week progress. It is possible that within a four-week period of time you will lose two pounds the first week, half a pound the second week, two and a half pounds the third week, and three pounds the fourth week. If you were to look at it on a weekly basis, the second week's weight loss of half a pound might be discouraging; the monthly average, however, is a respectable two pounds per week. As long as you carefully follow the program you have selected, the weight will eventually come off.

5. False. Repeating the same food is boring. In addition, it will minimize the efficiency of the weight loss. The key word to successful dieting is Variety—Variety—Variety.

6. False. According to many "old wives' tales," dieting has to be torture and the dieter must feel miserable and martyred. This is not so! The intent of losing weight of a sensible, well-balanced, nutritionally stable weight loss program is to teach the dieter the way that she/he should have been eating up to that point. The "diet" is just step one in changing to a new lifestyle and is, in effect, preparation for maintenance.

7. False. The best, most efficient way to consume a meal is "slowly" and with complete awareness of your body's signals. The appetite is controlled by a part of the brain called the appestat, which works very much like the thermostat in your house that turns the heat on and off. Our appestats are turned on and off by blood sugar level.

    If you have not eaten for a while, your blood sugar level goes down. This stimulates the appestat, which in turn triggers the hunger reflex. You begin to eat. As food is ingested, it tells the appestat to shut off the feeling of hunger. The problem is, this process takes at least twenty minutes from the time that food first enters the mouth until the feeling of satisfaction results. This means that all meals must be consumed slowly enough that you do not overeat before the appestat clicks off. It is, therefore, essential that all meals take at least twenty minutes to complete.

8. True. Eating all meals and snacks in the same place limits the number of situations with which you will be associating food. If you are psychologically adjusted to eating in just one environment, then the subconscious will not react with hunger to other situations. A perfect example of food/situation association is the popcorn/movie syndrome in which you somehow feel the need to stop at the candy counter when entering a movie theater, even though you just completed a five-course dinner.

   Eating should be an experience separate and apart from all other events. Never read or talk on the telephone while eating, for example, or you will interfere with your food awareness and your ability to "tune in" to the point of satisfaction.

9. True. There are several reasons why it is advisable to use a shopping list. First, you will be more likely to remember all the items you intend to purchase. From a financial point of view, the money expenditure will be directed toward only those items that are needed, rather than sundry unnecessary things. From a dieter's point of view, the need for the list is obvious. Only those items that are "legally" permitted on your program will be listed; thus, "illegal" foods will not be brought into the house.

   Another suggestion is to shop after eating rather than on an empty stomach.

10. False. Emotions play a major role in every phase of our lives. Food has been a tremendous "friend" to you in dealing with "crises," catastrophies, joys, and sorrows. Food has been a crutch, a comforter, a mother substitute. Perhaps this singular inappropriate behavior pattern has been the source of your weight problem.

    Learning to deal with life's events is part of successful weight loss and weight maintenance, and must not be ignored.

11. True. Very often the desire to eat something sweet is more psychological than physiological. Make your taste buds work for you. When that feeling comes on you, a sour pickle or lemon wedge will help dispel the craving.

12. True. When dieting, the key to success is perfection and discipline. Keeping a written diary is the only way you will be absolutely certain you are adhering to the prescribed regime. Very often, "a clear conscience is a result of a poor memory." Leave nothing to chance. *WRITE IT DOWN BEFORE YOU EAT IT!*

13. True. If you are water-retentive, foods such as sauerkraut, pickles, bouillon, diet soda, and so on should be avoided. Strangely enough, the best way to counteract water retention is to drink at least six eight-ounce glasses of water or seltzer each day, and to avoid foods high in salt content. Another suggestion is to eliminate the use of salt in cooking and at the table.

14. False. Although many of the traditional diet plans require abstention from such foods as cream cheese, peanut butter, and ice cream, one can lose weight very easily while eating these items if the foods are part of a specific, consistent weight-loss program. In fact, very few foods need to be eliminated from your diet as long as they are quantity-controlled.

15. False. Strenuous exercise is both unnecessary and unwise for an overweight individual. Before embarking on any exercise program, always consult your physician. If approval is given, then you may begin a program of simple basic exercises such as knee lifts, toe touches, half knee bends, and sit-ups. In addition, incorporating several "social" or informal exercises such as walking and bending will round out your exercise program.

16. True. A vitamin deficiency can cause serious health problems. Simply put, vitamins are organic compounds found in small quantities in all kinds of foods. Each serves a very specialized purpose in bodily functions. They are absolutely necessary for good health, growth, and maintenance. Vitamins A, D, E, and K are known as the fat-soluble vitamins, since they do not dissolve in water. B and C are water-soluble vitamins. They may lose some of their potency in cooking, but generally not enough to worry about. To be on the safe side, however, always use small amounts of water when cooking fresh produce. And be careful not to store it for too long or cook it too long. That can make them less potent, too. Whenever

CAN YOU DISTINGUISH THE FACTS FROM THE MYTHS IN DIETS?

you see dietary allowances for vitamins, keep in mind that they're only approximations. Your own personal needs depend on age, sex, and lifestyle. A well-varied diet will provide all the necessary vitamins you need for good health, which is the first step to a good-looking you.

17. False. Foods high in fiber play a critical role in proper body function and, in turn, aid in successful weight loss. Included in a sensible, balanced diet program are foods with high fiber content such as whole grain cereals, fruits, and vegetables.

    Fiber in the diet plays an important role in laxation, in controlling the absorption of fats from the digestive tract, and in insuring proper movement of the digestive tract. The latter is very important in preventing the lodging of food in the folds of the intestine, which could give rise to the production of toxic or irritating substances by bacteria. These, in turn, could cause difficulties or even cancer of the colon.

18. True. Water makes up over seventy percent of body weight. Even bone and teeth contain anywhere from ten to thirty percent water, so that a reducing program in which great care is not given to adequate water intake becomes a most dangerous program indeed. The obese patient may have additional problems brought on by a restricted water intake. One of these is the storage of water in the body as a result of improper function of endocrine glands. Only an adequate intake of water can prevent such storage and thus lead to a breakthrough in water loss, which so often compounds the problem of obesity and weight loss.

19. False. When a person is obese or simply overweight, there is no single reason for this condition. It is not merely that the person eats too much or does not exercise enough. While each person is unique, it is possible to describe a "fairly typical" overweight individual.

Behavior	Incorrect eating habits.
Affect (emotions)	Often depressed, agitated; easily angered or hurt.
Sensation	Tense. Most sensory pleasure is focused on food and eating.
Imagery	No clear mental picture of being slim and staying slim.
Cognition (attitudes & beliefs)	Often demanding, self-downing. Filled with "I can't" and "I must."
Interpersonal	Lacking assertive skills.
Biological	Generally does not follow sound nutritional or health-and-fitness programs.

The foregoing profile is a cursory sketch that underscores the interactive effect across the personality profile. Of course, each person will vary in terms of the specific problems that exist in each modality, but the point being stressed is that any overweight person will have behavioral problems, affective difficulties, sensory disturbances, a poor self-image, faulty cognition, interpersonal difficulties, and will not be adhering to health-giving biological activities.

20. True. Most overweight individuals are "experts" at losing weight and have done it hundreds of times. Overweight people are deficient in the skills necessary to maintain a weight loss. For that reason, it is absolutely essential that certain behavioral and cognitive (attitude and belief) changes take place during the weight loss period. Learning to eat, think, act, and perform as thin people do will put the odds in your favor.

?

From *Lean Line Facts and Myths about Dieting* by Lolly Wurtzel and Toni Marotta, edited by Sharon Edelman. Copyright © 1979 by Lean Line, Inc., South Plainfield, New Jersey and reprinted with their permission.

Do You Need Psychotherapy?

TEN WAYS IN WHICH YOUR BEHAVIOR MIGHT BE SAYING YES

If you're like most people, you probably have ups and downs. You might even have wondered if you should see a psychiatrist. But how do you decide? What is the difference between the normal ups and downs that everyone experiences and the kind of emotional problems that call for psychotherapy?

Psychiatrists and psychologists say it's time to get help when you feel so bad you can't function: when your problems start interfering with your daily life, your job, or your marriage.

"Then," says Dr. Thomas A. Williams, chairman of the Department of Psychiatry and Behavioral Sciences at East Virginia Medical School, "the crucial question is, how long has it been going on? A week or a couple of months? If the answer is a couple of months or so, you probably could use some help. Unless, of course, something has happened that anyone would be upset about."

Emotional problems often start when people can't get back on their feet after a crisis—a death, divorce, or loss of a job. Sometimes, though, a person begins to show signs of emotional stress for no apparent reason. In either case, emerging emotional problems usually show themselves in some of the following ways.

Note: Don't think you have an emotional problem just because you might have *occasionally* felt or acted like this. With the person who could really use psychotherapy, these things happen very frequently, usually over a period of months and often to the point where they jeopardize a job or personal relationships.

1. Excessive rage over small problems.
2. Increasing difficulty in getting along with others.
3. Physical symptoms—dizziness, fatigue, chest pains—with no medical basis.
4. Inability to stop thinking about problems.
5. Increasing feelings of inadequacy and self-doubt.
6. Fearfulness of certain situations or people.
7. Suspicions of others, especially of those who may try to help you.
8. Erratic sleep patterns; loss of appetite.
9. Feelings of hopelessness about oneself or the future.
10. Inability to change unsatisfactory or destructive behavior.

TWENTY QUESTIONS TO HELP YOU DECIDE

From Dr. John S. O'Brien, clinical instructor of psychiatry, Tufts University, and staff psychologist, Psychiatry Department, St. Elizabeth's Hospital, Boston; and Dr. John H. Brennan, psychiatrist and chairman of the Massachusetts Medical Society Committee on Mental Health.

CHECK THE ANSWERS THAT APPLY TO YOU.

1. In new situations, such as a job interview or a party with people you don't know, are you afraid things will go badly for you?
   - __ a. All or most of the time.
   - __ b. Frequently.
   - __ c. Occasionally.
   - __ d. Rarely or never.

DO YOU NEED PSYCHOTHERAPY?

2. When asked to do something you don't want to do, like babysit for friends or work late, can you say no when you really want to?
   __ a. All or most of the time.
   __ b. Frequently.
   __ c. Occasionally.
   __ d. Rarely or never.

3. Do you ever completely lose your temper and realize afterward that you got much angrier than the situation deserved; for example, your husband gets stuck in traffic and is late for dinner or your usually reliable dry cleaner doesn't have your clothes ready?
   __ a. All or most of the time.
   __ b. Frequently.
   __ c. Occasionally.
   __ d. Rarely or never.

4. When you're with another person or with a group of friends, can you get them to listen when you have a suggestion—like picking a restaurant or a movie?
   __ a. All or most of the time.
   __ b. Frequently.
   __ c. Occasionally.
   __ d. Rarely or never.

5. Do you have a lot of difficulty making decisions, such as what to do on vacation or in selecting a new coat?
   __ a. All or most of the time.
   __ b. Frequently.
   __ c. Occasionally.
   __ d. Rarely or never.

6. Do you hesitate to become involved in group activities? For instance, do you find yourself standing alone at parties?
   __ a. All or most of the time.
   __ b. Frequently.
   __ c. Occasionally.
   __ d. Rarely or never.

7. Do you constantly seek approval or encouragement for things you do all the time, such as your daily tasks at work or preparing a meal for your family?
   __ a. All or most of the time.
   __ b. Frequently.
   __ c. Occasionally.
   __ d. Rarely or never.

8. Can you express your displeasure when people take advantage of you—push ahead of you in line, for example?
   __ a. All or most of the time.
   __ b. Frequently.
   __ c. Occasionally.
   __ d. Rarely or never.

9. Do you feel satisfied with your closest relationships?
   __ a. All or most of the time.
   __ b. Frequently.
   __ c. Occasionally.
   __ d. Rarely or never.

10. Do you take a drink or tranquilizer to give you confidence before a job interview or a party?
    __ a. All or most of the time.
    __ b. Frequently.
    __ c. Occasionally.
    __ d. Rarely or never.

11. Do you have habits like smoking, nail biting or overeating that you are unable to control?
    __ a. Habit(s) I can't control all or most of the time.
    __ b. Habit(s) I frequently can't control.
    __ c. Habit(s) I occasionally can't control.
    __ d. None.

12. Do you have fears—such as a fear of flying or of small places or of certain animals or of knives, and so on—that you are unable to control or that keep you from doing many things that you really want to do?
    __ a. Fear(s) I can't control all or most of the time.
    __ b. Fear(s) I frequently can't control.
    __ c. Fear(s) I occasionally can't control.
    __ d. None.

13. When you leave the house, do you often find it necessary to go back to make sure the door is locked, stove off, iron unplugged, and so on?
    __ a. All or most of the time.
    __ b. Frequently.
    __ c. Occasionally.
    __ d. Rarely or never.

14. How often are your sexual activities unsatisfactory for you or your partner?
    __ a. All or most of the time.
    __ b. Frequently.
    __ c. Occasionally.
    __ d. Rarely or never.

15. Does it take you more than an hour to go to sleep, or do you wake up more than an hour earlier than you want to?
    __ a. All or most of the time.
    __ b. Frequently.
    __ c. Occasionally.
    __ d. Rarely or never.

16. Have you lost weight recently without a medical reason or without going on a diet?
    __ a. Very little, if any.
    __ b. More than five pounds.
    __ c. More than ten pounds.
    __ d. More than fifteen pounds.

17. Are you very concerned with cleanliness or contamination, particularly of yourself or objects you might touch?
    __ a. All or most of the time.
    __ b. Frequently.
    __ c. Occasionally.
    __ d. Rarely or never.

18. Do you think the future is completely hopeless, or do you ever think of hurting yourself or commiting suicide?
    __ a. All or most of the time.
    __ b. Frequently.
    __ c. Occasionally.
    __ d. Rarely or never.

19. Do you ever see, hear, or feel things that nobody else is aware of?
    __ a. All or most of the time.
    __ b. Frequently.
    __ c. Occasionally.
    __ d. Rarely or never.

20. Do you think you have superior powers or that other people have superior powers and are using them against you?
    __ a. All or most of the time.
    __ b. Frequently.
    __ c. Occasionally.
    __ d. Rarely or never.

??

WHAT YOUR ANSWERS MEAN

This is *not* a test where there are right or wrong answers. We all lose our temper now and then over something trivial, or we occasionally feel dissatisfied with our closest relationships. But with the person who could benefit from psychotherapy, these things happen very frequently—usually over a period of months—and very often reach a point where they threaten one's job or personal relationships.

In normal circumstances, the well-adjusted person will usually give the following answers:

1. c or d	8. a or b	15. c or d
2. a or b	9. a or b	16. a or b
3. c or d	10. c or d	17. c or d
4. a, b, or c	11. c or d	18. d
5. c or d	12. c or d	19. d
6. c or d	13. c or d	20. d
7. c or d	14. c or d	

DO YOU NEED PSYCHOTHERAPY?

Questions 1 to 10 evaluate how well you are able to express your feelings and how much self-confidence you have. If many of your answers are different from the ones indicated above, it simply means that you have trouble expressing your feelings or that you aren't very sure of yourself and could use more self-esteem. If you want to change any of these feelings or behavior, psychotherapy would probably help you.

Questions 11 to 14 involve some of the behavior that usually accompanies an emotional problem. If many of your answers are different from the ones listed, and if you think your problems are interfering with your daily life, it might be a good idea to see a professional and get an opinion. You might benefit from therapy.

Questions 15 to 20 also involve behavior that usually accompanies an emotional problem. If some or many of your answers are different from the ones we've given, they could be important early warning signs of an emotional problem. If you think this is a possibility, get a professional opinion right away. If therapy is needed, it will be easier if you don't delay.

IF YOU THINK YOU NEED HELP . . .

- First, see if your local hospital runs or can recommend a mental-health clinic. The advantage of a clinic is that a professional will do an intake interview, determine what kind of help you need, and then find the therapist best suited to you.
- If you prefer to get help privately, ask your physician to recommend a therapist or call the chairman of the psychiatry department at the nearest medical school for a recommendation. You can also call the local branch of the Mental Health Association. They will know of both clinics and individual therapists.

Reprinted from the May 19, 1978 issue of *Family Circle Magazine.* © 1978 THE FAMILY CIRCLE, INC.

?

?????????????????????
Can You Administer First Aid?
?????????????????????

First aid techniques should not be practiced by everyone. If you don't know what you are doing, you could cause more harm than good. Helping others—administering temporary treatment until a doctor is available—can be beneficial only if you know exactly what to do. Your answers to the following test will show whether or not you are adequately prepared to give first aid.

?

1. To stop severe bleeding from an open wound
    a. apply a tourniquet.
    b. apply direct pressure to the wound, elevate the limb, and if necessary, apply pressure to a pressure point in the major artery of the limb.
    c. apply an ice pack.

2. After you have applied an emergency bandage, you should
    a. change it frequently and cleanse the wound.
    b. remove any blood clots.
    c. never disturb the wound if there has been severe bleeding.

3. The symptoms of shock include
    a. weakness; a rapid but faint pulse; skin that is pale, cold, and sometimes moist and clammy; rapid and often shallow breathing; and sometimes nausea.
    b. weakness, a slowed pulse, flushed skin that feels warm to the touch, deep slow breathing, and sometimes nausea.
    c. convulsions, fever, and vomiting.

4. A victim of heat exhaustion
    a. has an abnormally high temperature, does not sweat, and may be unconscious.
    b. has a normal temperature, perspires a lot, and seems weak and exhausted.
    c. has a lower-than-normal temperature and feels cold and clammy to the touch.

5. An injury to a joint ligament or a muscle tendon in the area near a joint is called
    a. a sprain.
    b. a strain.
    c. a fracture.

6. A compound fracture is one in which
    a. the bone is broken in two or more places.
    b. the skin is broken.
    c. the bone is cracked rather than broken.

7. After an automobile accident or a similar accident in which there is danger of fractures or internal injuries, the most important thing to remember is
    a. do not move the victim unless doing so is clearly necessary to save his or her life.
    b. move the victim to a safe place and apply artificial respiration.
    c. move the victim to a safe place, cover him or her with a blanket, and apply a splint.

8. If a person has swallowed a strong alkali such as drain cleaner, you should
    a. neutralize it with lemon juice or vinegar.
    b. neutralize it with milk of magnesia.
    c. induce vomiting.

CAN YOU ADMINISTER FIRST AID?

9. Poison should be diluted with water or milk
   a. in all cases of poisoning.
   b. in all cases except when the victim is unconscious, in convulsions, or suffering from exhaustion.
   c. only when the poison is lye.

10. If someone is choking on a piece of food
    a. pound the victim on the back.
    b. try to remove the object with your fingers.
    c. stand behind the victim, put your arms around him, make a fist with one hand beneath his rib cage, clasp the fist in your other hand, push sharply inward and upward against his diaphragm.

11. A person may die if his or her oxygen flow is cut off for
    a. six minutes.
    b. ten minutes.
    c. twelve minutes.

12. The best treatment for mild burn is
    a. cold water.
    b. ice water.
    c. butter or grease.

13. In cases of snakebite, you should immobilize the part that has been bitten and
    a. keep it below the level of the heart.
    b. keep it above the level of the heart.
    c. apply an ice pack.

14. Which of the following bites usually causes the most severe reaction?
    a. Black widow spider.
    b. Tarantula.
    c. Scorpion.

15. Vomiting should be induced
    a. in all cases of poisoning.
    b. in all cases of poisoning except those in which the victim has swallowed a strong acid, an alkali, or a petroleum product.
    c. only when the victim has taken an overdose of barbiturates, tranquilizers, or sleeping pills.

16. If you think you are about to faint
    a. lie down or bend over with your head between your knees.
    b. breathe into a paper bag.
    c. order some coffee or tea.

17. The principal symptoms of a heart attack are
    a. nausea, indigestion, and vomiting.
    b. pain in the chest, upper abdomen, or left arm and shoulder and shortness of breath.
    c. chest pain and a bluish discoloration of the skin.

18. The best way to thaw a body part affected with frostbite is to
    a. rub the part.
    b. immerse the part in water that is as hot as possible.
    c. immerse the part in warm water—102°-105°F—unless the part has been thawed and then refrozen, in which case it should be warmed at room temperature.

19. The most severe type of burn is
    a. first degree.
    b. third degree.
    c. the most painful.

20. People who drown usually die because
    a. their lungs fill with water.
    b. their stomachs fill with water.
    c. they are asphyxiated from lack of air.

21. If a person is drowning, you should do the following:
    a. remove as much of your clothing as possible, swim out, and drag the victim back to shore.
    b. don't stop to remove any clothing—every moment counts.
    c. don't get into the water yourself; reach out with your hand or foot, or extend some object, such as a towel, stick, branch, or chair, and pull the victim to safety.

22. The second leading cause of accidental death is
    a. falling.
    b. motor-vehicle accidents.
    c. fires.

HEALTH/BEAUTY

23. If someone has an epileptic seizure, you should
    a. put something between the victim's teeth to prevent him from biting himself or you.
    b. keep him lying down, be sure he can breathe, and turn his head to one side or lay him on his stomach to prevent inhalation of vomit.
    c. cover him with a blanket and administer fluids.

ANSWERS

1. b	9. b	17. b
2. c	10. c	18. c
3. a	11. a	19. b
4. b	12. a	20. c
5. a	13. a	21. c
6. b	14. c	22. a
7. a	15. b	23. b
8. a	16. a	

???

EVALUATION

A score of 18 or above shows that you know your first aid. If you answered 14 to 17 questions correctly you've indicated that you have a knowledge of first aid but could use a little more background, information, and practice. If you scored lower than 14, your presence can be beneficial to an injured person but don't attempt emergency treatment.

Don't attempt to help an injured person unless you know what you're doing. And above all, whether or not you can give aid, call for professional help as early as you can.

?

Do You Know What to Do When You Get a Headache?

People have been getting headaches since the beginning of time. The first brain surgeons—prehistoric humans—cut holes in each other's heads to relieve the pain of headaches in an operation known as trephination. Fossil remains show that many of the patients (perhaps victims would be a more accurate term) survived for years after the operation. Medical science has come a long way since then, and, although certain types of chronic headaches resist cures, specialists now obtain excellent results with most types of headaches.

?

1. When you have a headache, it isn't really your brain that hurts.
   _____ True.   _____ False.

2. Headaches are among the usual symptoms of brain tumors.
   _____ True.   _____ False.

3. People have committed suicide because of headaches.
   _____ True.   _____ False.

4. The worse the pain, the more serious the condition.
   _____ True.   _____ False.

5. More than half of the visits to doctors' offices are for headaches.
   _____ True.   _____ False.

6. Migraine is the most painful kind of headache.
   _____ True.   _____ False.

7. Headaches afflict both sexes in approximately equal proportions.
   _____ True.   _____ False.

8. Headaches can cause hallucinations.
   _____ True.   _____ False.

9. Migraine may be painful, but it is not serious.
   _____ True.   _____ False.

10. Surgery has been known to cure migraines.
    _____ True.   _____ False.

11. Migraine tends to afflict people of above-average intelligence.
    _____ True.   _____ False.

12. It is possible to have a headache without any pain.
    _____ True.   _____ False.

13. A possible side effect of birth-control pills is a headache.
    _____ True.   _____ False.

14. Sex can cause headaches.
    _____ True.   _____ False.

15. Coffee is an effective treatment for headache.
    _____ True.   _____ False.

16. All types of alcoholic beverages are equally likely to cause hangovers.
    _____ True.   _____ False.

HEALTH/BEAUTY

17. The best cure for a hangover is "a hair of the dog that bit you."
_____ True. _____ False.

18. Headaches may be an indication that you need glasses or need your prescription changed.
_____ True. _____ False.

19. Eating in Chinese restaurants can cause headaches.
_____ True. _____ False.

20. Infected sinuses often cause headaches.
_____ True. _____ False.

???

ANSWERS

1. True. Both the brain and the cranium are insensitive to pain. The pain of headaches is felt in the scalp, muscles, veins, and especially the arteries inside and outside the cranium.
2. False. A brain tumor itself doesn't hurt; the pain, when there is any, is caused by the tumor's pressing against intracranial tissues, blood vessels, or nerves.
3. True. The two most severe types of headaches, cluster headache and tic douloureux (a facial neuralgia), considered to be among the worst pains that human beings suffer, have caused many suicides.
4. False. There is no correlation between severity of pain and seriousness of the condition.
5. True. More than half of all visits to doctors are for headaches.
6. False. The types of headache that usually cause the worst pain are cluster headache and tic douloureux.
7. False. Sufferers from migraine and tic douloureux are more likely to be women; sufferers from cluster headaches are more likely to be men.
8. True. Migraine sufferers have experienced hallucinations and distorted vision.
9. True. Migraine is not life-threatening and hardly ever causes any permanent damage.
10. False. Surgery seems to have no effect on migraine.
11. False. There is no correlation between IQ and migraine.
12. True. Migraines sometimes occur without pain. The symptoms of migraine, known as the aura, include distortion of vision and hallucinations.
13. True. Birth-control pills have been known to cause headaches.
14. True. Some people suffer from postcoital headaches.
15. True. Don't overdo the coffee, however; withdrawal from caffeine addiction can *cause* headaches.
16. False. Research indicates that hangovers are caused not so much by the alcohol itself as by congeners—substances that are added to impart color, flavor, and so forth, to alcoholic beverages. Bourbon, which has a high congener content, seems to cause more severe hangovers than vodka, which has a very low congener content. Incidentally, excitement and lack of sleep are thought to contribute to hangovers.
17. False. The best cure for a hangover headache (or any headache) is plain aspirin. For a stomach upset, an antacid should be taken (preferably the night before), and solid food will help if you can keep it down.
18. False. Headaches are rarely caused by eye problems.
19. True. What doctors refer to as "Chinese restaurant syndrome" is caused by monosodium glutamate, an ingredient of soy sauce.
20. False. Sinus conditions rarely produce headaches.

?

EVALUATION

If you scored between 18 and 20, you understand that headaches have many different causes, some of which are traceable to environmental factors and some not. A score between 15 and 17 shows that you have some misconceptions about headaches; if headaches are a problem for you, a discussion with your doctor would help. Less than 15 on this test indicates that you are in a state of blissful ignorance, untroubled by more than an occasional headache.

Such headaches as caffeine-withdrawal, Chinese restaurant syndrome (MSG syndrome), hot dog headache, and ice-cream headache can be cured by simply avoiding the headache-causing substance. Sometimes, too, headaches are caused by conditions on the job. Some headaches with psychological origins have been helped by psychotherapy or hypnosis. But for the occasional headaches that most of us get, the best remedy is plain aspirin, or better still a short rest in a dark quiet room.

For the most serious chronic headaches, such as migraine and cluster, a visit to a doctor or to a headache clinic may offer the best hope of relief. A clinic can give you a complete workup, including examination of your environment and living habits, and a physical checkup. Treatment may run the gamut from psychotherapy to wonder drugs to biofeedback methods.

Schedule of Recent Experience [SRE]

Dr. Thomas H. Holmes, of the University of Washington School of Medicine, Department of Psychiatry and Behavioral Sciences, developed the following life stress test in an effort to study a person's ability to handle stress and stressful life situations.

It is important to understand that events in your life, such as divorce, moving, or even taking out a loan, can affect your physical health. Alleviating the stressful situations, or preparing for those you cannot avoid, could save you from illness brought on by the pressures of daily life.

For each life event item listed below please do the following:

Think back on the event and decide if it happened during the last 12 months. If the event did happen, indicate the *number of times* it happened by placing a number in the column labeled "0 to 12 months ago." If the event did not happen during the last 12 months, check under "Does not apply."

	0 to 12 months ago	Does not apply
1. A lot more or a lot less trouble with the boss.	___	___
2. A major change in sleeping habits (sleeping a lot more or a lot less, or change in part of day when asleep).	___	___
3. A major change in eating habits (a lot more or a lot less food intake, or very different meal hours or surroundings).	___	___
4. A revision of personal habits (dress, manners, associations, etc.).	___	___
5. A major change in your usual type and/or amount of recreation.	___	___
6. A major change in your social activities (e.g., clubs, dancing, movies, visiting, etc.).	___	___
7. A major change in church activities (e.g., a lot more or a lot less than usual).	___	___
8. A major change in number of family get-togethers (e.g., a lot more or a lot less than usual).	___	___
9. A major change in financial state (e.g., a lot worse off or a lot better off than usual).	___	___
10. In-law troubles.	___	___
11. A major change in the number of arguments with spouse (e.g., either a lot more or a lot less than usual regarding child-rearing, personal habits, etc.).	___	___
12. Sexual difficulties.	___	___
13. Major personal injury or illness.	___	___
14. Death of a close family member (other than spouse).	___	___
15. Death of spouse.	___	___
16. Death of a close friend.	___	___
17. Gaining a new family member (e.g., through birth, adoption, oldster moving in, etc.).	___	___
18. Major change in the health or behavior of a family member.	___	___
19. Change in residence.	___	___
20. Detention in jail or other institution.	___	___
21. Minor violations of the law (e.g., traffic tickets, jaywalking, disturbing the peace, etc.).	___	___
22. Major business readjustment (e.g., merger, reorganization, bankruptcy, etc.).	___	___
23. Marriage.	___	___
24. Divorce.	___	___
25. Marital separation from spouse.	___	___
26. Outstanding personal achievement.	___	___
27. Son or daughter leaving home (e.g., marriage, attending college, etc.).	___	___
28. Retirement from work.	___	___

SCHEDULE OF RECENT EXPERIENCE (SRE)

29. Major change in working hours or conditions. _____ _____
30. Major change in responsibilities at work (e.g., promotion, demotion, lateral transfer). _____ _____
31. Being fired from work. _____ _____
32. Major change in living conditions (e.g., building a new home, remodeling, deterioration of home or neighborhood). _____ _____
33. Wife beginning or ceasing work outside the home. _____ _____
34. Taking on a mortgage greater than $10,000 (e.g., purchasing a home, business, etc.). _____ _____
35. Taking on a mortgage or loan less than $10,000 (e.g., purchasing a car, TV, freezer, etc.). _____ _____
36. Foreclosure on a mortgage or loan. _____ _____
37. Vacation. _____ _____
38. Changing to a new school. _____ _____
39. Changing to a different line of work. _____ _____
40. Beginning or ceasing formal schooling. _____ _____
41. Marital reconciliation with mate. _____ _____
42. Pregnancy. _____ _____

To score the Schedule of Recent Experience (SRE), multiply the number of times each event occurred by the value listed below for each of these events. Then total the results for the overall score.

Values of Questions on Schedule of Recent Experience (SRE)

No.	SRE Question	Mean Value
1	Trouble with boss	23
2	Change in sleeping habits	16
3	Change in eating habits	15
4	Revision of personal habits	24
5	Change in recreation	19
6	Change in social activities	18
7	Change in church activities	19
8	Change in number of family get togethers	15
9	Change in financial state	38
10	Trouble with in-laws	29
11	Change in number of arguments with spouse	35
12	Sex difficulties	39
13	Personal injury or illness	53
14	Death of close family member	63
15	Death of spouse	100
16	Death of close friend	37
17	Gain of new family member	39
18	Change in health of family member	44
19	Change in residence	20
20	Jail term	63
21	Minor violations of the law	11
22	Business readjustment	39
23	Marriage	50
24	Divorce	73
25	Marital separation	65
26	Outstanding personal achievement	28
27	Son or daughter leaving home	29
28	Retirement	45
29	Change in work hours or conditions	20
30	Change in responsibilities at work	29
31	Fired at work	47
32	Change in living conditions	25
33	Wife begin or stop work	26
34	Mortgage over $10,000	31
35	Mortgage or loan less than $10,000	17
36	Foreclosure of mortgage or loan	30
37	Vacation	13
38	Change in schools	20
39	Change to different line of work	36
40	Begin or end school	26
41	Marital reconciliation	45
42	Pregnancy	40

Copyright © 1979 by Thomas H. Holmes, M.D., Department of Psychiatry and Behavioral Sciences, University of Washington School of Medicine, Seattle, Washington 98195.

EVALUATION

Every change in your life will affect your mind and body. The more changes you undergo, the more likely you will physically and mentally react to the change. The emotional and physical stress you endure is measured by Life Change units. Stress, for some people, will result in minor illnesses, time off from work, or the purchase of over-the-counter or prescription drugs. Others have stronger, more adverse reactions and are more susceptible to disease, accident, or criminal action.

Of those people with over 300 Life Change units for the past year, almost eighty percent will be physically and emotionally affected in the near future; for those with 150 to 299 Life Change units, about fifty percent will be adversely affected in the near future; and, for those with less than 150 Life Change units, about thirty percent will be affected in the near future. So the higher your Life Change score, the harder you must work to alleviate stress and stay healthy.

The following suggestions from Dr. Thomas Holmes will help you decrease your Life Change units:

1. Become familiar with the life events and the amount of change they require.

HEALTH/BEAUTY

2. Put the Values Scale where you and the family can see it easily several times a day.
3. With practice you can recognize when a life event happens.
4. Think about the meaning of the event for you and try to identify some of the feelings you experience.
5. Think about the different ways you might best adjust to the event.
6. Take your time in arriving at decisions.
7. If possible, anticipate life changes and plan for them well in advance.
8. Pace yourself. It can be done even if you are in a hurry.
9. Look at the accomplishment of a task as a part of daily living and avoid looking at such an achievement as a "stopping point" or a time for letting down.

?

Stress: Are You Coping?

Considering the number of prescriptions written for tranquilizers every year, it doesn't seem likely that people are learning to cope with stress. Yet, in our fast-paced society, learning to deal with tension and anxiety is almost a necessity. Work responsibilities and personal problems all cause stress. Though some amount of stress may be beneficial—to keep people adapting and responding to challenges—keeping stress under control is important.

?

1. Do little things annoy you or irritate you?
   _____ Yes.   _____ No.

2. Do you have trouble getting along with people?
   _____ Yes.   _____ No.

3. Do you have trouble sleeping at night?
   _____ Yes.   _____ No.

4. Are you under constant pressure at work?
   _____ Yes.   _____ No.

5. In your work, do you have responsibility for the welfare or safety of others?
   _____ Yes.   _____ No.

6. Might a mistake by you have serious or even fatal consequences?
   _____ Yes.   _____ No.

7. Is your work unpredictable, so that you are never sure what your responsibilities will be from day to day?
   _____ Yes.   _____ No.

8. Are you usually worn out or exhausted at the end of the day?
   _____ Yes.   _____ No.

9. Do you always have more work than you can get done within the time alloted?
   _____ Yes.   _____ No.

10. Do you have to work on many tasks at once?
    _____ Yes.   _____ No.

11. Are you held responsible for the success of many projects although you do not have the authority to carry them out?
    _____ Yes.   _____ No.

12. Do you often feel tired and depressed?
    _____ Yes.   _____ No.

13. Do you often feel tense or anxious but unable to slow down or relax?
    _____ Yes.   _____ No.

14. Do you become upset in situations that never used to bother you?
    _____ Yes.   _____ No.

15. Have you been using drugs or alcohol much more frequently than usual lately?
    _____ Yes.   _____ No.

HEALTH/BEAUTY

EVALUATION

If you answered "yes" to at least five questions, you are aware of the possible dangers of stress. Learning to control stress may bring relief to your particular circumstances. Ten or more "yes" answers indicate that you are accustomed to stress in your daily life. Yet controlling the stressful situations is important. Try to discover the ways of coping that work best for you. And don't neglect the possibility of getting professional help if a problem becomes too overwhelming.

?

??????????????????????????
Do You Have Trouble Sleeping?
??????????????????????????

Do you have trouble sleeping? For those people who have never had trouble falling asleep, the question seems incomprehensible. But for others, falling asleep isn't a simple matter—it's something to worry about.

Insomnia is the inability to obtain adequate sleep. Job worries, personal problems, and other burdens keep the insomniac up late at night. To find out if you really are a problem sleeper, take this test and see if you can do anything about it.

?

1. How many hours of sleep do you usually get at night?
    a. Less than four.
    b. Between four and seven.
    c. More than seven.

2. Do you always go to bed at the same time?
    a. Yes.
    b. No.
    c. Almost always.

3. Do you think you get enough sleep?
    a. Yes.
    b. No.
    c. Sometimes.

4. How long does it take you to fall asleep?
    a. 10 to 15 minutes.
    b. 15 to 60 minutes.
    c. More than one hour.

5. Do you ever wake up during the night?
    a. Never.
    b. Sometimes.
    c. Many times.

6. Do you ever wake up before your alarm goes off and find yourself unable to get back to sleep?
    a. Often.
    b. Sometimes.
    c. Never.

7. How do you feel when you get up in the morning?
    a. Awake and alert.
    b. Awake.
    c. Still half asleep.

8. Do you go to bed earlier or later than you did a year ago?
    a. Earlier.
    b. Later.
    c. At the same time.

9. Do you get up earlier or later than you did a year ago?
    a. Earlier.
    b. Later.
    c. At the same time.

10. When you can't sleep, what do you do?
    a. Stay in bed and keep trying.
    b. Take a sleeping pill.
    c. Read or get up and do something.

11. Do you snore?
    a. Yes.
    b. No.
    c. Don't know.

HEALTH/BEAUTY

12. Do you worry about whether you will be able to sleep at night?
    a. Often.
    b. Sometimes.
    c. Never.

13. Does your spouse ever complain of being kicked during the night?
    a. Often.
    b. Sometimes.
    c. Never.

14. Do you ever get tired during the day and have to take a nap?
    a. Often.
    b. Sometimes.
    c. Never.

15. How often do you exercise?
    a. Every day.
    b. Two or three times a week.
    c. Once a week or less.

16. Do you take sleeping pills?
    a. Often.
    b. Sometimes.
    c. Never.

17. How much coffee do you drink in one day?
    a. Two cups or less.
    b. Three to five cups.
    c. More than five cups.

18. Is your general health good?
    a. Yes.
    b. No.
    c. Don't know.

19. Are you worried or depressed?
    a. Often.
    b. Sometimes.
    c. Never.

20. Are you under a great deal of stress?
    a. Yes.
    b. No.
    c. Occasionally.

???

ANSWERS

1. a—5; b—3; c—0
2. a—0; b—3; c—0
3. a—0; b—5; c—3
4. a—0; b—2; c—5
5. a—0; b—2; c—5
6. a—5; b—2; c—0
7. a—0; b—2; c—5
8. a—3; b—3; c—0
9. a—3; b—3; c—0
10. a—5; b—5; c—0
11. a—5; b—0; c—0
12. a—5; b—3; c—0
13. a—5; b—4; c—0
14. a—5; b—2; c—0
15. a—0; b—2; c—5
16. a—5; b—4; c—0
17. a—0; b—2; c—5
18. a—0; b—5; c—3
19. a—5; b—2; c—0
20. a—5; b—0; c—2

EVALUATION

If your score was between 0 and 30, you have no sleep problems. If your score was between 31 and 50, you have an occasional problem rather than a chronic one. You should be aware that sleep is only one part of your life and that it reflects the general state of your mental and physical health; if you aren't reasonably healthy, you cannot expect to sleep soundly. Exercise and proper nutrition may help; reducing your intake of caffeine by drinking less coffee, tea, and cola is also a good idea. Never take sleeping pills; they interfere with REM (rapid eye movement) stage sleep and inhibit dreaming, both of which seem to be essential for efficient sleep. If your score was over 50, you are a frequent insomniac who would benefit from medical advice, and perhaps you ought to consider a visit to a sleep clinic. In any case, try to convince yourself that it really isn't that important whether you sleep or not—when your body is exhausted enough, it will fall asleep by itself. Don't *try* to sleep—just *let* it happen.

??????????????????????? What Are the Signs of Alcoholism? ???????????????????????

The National Council on Alcoholism, Inc., is the only national voluntary health agency founded to combat the disease of alcoholism. The following questions will help a person learn if he or she has some of the symptoms of this disease. Use the questionnaire as a rough guide to help you determine if you, a member of your family, or someone you know may need help.

?

1. Do you occasionally drink heavily after a disappointment, after a quarrel, or when the boss gives you a hard time?
   _____ Yes.   _____ No.

2. When you have trouble or feel pressured, do you always drink more heavily than usual?
   _____ Yes.   _____ No.

3. Have you noticed that you are able to handle more liquor than you could when you were first drinking?
   _____ Yes.   _____ No.

4. Do you ever wake up with that "morning after" feeling and discover that you could not remember part of the evening before, even though your friends tell you that you did not "pass out"?
   _____ Yes.   _____ No.

5. When drinking with other people, do you try to sneak in a few extra drinks when others are not watching?
   _____ Yes.   _____ No.

6. Are there certain occasions when you feel uncomfortable if alcohol is not available?
   _____ Yes.   _____ No.

7. Have you recently noticed that when you begin drinking you are in more of a hurry to get the first drink than you used to be?
   _____ Yes.   _____ No.

8. Do you sometimes feel a little guilty about your drinking?
   _____ Yes.   _____ No.

9. Are you secretly irritated when your family or friends discuss your drinking?
   _____ Yes.   _____ No.

10. Have you recently noticed an increase in the frequency of your memory "blackouts"?
    _____ Yes.   _____ No.

11. Do you often find that you wish to continue drinking after your friends say they have had enough?
    _____ Yes.   _____ No.

12. Do you usually have a reason for the occasions when you drink heavily?
    _____ Yes.   _____ No.

13. When you are sober, do you often regret things you have done or said while drinking?
    _____ Yes.   _____ No.

14. Have you tried switching brands or following different plans for controling your drinking?
_____ Yes.   _____ No.

15. Have you often failed to keep the promises you have made to yourself about controlling or cutting down on your drinking?
_____ Yes.   _____ No.

16. Have you ever tried to control your drinking by making a change in jobs, or moving to a new location?
_____ Yes.   _____ No.

17. Do you try to avoid family or close friends while you are drinking?
_____ Yes.   _____ No.

18. Are you having an increasing number of financial and work problems?
_____ Yes.   _____ No.

19. Do more people seem to be treating you unfairly without good reason?
_____ Yes.   _____ No.

20. Do you eat very little or irregularly when you are drinking?
_____ Yes.   _____ No.

21. Do you sometimes have the "shakes" in the morning and find that it helps to have a little drink?
_____ Yes.   _____ No.

22. Have you recently noticed that you cannot drink as much as you once did?
_____ Yes.   _____ No.

23. Do you sometimes stay drunk for several days at a time?
_____ Yes.   _____ No.

24. Do you sometimes feel very depressed and wonder whether life is worth living?
_____ Yes.   _____ No.

25. Sometimes after periods of drinking, do you see or hear things that aren't there?
_____ Yes.   _____ No.

26. Do you get terribly frightened after you have been drinking heavily?
_____ Yes.   _____ No.

?

If you answered "yes" to any of the questions, you have some of the symptoms that may indicate alcoholism.

"Yes" answers to several of the questions indicate the following stages of alcoholism:
Questions 1–8: Early stage.
Questions 9–21: Middle stage.
Questions 22–26: The beginning of final stage.

EVALUATION

This test was divided, in effect, into three sections, representing the early, middle, and late stages of alcoholism. If you answered "yes" to even one question, you have at least one of the symptoms associated with alcoholism. If you answered "yes" to several questions, the distribution of the questions will tell you how far advanced your problem is. "Yes" answers to several of the questions from 1 to 8 indicate that you may be in the early stage of alcoholism. At this stage it is relatively easy to control your drinking if you give some sober thought to the possible consequences. "Yes" answers to several of the questions from 9 to 21 are a sure sign that you may have entered the middle stage of alcoholism, the stage in which alcohol becomes a serious problem—although the alcoholic isn't ready to admit it yet. "Yes" answers to one or more of the questions from 22 to 26 may mean that you are entering the final stage of alcoholism, the stage of actual addiction. If you believe that you or someone close to you may be entering this stage, seek professional help immediately. Alcoholism in its final stage is almost impossible to cure without outside help.

Courtesy of National Council on Alcoholism, Inc.

?

?????????
FINANCES
?????????

Are You a Good Money Manager?

Having a high income is one factor in achieving financial security, but the ability to live within your income, whatever it is, is just as important. Effective budgeting, no matter how small your paycheck, is not difficult, but it takes practice. It also takes efficiency, organization, and discipline. Your test results should tell whether you're able to manage your money successfully, and whether or not, in these times of inflation, high interest rates, and skyrocketing gas prices, you can achieve financial equilibrium.

1. What percentage of your monthly income do you save?
   a. At least 10 percent.
   b. At least 5 percent.
   c. Less than 5 percent.

2. What percentage of your monthly income is spent on rent or mortgage payments?
   a. 25 percent.
   b. 35 percent.
   c. 50 percent.

3. Do you calculate your net worth
   a. once a year?
   b. less often than once a year?
   c. never?

4. Do you set aside a little each month for expenses that must be paid quarterly or annually?
   a. Always.
   b. Sometimes.
   c. Never.

5. Do you keep a file of your financial records such as canceled checks, bank statements, receipts, warranties, insurance policies, tax records, etc.?
   a. Always.
   b. Sometimes.
   c. Rarely.

6. Have you chosen a bank that gives you the maximum rate of interest on your savings account and either free checking or interest on your checking account?
   a. Yes.
   b. Maximum interest yes, free checking no.
   c. Neither.

7. Do you make it a point to save a part of your income each month even if it's only a small amount?
   a. Always.
   b. Sometimes.
   c. Rarely.

8. How much money do you keep in your checking account?
   a. Only enough to pay your monthly expenses.
   b. Enough for two or three months' expenses.
   c. None; you write checks and then deposit money to cover them.

9. How much money do you keep in your savings account?
   a. Only what you need for an emergency fund.
   b. All your savings.
   c. None of your savings.

10. Do you pay your department-store bills within thirty days to avoid interest charges?
    a. Always.
    b. Sometimes.
    c. Never.

11. Do you balance your checkbook every month as soon as you receive your statement?
    a. Always.
    b. Sometimes.
    c. Never.

12. If you have enough money left over to invest some of it after you have paid your bills, where do you invest it?
    a. Stocks, bonds, or mutual funds.
    b. A savings account.
    c. Extra life insurance.

13. Do you ever make purchases that you later regret?
    a. Never.
    b. Sometimes.
    c. Often.

14. Do you check your bills before paying them?
    a. Always.
    b. Sometimes.
    c. Never.

15. Do you ever run out of money before the end of the month and have to use your savings to pay bills?
    a. Never.
    b. Occasionally.
    c. Frequently.

16. Have you ever been refused credit?
    a. No.
    b. Occasionally.
    c. Frequently.

17. Have you ever overdrawn your checking account?
    a. Never.
    b. Rarely.
    c. Frequently.

18. How do you handle your income-tax exemptions?
    a. You claim one exemption for yourself and each of your dependents.
    b. You claim extra exemptions so that less tax money will be withheld.
    c. You claim fewer exemptions so that you will get a large refund the next year.

19. Do you ever try to deal with many small debts by taking out one big loan to cover them?
    a. Never.
    b. Rarely.
    c. Sometimes.

20. Have creditors been dunning you for overdue bills?
    a. Never.
    b. Rarely.
    c. Sometimes.

EVALUATION

Give yourself 5 points for each question for which you checked **a**. Give yourself 3 points for each **b** answer. Add the total number of points to determine your score.

If you are an excellent money manager you probably attained a score of 90 or better, which would indicate that you are living within your means. A score between 75 and 89 shows a wise spender and saver who would probably benefit from keeping a relatively detailed monthly budget. If you scored below 75, you need practice in budgeting, and you may need to change some of your fundamental ideas about spending, saving, and borrowing.

What's Your Credit Rating?

There are an estimated 600,000,000 credit cards in circulation in the United States. These cards are costing Americans over 300 billion dollars in installment debts.

Buying on credit has practically become second nature, but it's not without its risks. Not knowing how to use your credit card wisely can make you a candidate for serious financial trouble.

The Consumer Credit Counseling Service of New York City, created to help consumers with preventive budget and credit counseling as well as actual debt management assistance, compiled the following test.

?

1. You can establish a credit rating by
    a. always paying for your purchases in cash.
    b. getting a steady job.
    c. taking a small loan and repaying it.

2. A Credit Bureau is
    a. an organization that calls your friends and neighbors to find out if you pay your bills.
    b. a company that decides whether or not you should get credit.
    c. an agency that collects and assembles information on users of credit.

3. Your credit rating
    a. is absolutely confidential and may not be viewed by anyone, including yourself.
    b. may be reviewed by you only, on request.
    c. is open to the public and may be reviewed by anyone.

4. You can challenge the information in your credit report
    a. by notifying the Credit Bureau and providing the correct information.
    b. by providing correct information to the creditor.
    c. never. Information in your file is virtually impossible to change.

5. What is the limit on the number of credit cards one can own?
    a. Twelve.
    b. Three for each member of the family.
    c. No limit.

6. How much debt is "too much"?
    a. 10 percent of disposable income.
    b. 20 percent of disposable income.
    c. 50 percent of disposable income.

7. By law, you may not be refused credit as a result of
    a. being in debt.
    b. receiving welfare payments.
    c. unfavorable information on your Credit Bureau records.

8. It is possible to get "free" credit if you
    a. convince your creditor that you need it for a worthy cause.
    b. pay your bills on time.
    c. borrow from one source to pay another.

FINANCES

9. Truth in lending means
    a. a creditor must tell you his reasoning if he increases your line of credit.
    b. points are taken off your credit rating if you give incorrect information when you apply for credit.
    c. a creditor must state credit charges in a uniform way so you can understand them and make comparisons.

10. Husbands and wives applying for credit should
    a. put all credit cards in one name.
    b. each have a card in his or her own name.
    c. have joint cards that can be used by both.

11. If you lose your credit card, you are responsible for
    a. a maximum of $50 charged before notification of loss.
    b. anything over the first $100 charged after the loss.
    c. 25 percent of all subsequent charges against the card.

12. Which of the following should not be bought on credit?
    a. A new couch for your living room.
    b. Those smart new shoes you've had your eye on.
    c. Your weekly grocery bill at the supermarket.

13. You are required to provide the following information when applying for a housing loan:
    a. a property appraisal that considers the racial makeup of the neighborhood.
    b. your intentions on increasing the size of your family.
    c. records on your family income, expenses, debt, and credit reliability.

14. A woman applying for credit cannot be asked about
    a. her plans for having children.
    b. alimony, child support, or separate maintenance payments she receives.
    c. her husband's job.

15. Personal bankruptcy can be declared by
    a. sending a letter to your creditors telling them you can't pay.
    b. running a notice in the newspapers.
    c. filing a petition in Federal Court.

16. If you've been incorrectly billed by your credit card company you can
    a. ask your Credit Bureau to make the necessary correction.
    b. notify the credit card company by mail.
    c. call the seller and request that he or she straighten it out with the credit card company.

17. Why are some interest rates higher than others?
    a. Interest rates are a reflection of what the market can bear.
    b. Some creditors are more profit-conscious than others.
    c. The degree of risk differs from one loan to another.

18. When your salary is garnished
    a. your employer can fire you.
    b. 10 percent of your gross salary goes directly to the creditor suing you for nonpayment.
    c. all your creditors can attach your salary simultaneously until their debts are paid.

19. The best way to get out of debt is to make more money.
    a. True
    b. False
    c. Both of the above.

20. You've just been notified that your bank has doubled your overdraft limit from $1,500 to $3,000. What do you do?
    a. Feel free to spend the additional $1,500. The bank obviously has faith in your ability to repay.
    b. Ignore it. Assume the bank has made a mistake.
    c. Spend it only if absolutely necessary.

21. Collection companies representing your creditors can
    a. call you whenever they want to about the money you owe.
    b. not call at all, but must contact you in writing.
    c. be limited as to the time and frequency they can call.

WHAT'S YOUR CREDIT RATING?

22. If you think you are being harassed, you should
    a. call your lawyer and file a harassment suit.
    b. seek the protection of your local police department.
    c. contact the Federal Trade Commission.

23. The best way to solve your debt problem is to
    a. stop buying on credit until you pay off your outstanding debts.
    b. take a consolidation loan and make one payment instead of several.
    c. limit your credit purchases to the bare necessities.

24. A cosigner of a loan
    a. cannot be a member of your family.
    b. can be anyone who wants to assume the risk.
    c. must have a good credit rating.

25. "Neither a borrower nor a lender be"
    a. still makes sense today.
    b. went out with the invention of plastic.
    c. should be considered on the merits of the situation.

?

ANSWERS

1. *c.* A potential creditor wants to have some indication that you are a good risk. A small bank loan or installment purchase *paid off promptly* establishes a credit history that can be your entry into the world of credit.
2. *c.* A Credit Bureau makes neither inquiries nor judgments to determine your qualifications for credit. Its function is to compile the records on your credit performance. When you apply for new lines of credit, this credit history may be used by the creditor to judge your ability to use credit.
3. *b.* The Fair Credit Reporting Act gives you the right to know what your credit file contains. You can find your Credit Bureau in your local phone book. There may be a fee. You should not have to pay a fee, however, if you have been turned down for credit within the preceding thirty days and if the reason for the credit rejection was a poor credit history as reported by the Credit Bureau.
4. *a.* When you notify the Credit Bureau that you dispute the accuracy of their information, it must reinvestigate and modify or remove inaccurate data. If still not satisfied, you may enter your own statement of up to one hundred words, which will be included in your record. If you feel that the Credit Bureau has not been responsive, you should contact the local office of the Federal Trade Commission.
5. *c.* Although there is technically no limit on the number of credit cards a person can own, let the buyer beware. Too frequent overuse of credit has a way of sneaking up on you.
6. *a.* Studies have shown that the average family can safely devote 10 percent of monthly take-home pay available after the necessities (food, clothing, and shelter) have been paid for, to pay off installment credit charges. At 20 percent the burden is unmanageable for most families.
7. *b.* A creditor may inquire as to whether an applicant receives welfare payments, but credit cannot be denied solely on that basis.
8. *b.* Credit card companies exist on monthly carrying charges, which commence if you don't pay the total bill before the grace period ends. If you keep your account up-to-date, you avoid these charges and, in effect, get "free" credit.
9. *c.* Creditors must provide information on both the finance charges and the annual percentage rate (which provides a comparison regardless of dollar amount or length of time to repay) when you apply for credit.
10. *b.* Each partner in a marriage should have his or her own credit cards and credit record. In that way, should your marital status change, it will be much easier to establish your own credit rating based on your own credit history.
11. *a.* The Truth in Lending Law protects you against unauthorized use of your credit card. If lost or stolen, the maximum amount you have to pay for charges made by someone else is $50. You will not be responsible for even that amount if the charges occur *after* you notify the issuer of the loss.
12. *c.* As a rule, don't pay for recurring basics (such as food) with credit. Credit buying is more appropriate for major purchases that are likely to have a life span exceeding the length of time it takes to pay for them.
13. *c.* Lenders may consider your sources of income and debts but they must apply these tests

FINANCES

fairly and without discrimination, according to the Equal Credit Opportunity Act.

14. *a.* Although the Equal Credit Opportunity Act protects a woman from discrimination in the issuance of credit, she may have to provide information about her sources of income (including her husband's) *if* she intends to rely on this income to repay her debt.

15. *c.* A personal bankruptcy claim must be filed in Federal Court. It is important to get good legal advice first, so that you can understand your various options and find out which of your possessions you can or cannot keep.

16. *b.* All billing adjustments should be requested in writing to your credit card company. Enclose copies of bills, receipts, etc., to substantiate your case.

17. *c.* A passbook bank loan will have a low rate of interest because the bank already has your money on deposit as security against your loan. A credit card carrying charge will be at a much higher rate because the creditor is relying on your good faith in repaying the money he has let you use.

18. *b.* Part of your salary goes directly to your creditor, but no more than one creditor at a time until they are all satisfied.

19. *c.* Some people might be able to discipline themselves to use income increases to pay off their bills. For others, these income increases often encourage further use of debt. Know thyself.

20. *c.* You are the best person to decide if you have legitimate need for the additional money and if you have the ability to repay the additional debt, should you incur it. Never assume that the bank knows more about your personal finances than you do.

21. *c.* The Fair Debt Collection Practices Act prohibits debt collectors from harrassing you or contacting you at inconvenient times. This law covers persons who regularly collect debts for others, but not the creditor himself or his lawyer.

22. *c.* Before going to the expense of using a lawyer, the Federal Trade Commission can provide free advice. Write to: Federal Trade Commission, Debt Collection Practices, Washington, D.C. 20580, or your local FTC office.

23. *a.* It costs money to use someone else's money. Consolidation loans are just another way of adding more debt to your already overextended finances. Never buy the bare necessities on credit. Pay cash.

24. *b* and *c.* A cosigner simply agrees to repay your debt if you don't. Therefore, the cosigner's rating must be good.

25. *c.* Intelligent use of credit can improve the quality of your life. Credit privileges are basically the temporary permission to use someone else's money. It's not free. You are the best judge of how much credit you can afford.

?

EVALUATION

If you had 20 or more correct answers, you have excellent credit sense; you know that there are times when buying on credit is to your advantage, but you also know how to minimize installment buying in order to save yourself money. You can give yourself credit for good judgment where credit is concerned with a score of 15 to 20; you know how to make credit work for you, but don't abuse it. Fewer than 15 correct answers shows that you may need help with your finances. You should remember that when you buy on credit you are paying for the privilege of using someomne else's money to buy something that you could not as easily buy otherwise, and that, when you put off paying for these items by using installment plans, you are paying much more for them in the long run.

Courtesy of the Consumer Credit Counseling Service, New York, New York.

?

Are You a Smart Shopper?

??????????????????
??????????????????

Knowing how to buy on sale, when to buy, and how to go about comparison-shopping are the "weapons" you need to get the most buying power out of a dollar in today's market. Without such knowledge you may waste a considerable amount of money. It's not too difficult to know how to shop; this test will determine how smart a shopper you are, and will give you a few valuable tips.

1. The best time of year to buy a new car is
    a. early spring.
    b. late summer.
    c. mid-winter.

2. When buying a new car you can expect to pay
    a. the sticker price.
    b. more than the sticker price.
    c. less than the sticker price.

3. Discount stores usually
    a. do not have enough parking.
    b. do not have the lowest prices.
    c. do not give shoppers much individual attention.

4. There are usually no _____ on items bought on sale.
    a. warranties
    b. return privileges
    c. sales taxes

5. The best time to shop for food is
    a. Friday evening.
    b. Saturday afternoon.
    c. Monday afternoon.

6. The best time to find bargains is often
    a. the first day of a sale.
    b. the last day of a sale.
    c. both of the above.

7. "Borax" is
    a. a line of inexpensive furniture.
    b. the house brand of any product.
    c. the lowest-priced brand of food.

8. You should never buy an electrical appliance that does not have
    a. the Good Housekeeping seal.
    b. the Underwriters Laboratories seal.
    c. the Parents' Magazine seal.

9. The technique of telling a customer that an advertised special is sold out, or of disparaging it and then pushing a higher-priced item, is called
    a. bait and switch.
    b. hit and run.
    c. supply and demand.

10. The best place to buy aspirin or toothpaste is probably a
    a. drugstore.
    b. discount store.
    c. grocery store.

11. The average refrigerator can be expected to last
    a. fifteen years.
    b. twenty years.
    c. twenty-five years.

FINANCES

12. It is probably safe to buy a _____ that has been a floor model.
    a. clothes washer
    b. coffee table
    c. stereo

13. You should never buy canned goods in _____ cans.
    a. dented
    b. rusty
    c. leaking

14. The highest grade of meat is
    a. USDA Choice
    b. USDA Prime
    c. USDA Good

15. Ground beef may not contain more than
    a. 10 percent fat.
    b. 20 percent fat.
    c. 30 percent fat.

16. When you buy a steak or some other prepackaged item sold by the pound, you should
    a. take it for granted that the weight is correct.
    b. check the weight by placing the item on the store's vegetable scale.
    c. ask the meat manager whether the weight is correct.

17. Listing on the label the nutritional content of a food is
    a. mandatory.
    b. voluntary.
    c. voluntary (with a few exceptions).

18. Loss leaders are
    a. specials on which a store takes a loss in hopes of attracting customers who will buy other things while they're in the store.
    b. specials that are not really reduced because they're marked up before they're marked down.
    c. advertised specials that the store doesn't really have; if you ask for one you will be told that the last one has just been sold.

19. _____ have slight flaws that do not affect their use.
    a. Firsts
    b. Seconds
    c. Irregulars

20. _____ have more pronounced flaws that may affect their use.
    a. Firsts
    b. Seconds
    c. Irregulars

21. If you are buying a way-out fashion that may soon go out of style, you will probably choose the
    a. highest-priced item.
    b. medium-priced item.
    c. lowest-priced item.

22. If you are buying clothing for a growing child, you will probably choose the
    a. highest-priced item.
    b. medium-priced item.
    c. lowest-priced item.

23. When buying clothing, you should figure the cost of _____ in the net cost.
    a. sales tax
    b. alterations
    c. dry cleaning

24. Children's _____ should not be handed down to their younger siblings.
    a. jackets
    b. slacks
    c. shoes

25. A garment marked "Sanforized" will not shrink more than
    a. 1 percent
    b. 3 percent
    c. 5 percent

ANSWERS

1. b	6. c	11. a	16. b	21. c
2. c	7. a	12. b	17. c	22. c
3. c	8. b	13. c	18. a	23. c
4. b	9. a	14. b	19. c	24. c
5. c	10. b	15. c	20. b	25. a

ARE YOU A SMART SHOPPER?

EVALUATION

A score between 22 and 25 is the mark of a good bargain hunter. Being aware of consumer fraud and rip-offs as well as unadvertised sales and limited specials will make you the shopper who will not be easily victimized. If you scored between 18 and 21 you might be headed for some trouble. Keep your eyes open and your wallet shut, so that merchants won't be able to take advantage of you. When you shop be sure you are shopping for something you need, and don't be taken in by bargains and sales if you aren't looking for that particular item. A score below 18 shows that you aren't getting your money's worth. Taking the time to look around for places and times to shop will save you money in the long run. You need to become more aware of how to get the most for your money and make your dollar go as far as it can in today's market.

?

??????????????????????? Do You Need a Tax Accountant? ???????????????????????

Having to pay taxes is bad enough, but having to endure the annual rite of tax-return preparation adds insult to injury. And every year you probably say you will get them done early, and then April 15 rolls around.

The Internal Revenue Service, the mastermind behind this taxing situation, agreees that every taxpayer should claim every deduction, exemption, and credit to which he or she is legally entitled, so it seems to make sense to get professional help if your financial affairs are at all complicated and you don't have an accounting background. On the other hand, you may be quite capable of listing your own income and deductions, and thereby saving yourself a tax-preparer's fee.

?

1. You income tax must be calculated from January 1 to December 31.
   _____ True. _____ False.

2. If after filing your tax return you discover that you could have saved money by itemizing your deductions you may change your mind by filing an amended return.
   _____ True. _____ False.

3. Unemployment compensation is not taxable.
   _____ True. _____ False.

4. By checking a box on your tax return, you may earmark $1 of your tax for a general fund for presidential campaign expenses.
   _____ True. _____ False.

5. In the cash method of accounting, you report income in the year you receive it and expenses in the year you pay them.
   _____ True. _____ False.

6. You can claim exemptions for members of your household only if they are related to you.
   _____ True. _____ False.

7. If you are self-employed or have income from alimony, pensions, annuities, interest, dividends, rent, or capital gains from which no federal income tax is withheld, you must file a declaration of estimated tax for the current year.
   _____ True. _____ False.

8. You must report all tips you receive to your employer.
   _____ True. _____ False.

9. If you perform a service for someone and are paid in the form of barter rather than money, you don't have to report this on your tax return.
   _____ True. _____ False.

10. If you itemize deductions, you may deduct state and local taxes on all the gasoline you buy.
    _____ True. _____ False.

11. You may apply for an extension of time to file your income-tax return.
    _____ True. _____ False.

12. You may deduct bad debts from your taxable income.
    _____ True. _____ False.

13. If you buy a new car and receive a $400 rebate from the dealer, you don't have to report the $400 as income.
    _____ True. _____ False.

14. You must keep records of your income and deductions until the end of the next tax year.
    _____ True. _____ False.

15. Dependent children don't have to file income-tax returns.
    _____ True. _____ False.

16. A married couple may file a joint return even if one partner had no income during the tax year.
    _____ True. _____ False.

17. If you and your spouse file a joint return, you cannot change your mind and file separate returns for that year.
    _____ True. _____ False.

18. If your doctor says that a vacation in a warm climate would improve your health, you may deduct the cost of transportation and lodging during this vacation.
    _____ True. _____ False.

19. You may deduct only those medical expenses that total more than three percent of your adjusted gross income.
    _____ True. _____ False.

20. You may deduct commuting expenses to and from work.
    _____ True. _____ False.

ANSWERS

1. False. You may use either a calendar year or a fiscal year (a twelve-month period ending on the last day of any month).
2. True. On Form 1040X, *Amended U.S. Individual Income Tax Return,* you can change your mind about itemizing, report income that should have been reported on your original return, or claim deductions or credits that you could have claimed but did not. An amended return must be filed within three years from the date of the original return or within two years from the date on which the tax was paid, whichever is later. (A return that was filed early is considered to have been filed on the due date.)
3. False. Beginning with tax year 1979, you may have to include some or all of the employment compensation you receive as taxable income. See the instructions with your tax return for details.
4. True. Checking this box will not change the amount of your tax; it simply allows you to specify where this dollar will go.
5. True. In the cash method of accounting, income is reported when it is either actually or constructively received—that is, when it is credited to your account, whether or not you have physical possession of it. In the accrual method, you report income when you earn it, whether or not you have it, and expenses as they occur rather than when you actually pay them.
6. False. You can claim an exemption for a person who was a member of your household for the entire year whether or not that person was related to you.
7. True. You must file a declaration of estimated tax if your estimated tax is $100 or more and your expected gross income includes more than $500 that is not subject to withholding. The declaration must be filed by the due date for the previous tax year. The estimated tax may be paid in four equal installments or all at once, but at least the first installment must accompany the declaration.
8. False. You must report tips to your employer only if you make more than twenty dollars in tips during a month while working for one employer. These tips are subject to withholding of income tax and Social Security or Railroad Retirement tax. If you receive less than twenty dollars in any month while working for one employer, you need not report these tips to your employer, but you must include them as part of your gross income. Thus, only income tax will be paid on these tips.
9. False. You must report the fair market value of whatever you received in trade.

10. False. State and local taxes on gasoline and other motor fuels for non-business use are no longer deductible.
11. True. You can file for an automatic extension of two months. If you do this, you must pay your estimated tax with the application for extension. If it turns out that you underestimated your tax, you will have to pay interest on the unpaid balance, and, if you underestimated by more than ten percent, a penalty will be assessed. If you file for an extension, you cannot use Form 1040A or ask the IRS to figure your tax.
12. True. The debt must be a total loss—it cannot be partially uncollectible—and you must show that you took reasonable steps to collect it. Bad debts are considered short-term capital losses.
13. True. The $400 is not considered as income, but simply as a reduction in the price of the car.
14. False. You must keep records that support your return until the statute of limitations expires—usually three years from the date the return was filed or two years from the date the tax was paid, whichever is later.
15. False. A dependent child must file a return if he or she had a gross income of $3,300 or more, unearned income of $1,000 or more, or self-employment income of $400 or more.
16. True. A married couple may file either a joint return or separate returns even though one partner had no income or deductions. Married couples should figure their taxes both ways to see which is lower.
17. True. If you and your spouse file separate returns, you may change to a joint return for that tax year by filing an amended return within three years of the due date. If you file a joint return originally, however, you're stuck with it.
18. False. Even if the vacation is recommended by the doctor, it is not deductible. Some transportation costs connected with treatment for a specific medical reason *are* deductible, however.
19. True. Only medical expenses in excess of 3 percent of your adjusted gross income are deductible.
20. False. Commuting expenses are not deductible. Only if travel is a necessary part of your work are transporation expenses deductible.

EVALUATION

Congratulations to those who scored between 17 and 20. You should look forward to doing your taxes and claiming deductions that would surprise the IRS. For those who know how to fill out a short form but hesitate on the longer forms, your score of 15 or 16 should tell you something: you might want to obtain a professional tax accountant. Remember, if the government wants you to claim all the deductions you can, you may as well get help to find out what they are. For those who scored below 15, you are probably lost when confronted by any tax form. Seek help from a professional accountant and from the Free Information Offices of the IRS. With your financial records and knowledge in a shambles, you are only cheating yourself and not Uncle Sam.

?

Are You Financially Prepared for Retirement?

Unless you are unusually well prepared, you will have to lower your standard of living when you retire. This information may shock you since you've spent the better part of your life contributing to Social Security and pension funds so that you would have a little something tucked away when you retired. And today, a little something is all you are going to have.

With the present rate of inflation, one can barely live on Social Security and pension benefits. If this is the case then retiring isn't all it's cracked up to be. Because fixed incomes are unresponsive to inflation, it is very important for you to think seriously about retirement and the nest egg you will be forced to live on. The Social Security Administration recommends that you register for Social Security payments three months before you retire, but that you start to think about financial retirement now.

In order to safeguard your future happiness, you've got to start planning now.

?

1. Unless you are self-employed, you will have to retire when you reach sixty-five.
   _____ True. _____ False.

2. A private pension plan is a better risk, a safer source of retirement income, than Social Security.
   _____ True. _____ False.

3. Once you retire, all you have to look forward to is fishing trips and chess.
   _____ True. _____ False.

4. In order to maintain your standard of living, you will need the same income after you retire that you made before you retired.
   _____ True. _____ False.

5. You can collect Social Security retirement benefits if you have worked for ten years.
   _____ True. _____ False.

6. Social Security benefits begin at sixty-five.
   _____ True. _____ False.

7. There is a good possibility that, after contributing to your company's pension plan, you will never collect benefits from it because the funds will be inadequate.
   _____ True. _____ False.

8. If you are under seventy-two and earn more than $3,000 per year, your Social Security retirement benefits are reduced.
   _____ True. _____ False.

9. If you are a married woman who works, you can collect only from your own Social Security account.
   _____ True. _____ False.

10. If a divorced man who has remarried dies, only his second wife may collect.
    _____ True. _____ False.

11. Income from Social Security is not taxable.
    _____ True. _____ False.

FINANCES

12. If you choose to retire at sixty-two instead of at sixty-five you will always get smaller checks than if you had waited until you were sixty-five.
    _____ True.   _____ False.

13. The Social Security system guarantees a minimum monthly income to every American over sixty-five.
    _____ True.   _____ False.

14. Although civil service employees usually are not eligible for Social Security because the civil service has its own retirement fund, it is possible for some people to collect both civil service benefits and Social Security benefits.
    _____ True.   _____ False.

15. Medicare provides free hospital and medical insurance for anyone who is eligible.
    _____ True.   _____ False.

16. As long as you have Medicare, you don't need other health insurance.
    _____ True.   _____ False.

17. Although Medicare is administered under the Social Security system, you don't have to retire to be eligible for Medicare.
    _____ True.   _____ False.

18. In addition to Medicare, there are state programs that can help with your medical bills.
    _____ True.   _____ False.

19. Medicare does not pay for prescription drugs.
    _____ True.   _____ False.

20. Medicare won't pay any nursing-home bills.
    _____ True.   _____ False.

21. It is possible to build up pension benefits in the same plan while working for more than one employer.
    _____ True.   _____ False.

22. If you leave your company before you retire, you will not be able to collect benefits from your pension plan.
    _____ True.   _____ False.

23. Most pension plans are financed by employer contributions.
    _____ True.   _____ False.

24. Life insurance should be considered primarily as insurance rather than as an investment.
    _____ True.   _____ False.

25. If your employer doesn't have a pension plan, you're out of luck; you'll have to depend on Social Security and investments.
    _____ True.   _____ False.

26. If you are self-employed, you may choose either an IRA or a Keogh Plan.
    _____ True.   _____ False.

27. For someone who wants to invest in real estate, a real estate investments trust (REIT) is a good, safe source of income comparable to mutual funds.
    _____ True.   _____ False.

28. An annuity, which may be sold only by a life-insurance company, is the opposite of a life-insurance policy.
    _____ True.   _____ False.

29. A no-load mutual fund is one that doesn't load you down with a lot of unprofitable stocks.
    _____ True.   _____ False.

30. Common stocks are the best hedge against inflation.
    _____ True.   _____ False.

?

ANSWERS

1. False. The Age Discrimination in Employment Act of 1978 raised the mandatory-retirement age to seventy, and some states have eliminated the age limit entirely. It is possible that the federal mandatory-retirement age may be raised again, since because of the recent lessening of the birthrate there are fewer young workers, and employers are beginning to appreciate the merits of older, more experienced people.

ARE YOU FINANCIALLY PREPARED FOR RETIREMENT?

2. False. The Social Security system is as stable as our government; it cannot fail unless the entire U.S. economy fails, in which case private pension funds will also be bankrupt. If Social Security funds run out, Congress can appropriate money through taxation. Also, private pensions usually do not provide cost-of-living adjustments, as does Social Security.
3. False. Many early retirees are taking advantage of the opportunity to continue their education, work part-time or full-time, or even begin a second career.
4. False. Because your expenses will be lower, you will need only 60 to 70 percent of your pre-retirement earnings. Unfortunately, however, many retired persons must live on less than 50 percent of their former incomes. The problem is compounded by inflation, because pensions, Social Security, and most investments do not respond to rises in the cost of living as readily as regular incomes.
5. True. The number of years varies according to your age but is never more than ten.
6. False. Full retirement benefits begin at sixty-five, but reduced benefits can be collected at sixty-two, or at sixty if you are a widow or widower. Also, disability and survivors' benefits are available before sixty-five. None of these benefits are paid automatically; you must apply for them.
7. False. Although this often happened in the past, the Employee Retirement Income Security Act (ERISA) of 1974 insures and regulates private pension plans, so that the workers who participate in these pension plans, about half of the total labor force, are assured of collecting when they retire.
8. True. This feature of the Social Security Act is known as the retirement test (or earnings test or work-income test). In 1982, the age at which you may collect regardless of earnings will be reduced to seventy.
9. False. You may collect retirement benefits whether from your own account or your husband's, whichever is more.
10. False. An ex-wife is sometimes able to collect widow's benefits if she is over sixty (or fifty if disabled) and was married for at least ten years or has children. Whether or not the man's second wife is also collecting has no bearing on the matter. Also, a divorced woman who is at least sixty-two and was married for ten years may collect benefits when her ex-husband retires.
11. True. There are no taxes on Social Security benefits.
12. True. The reduced rate applies for the rest of your life, unless you go back to work.
13. True. If you can meet certain conditions, you may be eligible for Supplemental Security Income (SSI) benefits, whether or not you are collecting regular Social Security checks.
14. True. If a person has worked for both the federal government and a private employer, he or she may be eligible for civil service retirement benefits and for Social Security.
15. False. Although Medicare hospital insurance is free, a monthly premium is charged for Medicare medical insurance.
16. False. Medicare pays less than half of the health-care costs of the average person who is sixty-five or older. If you can't afford to pay for the other half, a private health-insurance plan might be a good idea.
17. True. With a few exceptions, anyone who is at least sixty-five (less than sixty-five if disabled) is eligible for Medicare hospital and medical insurance.
18. True. Almost all states have Medicaid, a state-operated program for people with low incomes regardless of age. Payments are made directly to the doctor or hospital that performs medical services for you. There are certain eligibility requirements, but you need not be eligible for Social Security. It is possible to collect from both Medicare and Medicaid.
19. True. Medicare medical insurance (Part B) covers doctor bills and outpatient care, but certain things, such as routine checkups, glasses, hearing aids, dentures, orthopedic shoes, and prescription drugs, are not covered.
20. False. Medicare Part A (hospital insurance) will pay for skilled nursing facilities—that is, a stay in a nursing home that begins within fourteen days of a hospital confinement for the same condition that lasted at least three days. Medicare does not pay for custodial nursing-home care, but in some states Medicaid will pay part of the costs.
21. True. Although most pension plans are administered by single employers, some unions, for instance, have *multiemployer pension plans,* in which an employee may accumulate credited service toward pension benefits working for

different employers in the same industry.
22. False. Sometimes you do lose benefits. If, however, you have been paying into a plan long enough to acquire the right to benefits (called *vesting*), you must receive the benefits you are entitled to even if you leave the company before retirement age.
23. True. Most pension plans are financed entirely by employers. Some, called *contributory plans,* are financed by the contributions of both employer and employees. A few union plans are financed by union dues.
24. True. Experts agree that, while life insurance is invaluable as protection for someone with dependents, other types of investment offer a much greater return on your investment dollar. In fact, retirees are often advised to stop paying the premiums on their life insurance policies in order to increase their income.
25. False. You can contribute to your own pension plan by setting aside up to 15 percent of your salary or $1500, whichever is less, to an Individual Retirement Account (IRA). No taxes are paid on this money until you retire.
26. True. If you are self-employed, you have your choice of an IRA or a Keogh Plan. Under the IRA, however, you are limited to a maximum of $1500 a year, while the Keogh Plan permits you to set aside 15 percent of your salary, up to a maximum of $7500 a year. Therefore, the Keogh plan is probably better for anyone who makes $10,000 or more.
27. False. At least one major real estate investment trust has gone bankrupt recently because of bad investments and high interest rates. A REIT is not a good bet for an inexperienced investor.
28. True. With life insurance, you pay annual premiums and your beneficiary collects a lump sum only if you die. With an annuity, you pay a lump sum and get in return a regular income for the rest of your life, no matter how long you live. Of course, some insurance policyholders will die before their policies are paid up, and some annuity holders will live long enough to collect more than they paid in, but the insurance company comes out ahead because its actuarial tables tell it how many people will die in a given year; all its life-insurance policies (or annuities) will even out and will give the same result statistically, whether a given policyholder dies at twenty or at seventy. Annuities are a steady, sure source of income, but because the amount of income is usually fixed the annuity holder is at the mercy of inflation.
29. False. A no-load mutual fund is one for which you pay no sales charge. When you buy shares in a load fund, a commission for the salesman or broker is deducted from the values of the shares. Obviously, this is an excellent reason to invest in no-load funds, but you should compare different funds and take into account the expected return for each. Your broker probably won't help you here; if you want to buy shares in a no-load fund, you will have to go directly to the fund itself.
30. True—as long as they keep going up and not down, that is! A common stock that is growing can give you a very high return on your investment because there is no limit to the value of your shares of stock. However, there is also a greater risk than with most other types of investment. Since you are part owner of the company in which you have bought stock, your fortunes rise or fall with those of the company.

EVALUATION

A well-prepared retiree would score between 25 and 30. Knowing what to expect from retirement will help safeguard your future happiness. Knowing a little about your approaching retirement (but not enough) will add up to a score between 20 and 24. Any score under 20 indicates that your knowledge and level of preparedness are deficient; unless you do something about it now, you may find it difficult to adjust to retirement.

?

Is Your Worth Insured?

Insurance has proven effective in many cases, in minimizing the cost of illnesses, accidents, and unexpected losses. But exorbitant premiums and involved claim reporting make people wary of dealing with insurance companies. In addition, the average person is undereducated when it comes to deciding just how much insurance is necessary. By spending too much money on insurance—making sure that everyone and everything around you is covered—you might overburden your budget and take away from other equally important needs.

Fear of economic loss is the major reason why people buy insurance, but just how much insurance coverage a person needs is a matter of individual choice. Test yourself and see if you know enough about insurance and if your coverage meets your needs.

1. Suppose your insurance salesman recommends that you cancel your life insurance policy and buy a different one, which he can sell you at a lower cost. Should you
    a. accept because you can save money without losing any benefits?
    b. refuse because there must be a catch; all insurance policies with the same coverage cost the same?
    c. ask him to put the proposal in writing and show it to your lawyer or accountant?

2. In which type of insurance is a specified amount paid to the policyholder after a certain number of years, after which insurance ends, while, if the policyholder dies before that time, the full amount of the policy goes to the beneficiary?
    a. Term insurance
    b. Endowment insurance
    c. Coinsurance

3. Which types of insurance accumulate cash value?
    a. Straight life and term insurance
    b. Term insurance and endowment
    c. Straight life and endowment

4. A general term for insurance that offers protection against loss of income because of illness, accident, or death is
    a. property and casualty insurance.
    b. liability insurance.
    c. personal insurance.

5. Which type of life insurance is cheapest?
    a. Term
    b. Straight life
    c. Endowment

6. Life insurance premiums for women are usually lower than for men because
    a. women live longer than men.
    b. men live longer than women.
    c. men usually have greater financial obligations and responsibilities.

7. In which type of life insurance are premiums paid for a specified number of years, after which the policy is paid up for life?
   a. Term insurance
   b. Limited-payment insurance
   c. Temporary insurance

8. Term insurance
   a. is permanent insurance.
   b. is not permanent but may be renewed at any time at the same rate.
   c. may be exchanged for permanent insurance if it is of the convertible type.

9. After about two years (depending on the policy), a life insurance policy becomes incontestable—that is
   a. the policyholder may not cancel without forfeit.
   b. the insurance company may not cancel under any circumstances.
   c. neither the policyholder nor the insurance company may cancel.

10. If you are unable to keep paying the premiums on a permanent life insurance policy, you
    a. forfeit the policy.
    b. must cash in the policy for its face amount or forfeit the policy.
    c. may convert the policy to paid-up insurance in a reduced amount or to extended term insurance.

11. Settlement options are
    a. alternative methods of payment of the proceeds of a life insurance policy.
    b. the insurance company's option to drop the policy if the insured becomes too great a risk.
    c. the result of an insurance company's investigation after the death of the policyholder.

12. A feature by which overdue premiums may be paid by a loan against the policy's cash value is called
    a. a waiver of premium.
    b. an automatic premium loan.
    c. a cash value loan.

13. Participating insurance, a type of insurance in which the policyholders share in the actual cost of their insurance and receive policy dividends if their premiums exceed those costs, is issued mainly by
    a. stock life insurance companies.
    b. mutual life insurance companies.
    c. legal reserve life insurance companies.

14. It is most economical to
    a. buy as much health insurance as you can afford.
    b. try to insure yourself against every possible medical expense.
    c. buy insurance only for major medical expenses and take care of other expenses yourself.

15. Which type of health insurance policy is usually cheapest?
    a. Group insurance
    b. Individual insurance
    c. Major medical insurance

16. The type of health insurance that pays for a physician's operating charges is
    a. major medical insurance.
    b. surgical expense insurance.
    c. disability income insurance.

17. Major medical insurance usually includes
    a. a deductible provision.
    b. a coinsurance clause.
    c. both a deductible provision and a coinsurance clause.

18. If an insurance salesman calls you on the phone and asks if you have life insurance, you should
    a. tell him to come to your house, even if you are already fully insured.
    b. tell him he's wasting your time, and hang up on him.
    c. politely tell him you're already insured, and end the conversation as soon as possible.

IS YOUR WORTH INSURED?

ANSWERS

1. c	10. c
2. b	11. a
3. c	12. b
4. c	13. b
5. a	14. c
6. a	15. a
7. b	16. b
8. c	17. c
9. b	18. c

EVALUATION

You're on the right track if you scored between 17 and 20. Knowing the principles behind life, home, medical, car, and other insurance policies, and putting such knowledge into practice, is well worth your time and money. For those who scored between 14 and 16, it's time to check you insurance coverage—it pays to make sure you know just what coverage you and your family have. There's no time like the present to plan for the future. A score below 14 shows that you had better plan now—so that your future needs are taken care of no matter what happens.

?

?????
HOME
?????

??????????????????????????
Are You Ready to Buy Your Own Home?
?????????????????????????

Buying a house is usually the largest single purchase and the greatest investment that a person will ever make. But too many people rush into this purchase without knowing what to look for. Many new homeowners are further surprised by the amount of work that owning and maintaining a home entails. There is a plumbing, heating, and electrical system to be maintained, walls to prepare and paint, and a yard and garden to keep up. Buying the right house in the first place can minimize the effort and expense of keeping these systems in working order, and can make home maintenance a lot less troublesome.

Your answers to the following test will help you determine what you need to know before opening the front door. After answering the questions, you will have a better idea of whether you are ready to purchase your own home; you will also know some of the factors that should be considered before making the investment.

???????????????????????????????????????

1. The best time to buy a house is
   a. early spring.
   b. summer.
   c. late fall.

2. Home buyers should plan to spend no more than _____ of their income for housing.
   a. 10 percent
   b. 30 percent
   c. 50 percent

3. You should not purchase a house that has a market value of more than _____ times your annual gross income.
   a. 2½
   b. 3½
   c. 5½

4. The most important thing to consider when buying a home is
   a. the total purchase price.
   b. the monthly cash flow (the cost of heating, electricity, taxes, insurance, mortgage payments, etc.).
   c. both of the above.

5. In the North, it's a good idea to look for a house with lots of
   a. southern exposure.
   b. northern exposure.
   c. western exposure.

6. You are considering the purchase of a home in an area where the schools are adequate but there are plans for a new school system. Which of the following is true?
   a. Taxes will rise and reduce property value.
   b. The new school will attract families with children and increase property value.
   c. Both of the above.

7. When shopping for a home, you find a two-story Colonial that you like, but the roof is in poor condition; some roofing material has rotted away, and the gutter and drainpipes are rusted. Should you
    a. refuse to buy the house?
    b. express interest but insist that the roof be replaced first?
    c. make an offer if you like the house otherwise?

8. You are considering two houses. One has some very solid-looking stone walls; there are a couple of four-foot cracks, but you could repair these easily. The other house has aluminum siding. Which would be the better choice?
    a. The house with stone walls.
    b. The house with aluminum siding.
    c. Neither.

9. Which is the best roofing material for a house in the Northeast?
    a. Wood shingles.
    b. Clay tile.
    c. Asphalt shingles.

10. The sturdiest type of wall construction is
    a. wet-wall construction.
    b. dry-wall construction.
    c. moist-wall construction.

11. Suppose you find cracks in the walls of an older house you are considering buying. Should you
    a. refuse to buy the house?
    b. plan to make the repairs yourself if the cracks are not extensive?
    c. insist that the present owner repair the wall?

12. An electrical heating system
    a. is safer than steam but requires more maintenance.
    b. does not require fuel.
    c. is usually the cheapest.

13. Circuit breakers
    a. are more convenient than fuses.
    b. indicate that the electrical system is more modern than one that uses fuses.
    c. suggest both of the above.

14. A real-estate broker is paid
    a. a salary by a real-estate agency.
    b. a commission by the seller.
    c. a commission by the buyer.

15. Signing a binder
    a. protects the buyer.
    b. protects the seller.
    c. should be avoided if possible.

16. A commitment letter is
    a. a letter from a prospective seller to a real-estate broker agreeing to pay the broker a commission.
    b. a letter from a buyer to a seller agreeing to purchase a house.
    c. a letter issued by a lender stating that the lender is willing to grant a purchaser a mortgage.

17. Which is the best type of deed to have for your house?
    a. A warranty deed.
    b. A bargain-and-sale deed.
    c. A quitclaim deed.

18. In *tenancy in common*
    a. each partner has an equal interest.
    b. the property may be divided either equally or unequally.
    c. a right of survivorship is included.

19. In *joint tenancy*
    a. if one of the owners dies, his or her interest in the property reverts to the other owner or owners.
    b. if one of the owners dies, his or her interest goes to his or her heirs.
    c. the deceased owner's interest goes to whoever is named in his or her will.

20. *Tenancy by the entirety* differs from joint tenancy in that
    a. there is no right of survivorship.
    b. neither owner may transfer an interest in the property without the consent of the other owner.
    c. on the death of either owner, his or her interest goes to the other owner.

ARE YOU READY TO BUY YOUR OWN HOME?

ANSWERS

1. *c.* Late fall is the end of the home-buying season. By that time most potential buyers will have found houses, and homeowners may be more anxious to sell and willing to settle for a lower price.
2. *b.* Buyers (and even renters) are usually advised not to spend more than 30 percent of their incomes for housing.
3. *a.* Usually, one should not purchase a house costing more than 2½ times your annual gross income. However, if you are a young professional whose income probably will be much higher in the next few years, you may want to consider purchasing a more valuable house.
4. *c.* Both items should be considered, although many buyers would rather purchase a house with a higher purchase price if the monthly cash flow will be low.
5. *a.* Since a southern exposure receives the most sunlight, a house with large windows on its southern side will receive light and heat from the sun and will cost less to heat. Conversely, a house in the South with a northern exposure will be cooler and will cost less to air-condition.
6. *c.* Probably both. Taxes almost certainly go up in the short run, but the new schools may make the area more attractive in the long run.
7. *c.* It isn't very expensive to replace a roof, so you shouldn't let that stop you from buying a house you like. However, you may want to lower your bid to allow for the cost of replacing or repairing the roof.
8. *b.* A stone house with cracks as long as four feet probably has an unsteady foundation. You should never purchase such a house without having it examined by a professional. Aluminum siding, on the other hand, is a very practical choice; it is durable and virtually maintenance free.
9. *c.* Wood shingles are a fire hazard. Clay is not suitable for colder climates because it cannot withstand exposure to snow and ice. Asphalt shingles, however, are a good all-purpose roof material.
10. *a.* Wet-wall construction (such as plastic, masonry, and brick) is usually stronger than dry-wall construction (such as gypsum board, sheetrock, and paneling).
11. *b.* In an older house, small cracks are to be expected and are not serious. Large cracks or whole sections that are loose, however, are a different story.
12. *b.* Because steam heat is potentially dangerous, it usually requires more maintenance than other systems. An electrical system, although it does not require you to supply it with fuel, can be the most costly in areas where electrical power is expensive.
13. *b.* Circuit breakers are both more modern and more convenient than fuses.
14. *b.* Because a real-estate broker is paid a commission by the seller, he or she is more interested in finding a buyer for a specific house than in finding the right home for you.
15. *c.* A binder is an agreement prepared by a real-estate broker to lock up a sale before the actual contract is signed. However, some binders are so specifically worded that they can be enforced as though they *were* contracts. Never sign one without consulting your attorney.
16. *c.* After a bank or other lending institution has investigated all aspects of a real-estate transaction, it will give the purchaser a letter of commitment stating that the mortgage has been approved.
17. *a.* A warranty deed or deed with full covenant pledges that the seller owns the property, has the right to sell it, and warrants that there are no defects in the title. In a bargain-and-sale deed, the seller conveys the title to the purchaser absolutely. In a quitclaim deed, the seller simply relinquishes all claim to the title.
18. *b.* The property may be divided equally or unequally, but there is no right of survivorship—if one of the owners dies, his or her interest goes to the heirs named in the will.
19. *a.* The deceased's interest in the property goes to the other owner or owners. Property owned by joint tenants cannot be given away in a will; it can, however, be given away while the owner is alive, in which case the joint tenancy is ended.
20. *b.* Tenancy by the entirety is designed for married couples only and is based on the idea that husband and wife are one. Therefore, neither partner may give away his or her interest without the consent of the other.

EVALUATION

20 to 17. *Broker.* Your knowledge of the real estate market and the ins and outs of home buying, make you a real estate expert. With this knowledge and the right amount of money, you cannot go wrong by investing in a house.

16 to 14. *Buyer.* Your overall understanding of the housing market isn't bad, but do a little more research before plunging into a deal. Learning the finer points of maintenance and repair can save you a lot in the long run.

Below 14. *Renter.* Don't buy or sell. Stay in your rented apartment, at least for the time being.

?

???????????????????????
Do You Know Your Rights as a Tenant?
???????????????????????

Do you know what to do if your sink backs up and you need professional service or what to do if your landlord withholds your security deposit? It may not be your house, but it is your home. As a tenant you can exercise your legal rights—if you know them.

?

1. The first thing you should do if your landlord refuses to make repairs is withhold the rent.
   _____ True. _____ False.

2. A suit by a tenants' organization is not much more effective than a suit by a single tenant.
   _____ True. _____ False.

3. A tenant is not liable for "normal wear and tear" to an apartment.
   _____ True. _____ False.

4. It is perfectly legal for you to refuse to pay your last month's rent when you move out and to tell the landlord to take it out of the security deposit.
   _____ True. _____ False.

5. In a few states, a landlord is legally required to pay a tenant the interest earned on the security deposit.
   _____ True. _____ False.

6. If, when you move into your apartment, you send your landlord a certified letter listing any defects in the apartment, you may make it easier to get back your security deposit when you leave.
   _____ True. _____ False.

7. Usually, depending on the terms of the lease, anything that is permanently attached (nailed, for instance) is the property of the landlord.
   _____ True. _____ False.

8. Usually, again depending on the terms of the lease, anything that is attached but can be removed without causing damage or leaving holes is the property of the tenant.
   _____ True. _____ False.

9. Before you paint your apartment, you should get permission in writing from your landlord.
   _____ True. _____ False.

10. In many states, you can make needed repairs and deduct the cost from your rent.
    _____ True. _____ False.

11. *Warranty of habitability* means that the tenant will keep the premises in the same condition in which they were rented.
    _____ True. _____ False.

12. A landlord cannot be held liable for injuries to a tenant that result from the landlord's negligence as long as there was no malice.
    _____ True. _____ False.

13. Your landlord is obligated to paint your apartment every year.
    _____ True. _____ False.

14. Before availing yourself of a repair-and-deduct provision in your state's tenants' law, you must notify your landlord and give him or her sufficient time to make the necessary repairs.
_____ True.   _____ False.

15. *Warranty of habitability,* a concept recognized in some states, means that the landlord warrants that the premises are and will remain fit to live in.
_____ True.   _____ False.

16. *Constructive eviction* refers to a tenant's having to leave an apartment because of intolerable living conditions.
_____ True.   _____ False.

17. Your landlord cannot be held liable for damages if your apartment is burglarized.
_____ True.   _____ False.

18. If a court finds in your favor in a breach-of-warranty suit, it may order your rent reduced until repairs are made.
_____ True.   _____ False.

19. Judges are usually more favorable to tenants than juries are.
_____ True.   _____ False.

20. If your landlord refuses to make reasonable repairs after you have requested them in writing, the next step is to call the housing authority and request an inspection; if the premises are found to be in violation of the housing code, you may be within your rights to sue or to withhold rent.
_____ True.   _____ False.

??

ANSWERS

1. True.	8. True.	15. True.
2. False.	9. True.	16. True.
3. True.	10. True.	17. False.
4. False.	11. False.	18. True.
5. True.	12. False.	19. False.
6. True.	13. False.	20. True.
7. True.	14. True.	

EVALUATION

If you had 18 or more correct answers, it is obvious that you are well-informed of your rights and responsibilities as a tenant. If you scored between 15 and 17, you should consider learning more about local rent laws and ordinances, in order to fully understand what courses of action are legally permitted. If you answered less than 15 questions correctly, you should seek help from some or all of the many sources available to today's tenant—from government agencies to tenant organizations to private lawyers.

Though landlord-tenant laws vary from state to state you can protect yourself, wherever you live, with a lease. Signing your name to a lease makes you and your landlord legally responsible for your home. Don't sign anything you don't understand, and try to have clauses you don't like removed from the lease. To make the laws work for you, you have to know what they are.

?

??????????????????
Are You Energy Conscious?
??????????????????

The present world situation and the gasoline shortages of the 1970s and '80s have brought home to us something that most Americans had previously known only on an intellectual level: the world has a limited amount of resources to support its growing population. World oil production is expected to peak some time in the 1990s if not sooner, while the demand for oil will continue to grow. Since the United States presently imports almost half of its oil, we are, as we all know, at the mercy of the oil-exporting countries. Other sources of energy, such as solar and coal, will help, but in the meantime the easiest, cheapest, and most effective means of achieving this goal of independence is simply to reduce the demand for energy through conservation.

There are also good selfish reasons for conserving energy. Through proper insulation and wise use of heating equipment and appliances, you can save hundreds or even thousands of dollars per year, and you may be able to claim tax credits for energy-saving alterations. But even without installing major equipment you can still achieve significant savings through sound energy-conservation practices such as those revealed in this test.

??

1. One of the best (and easiest) ways to reduce energy consumption in your home is to turn off lights and appliances that are not in use.
   _____ True.   _____ False.

2. Incandescent lighting is more energy efficient than fluorescent lighting.
   _____ True.   _____ False.

3. You can save energy by using three-way bulbs at their lowest level whenever possible.
   _____ True.   _____ False.

4. Long-life incandescent light bulbs are more energy efficient than regular bulbs.
   _____ True.   _____ False.

5. Light-colored walls reflect light and reduce the amount of artificial lighting needed.
   _____ True.   _____ False.

6. A self-defrosting refrigerator will save energy.
   _____ True.   _____ False.

7. A TV set with the "instant-on" feature wastes energy.
   _____ True.   _____ False.

8. It's not worth it to caulk and weatherstrip your doors and windows because the savings effected are minimal.
   _____ True.   _____ False.

HOME

9. If you install solar, wind, or geothermal heating, cooling, or hot-water equipment in your home, you may be eligible for a tax credit of up to $2200.
   _____ True.   _____ False.

10. A kitchen fan can waste heat by blowing away warm air.
    _____ True.   _____ False.

11. You should always keep your fireplace damper open.
    _____ True.   _____ False.

12. Burning a fire in your fireplace can be very wasteful unless it is done properly.
    _____ True.   _____ False.

13. One heavy sweater is warmer than two light-weight sweaters.
    _____ True.   _____ False.

14. A hat is a good way to keep warm in the winter, even indoors.
    _____ True.   _____ False.

15. The amount of water lost through most leaky faucets is minimal.
    _____ True.   _____ False.

16. Water boils faster in an open pan than in a kettle or a covered pan.
    _____ True.   _____ False.

17. A gas stove with electronic ignition uses much less energy than one with pilot lights.
    _____ True.   _____ False.

18. If your pilot light burns yellow instead of blue, it is not burning efficiently.
    _____ True.   _____ False.

19. With an electric stove, you can turn off the burners several minutes ahead of time and they will stay hot enough to finish cooking your food.
    _____ True.   _____ False.

20. If you keep opening your oven door to check whether something is done, it will take longer to cook and will use more energy.
    _____ True.   _____ False.

21. If your manual-defrosting refrigerator has more than a quarter-inch of frost built up, it will use more energy.
    _____ True.   _____ False.

22. The lint screen in your clothes dryer need not be emptied more than once or twice a month.
    _____ True.   _____ False.

23. Washing a load of dishes in your dishwasher takes about fourteen gallons of hot water.
    _____ True.   _____ False.

24. To save energy, you should let your clothes dryer cool off after each load before starting the next one.
    _____ True.   _____ False.

25. Taking a shower usually requires less water than taking a bath.
    _____ True.   _____ False.

26. It doesn't matter what time of day you choose to run your dishwasher or clothes washer or dryer.
    _____ True.   _____ False.

27. Most cars get about 20 percent better gas mileage at 55 MPH than at 70 MPH.
    _____ True.   _____ False.

28. Radial tires may last longer than bias tires, but they get lower gas mileage.
    _____ True.   _____ False.

29. Underinflated tires can lower your gas mileage.
    _____ True.   _____ False.

30. It takes so much gasoline to restart your car that, unless you have to wait for ten minutes or more, you should let your engine idle rather than turn it off.
    _____ True.   _____ False.

ARE YOU ENERGY CONSCIOUS?

ANSWERS

1. True.	11. False.	21. True.
2. False.	12. True.	22. False.
3. True.	13. False.	23. True.
4. False.	14. True.	24. False.
5. True.	15. False.	25. True.
6. False.	16. False.	26. False.
7. True.	17. True.	27. True.
8. False.	18. True.	28. False.
9. True.	19. True.	29. True.
10. True.	20. True.	30. False.

EVALUATION

25 to 30. *Energy miser.* You're not only doing your part but your energy bills are probably as low as can be.

19 to 24. *Energy consumer.* You are aware of the problem, and you are beginning to take steps to combat it.

18 to below. *Energy spendthrift.* You should understand that small sacrifices by everyone now will prevent greater privations for everyone later.

?

??????????????????????
How Good Is Your Decorating Ability?
??????????????????????

Designing a home that reflects your personality and style of living isn't as easy as it seems. We all know what we like, but putting everything together, whether for a studio apartment or a ten-room house, needs special care and attention. While many amateurs have created beautifully decorated homes, others have designed mismatched hodgepodges that can be depressing. Employing a professional decorator or an interior designer can be costly, but doing the job yourself can be a tremendous chore. Designing a style for living is a talent that can be acquired and nurtured; the following questions will test your decorating ability and tell you what you need to learn.

?

1. The style in which your rooms are decorated should harmonize with that of the house itself.
   _____ True.   _____ False.

2. You should never mix styles or periods—a room may be French Provincial or Early American, for instance, but not both.
   _____ True.   _____ False.

3. When choosing a color scheme for a room, you don't need to worry about the colors in the other rooms.
   _____ True.   _____ False.

4. There is time enough to decide on a color scheme after you have bought the first few pieces of furniture for a room.
   _____ True.   _____ False.

5. The most tastefully decorated rooms are those with pieces of furniture whose color and fabric match perfectly.
   _____ True.   _____ False.

6. If you are going to move, you should simply decide what furniture goes in each room and wait until you are actually in the new house to decide exactly where each piece will go.
   _____ True.   _____ False.

7. It usually isn't a good idea to use cool colors in a room that faces north.
   _____ True.   _____ False.

8. If you have a long, narrow hallway with no room for furniture, there isn't much you can do with it.
   _____ True.   _____ False.

9. Dark colors tend to make a room look smaller.
   _____ True.   _____ False.

10. If a ceiling is too high, it can be made to look lower by painting it a lighter color than the walls.
    _____ True.   _____ False.

11. If you wish to camouflage windows that are off-center or unattractive, you should use drapes of a subdued color.
    _____ True.   _____ False.

HOW GOOD IS YOUR DECORATING ABILITY?

12. If you decided to decorate your living room in shades of peach and tangerine but the room contains a large red-brick fireplace, you can disregard the fireplace because it is only one element of a whole room.
    _____ True. _____ False.

13. Although it is customary to decorate a room in two or three main colors and perhaps one accent color, a color scheme that consists of many different shades of the same color can also be effective.
    _____ True. _____ False.

14. If you have a favorite old chair that belonged to your grandfather but it just doesn't look right in your living room no matter where you put it, you should get rid of it.
    _____ True. _____ False.

15. Most rooms need both general background lighting and specific lighting for particular activities.
    _____ True. _____ False.

16. It's a good idea to balance heavy, "permanent" pieces of furniture with smaller, lightweight pieces that can be moved easily.
    _____ True. _____ False.

17. If your walls are beginning to crack or peel and replastering would be too expensive, you can hide the cracks by painting the walls a dark color.
    _____ True. _____ False.

18. An unattractive feature such as a radiator or air conditioner may be camouflaged by painting it the same color as the walls.
    _____ True. _____ False.

19. Furniture must be arranged symmetrically around a central point such as a fireplace, or simply arranged with half the furniture on each side of the room.
    _____ True. _____ False.

20. In decorating, it's sometimes a good idea to splurge on one piece of very high quality that pleases you, even if you have to economize on the rest of the furniture.
    _____ True. _____ False.

ANSWERS

1. True. This does not mean that the styles for house and furnishings must be exactly the same, but they should be compatible. Early American would not work in a contemporary house, for example, while it would be appropriate in a Colonial or Federal style building.
2. False. While a room that is done all in one period may be lovely, it isn't necessary for all the pieces to be of the same period; a room that mixes periods may be just as lovely but have the comfortable, lived-in look that distinguishes a home from a museum. A style that mixes periods is known as transitional or eclectic.
3. False. It is true that the rooms are separate, but jumping from one color scheme to another in adjacent rooms, especially in a small house or apartment, can be distracting. One method is to try to use one color from the first room's color scheme in the second room, then one color (not necessarily the same one) from the second room in the third room, etc.
4. False. It should be obvious why this statement is wrong: you can't choose the color of a piece after you've bought it. The time to plan a room is before you have begun to furnish it.
5. False. A room in which everything matches is usually dull.
6. False. You should draw up a layout beforehand. Measure the rooms and decide where each piece will go. Otherwise, you may discover that your sofa doesn't fit in your living room!
7. True. In general, cool colors will make a northward-facing room seem even more cold and forbidding.
8. False. This is a perfect display area for pictures, wall hangings, and spotlights to highlight them. If you hang mirrors along the walls, they will reflect the lighting and give an illusion of space.
9. True. Dark colors tend to make a room look smaller, light colors tend to make a room look larger.
10. False. A *darker* color than the walls would probably make the ceiling seem lower.
11. True. This is a good way to avoid drawing attention to an unattractive feature in a room.
12. False. You can't suspend the rules for one item. That red-brick fireplace will still be there,

clashing with the walls, unless you take it into account from the beginning.
13. True. Doing a room in different shades of the same color is tricky, however, and should not be attempted by the inexperienced.
14. True. If you can't bear to throw it away, move it to another room or give it to a friend.
15. True. Lighting should be adaptable for different uses. All rooms need background lighting, but some rooms will need different amounts of specific lighting depending on what the room will be used for.
16. True. The heavier pieces give a room stability, but the lighweight pieces can be more flexible for everyday living.
17. True. The imperfections will be less visible if the walls are painted a dark color. Another possibility would be covering them with fabric or paneling.
18. True. Similarly, you can draw attention to features that you want to emphasize by painting them a contrasting color.
19. False. A symmetrical arrangement is certainly one possibility, but an asymmetrical arrangement can be much more interesting. Pieces may be arranged diagonally with, for instance, a high object balanced by a low one farther from the center. The technique is similar to that of Japanese flower arranging.
20. True—within reason, of course. If you just *have* to have that sofa or wing chair, go ahead and splurge, but be sure that you save some of your budget for whatever else you need to buy. And be sure that you won't tire of your extravagant purchase in a year or two.

EVALUATION

If you answered between 17 and 20 questions correctly, you seem to know what it takes to put everything together; with such well-developed designing ability, you should be proud of your tastefully decorated home. A score between 13 and 16 shows that your desire exceeds your talent, but don't lose hope. Redoing an entire house requires a great deal of planning and discipline, as does a small apartment, and if you have the interest, a small amount of effort and study will improve your decorating skills immensely. If you had less than 13 correct answers, you are dreaming a little too much. With rigid ideas and no planning, your home won't come out the way you think. For those who didn't score well but who want to develop their own home environment, take time, plan ahead, and study, and you'll see the difference in your decorating efforts.

?

????????????????? Are You Safety Conscious? ?????????????????

The safety points in this checklist are important, but there's lots more to learn about home safety.

Are you alert—aware—safety conscious? If you are, you will want to see some of the National Safety Council's other materials. Do you want to do something about it? You can be instrumental in the development of a community-wide program for home safety in your town. The National Safety Council has program planning kits for home accident prevention. For information, write to them at 444 North Michigan Avenue, Chicago, IL 60611.

?

	Yes	No
1. Do you look for tripping hazards—toys left around, mops and brooms, other clutter? And put them away?	___	___
2. Do you light your way ahead of you into rooms, up and down stairs?	___	___
3. Do you look at the label before taking any medicine?	___	___
4. Do you seek out fire hazards—rubbish in attic or basement, bundles of oily rags? And clear them out?	___	___
5. Do you watch for cleaning supplies, insecticides, medicines, matches, etc., left where children can get at them? And put them away?	___	___
6. Do you look to see that all window screens, guards, storm sashes, etc., are securely fastened?	___	___
7. Do you see that cigarettes, matches, and so forth are really out?	___	___
8. Have you anchored small throw rugs and repaired worn carpets?	___	___
9. Are broken stairways, loose floor boards, wobbly railings, promptly repaired?	___	___
10. Do you have flues, pipes, and chimneys inspected regularly—and repaired?	___	___
11. Do you keep all electrical equipment in good repair and discard or repair worn cords?	___	___
12. Is there a secure and adequate hand hold or grab bar over bathtub or shower?	___	___
13. Are all gas burners properly adjusted, free from leaks, petcocks tight?	___	___
14. Do you always use a solid ladder (or step stool) instead of a makeshift, such as a pile of boxes or an unsteady chair?	___	___
15. A fairly universal rule of fire prevention authorities is: No smoking in bed! Do you always observe it?	___	___
16. Do you always disconnect electric appliances when not in use?	___	___
17. Do you always keep garage doors open when running the motor inside?	___	___
18. Do you always provide adaquate ventilation in any room where portable gas or oil heaters are used?	___	___
19. Do you always keep guns unloaded and locked up?	___	___
20. Do you keep the yard clear of broken glass, nail-studded boards, garden tools, and other litter?	___	___

SCORE BOX
Number answered "Yes." ___
Total points (count 5 points for each "Yes.") ___

EVALUATION

If your score is
80 to 100   It's in your bones!
55 to 75   Better wake up!
Under 55   Call the ambulance!

Courtesy of National Safety Council

??????????
JOB/CAREER
??????????

How Good Is Your Job Interview Technique?

As every job-hunter knows, the person who is hired for a job is not necessarily the one who can do the job best; the person who gets the job is the one who knows the most about how to get a job. Good job-hunting skills are crucial to success. Knowing how to conduct yourself during a job interview is the most important of these skills, because the impression you make on you interviewer is the greatest factor—often the only factor—in getting the job. Good interview techniques include such basics as being on time, being neat and well-groomed, and trying to look sharp even when you're nervous. But there is more; you must have the right answers to the interviewer's questions, and you must have some questions and comments of your own that will impress the interviewer. The key is careful planning; if you have done enough planning, nothing that happens during the interview will surprise you. The following test will show how well you are able to sell yourself for a job.

1. Suppose your employer notifies you several weeks (or even months) in advance that you are to be laid off. Do you
    a. spend a lot of time pounding the pavement?
    b. stay home so you won't miss any phone calls?
    c. ask your employer for the use of your old office for as long as possible so that you can take calls there?

2. You prepare for an interview by
    a. shining you shoes and getting a good night's sleep.
    b. looking up the company in Dun & Bradstreet's Directory, trade journals, its own annual report, etc.
    c. using Transcendental Meditation to calm yourself.

3. You rehearse for an interview in front of
    a. your bathroom mirror.
    b. your spouse.
    c. a friend who is in the same business.

4. When you walk into the interviewer's office you see that you have a choice of three chairs. The interviewer doesn't indicate which one is for you, so you take
    a. the one directly in front of the desk.
    b. the one on the side of the desk.
    c. the one behind the desk.

5. After you sit down, do you
    a. sit on the edge of your chair in order to look eager?
    b. sit back and cross your legs in order to look relaxed and confident?
    c. sit back and fold your arms in order to look tough and capable?

JOB/CAREER

6. If after you sit down the interviewer continues to talk on the telephone for several minutes, you
   a. sit quietly and try not to fidget.
   b. stare at the interviewer, hoping he or she will stop being so rude.
   c. quietly keep occupied by reading or taking notes.

7. While you are describing at length your experience at your last job, the interviewer casually looks out the window. You say,
   a. "Am I boring you?"
   b. "I've also been doing some volunteer work that I believe is relevant . . ."
   c. "Would you like to hear more about my experience?"

8. Should you lie during a job interview?
   a. Yes.
   b. No.
   c. No, but it doesn't hurt to present the truth in the best possible light.

9. If an interviewer offers you a cigarette, you say,
   a. "Yes, I'd love one."
   b. "No, thank you."
   c. "Are you kidding? Don't you know those things cause cancer?"

10. The attitude that you want to project is
    a. eager and enthusiastic.
    b. interested but relaxed.
    c. skeptical and superior.

11. You are being interviewed for a job with a much higher salary than your present one of $15,000. If the interviewer asks you how much you're making, you say,
    a. "Fifteen thousand."
    b. "Fifteen thousand, but I'm worth much more."
    c. "Seventeen thousand five."

12. If the interviewer asks rude or insulting personal questions, you can assume that
    a. he or she doesn't like you.
    b. he or she thinks you are incompetent.
    c. he or she has already decided to hire someone else.

13. If you are asked to fill out a job application, what do you write in the box marked "salary desired"?
    a. the salary you want
    b. the lowest salary you would accept
    c. the word "negotiable"

14. The job application asks for the "reason for leaving" a job from which you were fired. You write
    a. "terminated."
    b. "laid off."
    c. "quit."

15. If the interviewer asks you what you think of your present (or most recent) company, you say,
    a. "I love working there, and I wish I didn't have to leave."
    b. "They're a bunch of no-good chiselers."
    c. "I've enjoyed working there, but now I'm ready to move on."

16. If the interviewer asks, "Do you think a person of your extreme youth can handle a managerial position?" you say,
    a. "Yes, I think so."
    b. "I think my creativity and fresh ideas should offset my lack of experience."
    c. "You'll notice that I was president of several clubs in college, so I've had experience managing people."

17. Suppose the interviewer asks you, "Where do you want to be ten years from now?" You reply,
    a. "I'm after *your* job."
    b. "Doing the same type of work, but one or two levels higher."
    c. "I'd like to go into business for myself."

18. The interviewer asks you your greatest weakness. You reply,
    a. "Procrastination."
    b. "I'm too quick to lose my temper."
    c. "I'm a perfectionist."

HOW GOOD IS YOUR JOB INTERVIEW TECHNIQUE?

19. Toward the end of the interview, your interviewer asks whether you have any questions. You say,
    a. "No, I can't think of any."
    b. "Yes; what benefits does the company offer?"
    c. "If, in several years, I've done as good a job as I plan to, to what position might I expect to be promoted?"

20. Suppose the interviewer tells you that he or she is impressed with your qualifications but has no suitable openings. You say,
    a. "Well, thanks anyway for the interview."
    b. "I hope you'll keep me in mind if something does come up."
    c. "Do you know of any other companies in your business that might have openings?"

???

ANSWERS

1. c	8. c	15. c
2. b	9. b	16. b
3. c	10. b	17. b
4. a	11. a	18. c
5. b	12. c	19. c
6. c	13. c	20. c
7. b	14. a	

EVALUATION

You must be a terrific salesperson if you scored from 18 to 20. You should be able to walk in and out of an interview with complete confidence. Less than five wrong answers shows that you know how to put your best foot forward, but there is also room for improvement. You have to remember that only one person will be hired for each job, and you won't get the job by being second best. Any score lower than 15 shows that you have to rethink your interviewing strategy. Even if you are satisfied with your present job, you never know when you will have to use your job-hunting skills again.

?

The Harrington/O'Shea System for Career Decision-Making®

THOMAS F. HARRINGTON, PH.D.
NORTHEASTERN UNIVERSITY

ARTHUR J. O'SHEA, PH.D.
BOSTON STATE COLLEGE

The Harrington/O'Shea System for Career Decision-Making® is designed to help you learn more about yourself and the world of work and how you might fit into that world in the most satisfying way possible. In its complete form the Career Decision-Making® System takes a sophisticated look into a person's interests, value systems, abilities, talents, and current planning, integrates this lifestyle information, relates it to the world of work, and offers career options, decision-making strategies, and factual information to help the person in career planning.

What follows is an excerpt from the Harrington/O'Shea System. A word of caution. This excerpt cannot have the reliability of the total program. In view of this, your results should be taken as giving tentative career suggestions. Your open, honest responses are essential to your receiving valid direction. This is not a test in the strict sense. Relax and enjoy the experience.

A SAMPLE FROM THE CAREER DECISION-MAKING® SYSTEM

Directions: Many activities and occupations are listed below. Place a check mark in front of those that you would like to do. Do not be concerned about whether you have the ability or training for the activity or job. Just decide whether you would LIKE to do it. Work rapidly. Your first reactions will produce the best results.

Group 1—Scientific
☐ Carry out scientific experiments
☐ Be a doctor who specializes in preventing diseases
☐ Use math to solve scientific problems
☐ Examine the effects of air pollution on the environment
☐ Be a marine biologist
☐ Be a medical laboratory assistant
☐ TOTAL Scientific checks

Group 2—The Arts
☐ Be a jazz musician
☐ Write TV scripts
☐ Draw cartoons
☐ Arrange background music for movies
☐ Write book reviews as a literary critic
☐ Design ads for TV or magazines
☐ TOTAL Artistic checks

Group 3—Crafts
☐ Repair damaged toys
☐ Refinish furniture
☐ Plant and care for a vegetable garden
☐ Repair airplane engines
☐ Assemble parts for stereo equipment
☐ Repair things around the house
☐ TOTAL Crafts checks

Group 4—Social
☐ Give first aid assistance
☐ Teach and train adults
☐ Give legal advice to poor people
☐ Direct a playground sports program

THE HARRINGTON/O'SHEA SYSTEM FOR CAREER DECISION-MAKING®

☐ Help persons find jobs after their release from prison
☐ Be a social science instructor in a two-year college
☐ TOTAL Social checks

Group 5—Business
☐ Organize and direct the operations of a business
☐ Be a lawyer for a company
☐ Promote the development of a new community shopping center
☐ Be a real estate agent showing and selling houses
☐ Buy merchandise for a large department store
☐ Travel throughout the country selling products to companies
☐ TOTAL Business checks

Group 6—Clerical
☐ Make plane and hotel reservations in a travel bureau
☐ Keep the financial records for a company
☐ Supervise an office clerical staff
☐ Operate data processing equipment
☐ Be a bank teller
☐ Keep records of goods in stock and supplies received
☐ TOTAL Clerical checks

DIRECTIONS FOR INTERPRETING YOUR RESPONSES

1. For each interest group add up the checks and write the total number in the box at the bottom of the group.
2. In the boxes below write the interest group names of your two highest scores, for example, Social-Scientific. If a tie causes you to have more than two interest groups, go back to the survey questions in the tied groups and eliminate your check from the one question you feel least sure about liking. This will remove one group from the tie. If you still have more than two groups because of a tie, repeat the elimination process until you have only two highest scores.

Highest Interest Area   Second Highest

3. Find your pair of two highest interest groups in the list below and put a check in the box before it. The order of your groups is not important. Thus, two persons with their highest scores ordered Social-Scientific and Scientific-Social respectively would enter the list at the same point, that is, Scientific-Social. The pairs are listed alphabetically.

Your highest interest scores	Career clusters
The Arts-Business	Artistic, Business, Management
The Arts-Clerical	Artistic, Clerical, Data Analysis
The Arts-Crafts	Artistic, Skilled Crafts, Technical
The Arts-Scientific	Artistic, Math-Science, Medical-Dental
The Arts-Social	Social Service, Artistic Management, Data Analysis, Clerical
Business-Crafts	Management, Skilled Crafts, Customer Service
Business-Scientific	Management, Math-Science, Technical
Business-Social	Management, Social Service, Legal
Clerical-Crafts	Clerical, Data Analysis, Skilled Crafts
Clerical-Scientific	Data Analysis, Math-Science, Clerical
Clerical-Social	Clerical, Data Analysis, Social Service
Crafts-Scientific	Technical, Skilled Crafts, Math-Science
Crafts-Social	Customer Services, Skilled Crafts, Social Service
Scientific-Social	Medical-Dental, Math-Science, Social Service

4. Next to your pair of highest interest scores which you have checked above, you will find the names of Career Clusters, that is, jobs that a scientific analysis found to be related. Circle your Career Clusters. They are the Career Clusters that the Career Decision-Making® System is suggesting that you explore as areas of potential job satisfaction. Each cluster suggested to you should be given equal emphasis in your initial exploration.

?

CAREER EXPLORATION AND DECISION-MAKING

INTRODUCTION

The career clusters suggested to you for exploration are based on your interests. Your likes and dislikes for a number of job activites were scored against six major occupational environments or work settings—the arts, clerical, crafts, business, social, and scientific. Personality can also be described according to these six categories. Psychological research, especially that of Dr. John Holland, has shown that people tend to search out and find satisfaction in a work setting that is in agreement with their personality types. Thus, scientific-type persons will find their greatest satisfaction in a scientific work setting.

A word of caution about interests. They suggest jobs that you might find satisfying. They do not measure ability. As you explore your career options, you will have to consider ability, as well as values, training requirements, and employment outlook. The complete Career Decision-Making® System goes into much greater depth in examining these points.

A few more cautions. Career decision-making is a long process. Don't expect to make a final decision at once. You may change your mind often. What you are trying to do now is to organize your thinking about topics considered important in deciding on a career. This survey will not tell you the scientific career that you should pursue. Rather, careers will be suggested to you for your exploration, and some guidelines will be provided to help you to narrow down your choices.

CAREER CLUSTER CHART

The chart on the next pages displays the career clusters in this abbreviated form of the Career Decision-Making® System. These eleven clusters cover the world of work with reasonable thoroughness. Through this chart you are given basic information about each career cluster. You should pay particular attention to those which your survey scores suggested for careful exploration.

A few words to explain and integrate the information on the chart. For each cluster there are three major headings. First, there is a list of jobs typical of the hundreds of jobs that make up the cluster. The letter in front of each job gives the Department of Labor estimate of the job's employment outlook. An E means the outlook is excellent, G = Good, F = Fair, while NA signifies that the Department of Labor has not made a projection. You will find other letters above each job column. These refer to the level of education and training generally required of the jobs in the column. APP/OJT means that an apprenticeship or on-the-job training usually prepares the worker without the need for specialized education other than a general education. However, some college, specialized work experience, or training may prove helpful. V/T signifies the requirement of vocational or technical programs in high school and/or junior college and technical and business schools. C means that the job calls for a four-year college degree and at times a graduate degree.

Job Values, the second heading in the chart, tells you the kind of satisfactions people derive from each cluster. Job values are things that people look for in a job, things that provide fulfillment in a job. Some persons derive their greatest satisfaction from helping others, some from the prestige they win through their work, others from the opportunity to be creative.

Under the final heading, Required Abilities, you will find the abilities that each career cluster demands. Under these last two headings you will find a number of values and abilities listed for each career cluster. Each value and ability may not be related to every job in the cluster, but most will be.

USING THE CAREER CLUSTER CHART

It is now time to study your career clusters, the ones suggested by your high scores and which you circled in the right hand column on page 219. Study the list of typical jobs in your clusters. Circle those jobs that appeal to you and that you want to explore more deeply.

Read through the values that are associated with your clusters. Are the values listed what you are intent on gaining from your career? Remember that values are highly personal, that different persons will achieve different values doing the same job. However, certain values are commonly associated with a particular job cluster. If your values are totally different from those that are most often gained in a career cluster, you might well not find satisfaction in that cluster. We are talking here about the accountant with the talent and training for accounting who after five years on the job has less enthusiasm for the work, does some serious soul-searching, discovers a hierarchy of values in which a strong need for helping others holds primacy, and enrolls in a graduate school to prepare for a career in psychology.

Abilities are yet another piece in the career puzzle—an essential one. Interest is not enough. Study the abilities required in your career clusters. Be honest with yourself. Use your life experiences as criteria. Include school performance, work and volunteer experiences, hobbies, club involvement, home activities.

THE HARRINGTON/O'SHEA SYSTEM FOR CAREER DECISION-MAKING®

Career Cluster Chart

Cluster	Typical jobs			Job values	Required abilities
Artistic Work	APP/OJT F—Artist F—Photographer F—Dancer F—Actor/Actress	C and/or OJT F—Musician F—Singer V/T G—Industrial Design F—Interior Design	V/T F—Model F—TV/Radio Announcer C F—Clothes Designer F—Reporter F—Writer G—Representative	Creativity/Variety Work with Mind Independence High Achievement Prestige/Salary Leadership Work with People	Artistic Manual Spatial Persuasive Leadership Musical Social
Clerical Work	APP/OJT E—Bank Teller E—Cashier G—File Clerk G—Hotel Clerk E—Library Asst. F—Mail Carrier	APP/OJT NA—Mail Clerk E—Receptionist F—Telephone Operator G—Ticket Agent G—Typist	V/T F—Key Punch Operator E—Medical Record Clerk E—Secretary F—Stenographer	Routine Activity Supervised Work Security Work with People Work with Hands	Clerical Language Computation Social
Customer Services	APP/OJT F—Bus Driver G—Cleaner G—Correction Officer G—Flight Attendant E—Food	APP/OJT G—Counter Worker G—Gas Station Attendant E—Nurse's Aide/Orderly G—Police Officier E—Security Guard	APP/OJT G—Sales Clerk E—Taxi Driver G—Waiter/Waitress V/T F—Barber E—Beautician E—Physical Therapy Aide	Work with People Routine Activity Physical Activity Supervised Work Work with Hands	Social Manual Clerical Mechanical Computation Artistic
Data Analysis	APP/OJT G—Business Machine Operator G—Computer Operator G—Statistical Clerk	V/T G—Accountant G—Accounting Clerk G—Bookkeeper G—Payroll Clerk	C E—Bank Loan Officer G—Insurance Underwriter	Work with Mind Routine Activity Supervised Work Salary Security	Math Computation Clerical Language
Legal Work	APP/OJT G—Claim Adjuster E—Customs Inspector G—Detective	V/T E—Building Inspector E—Food and Drug Inspector	C G—FBI Agent NA—Judge F—Lawyer NA—Paralegal Asst.	Leadership Creativity/Variety Work with Mind Independence Work with People	Persuasive Leadership Social Language
Management/ Sales	APP/OJT E—Contractor G—Hotel Manager Manufacturer's Representative E—Restaurant Manager G—Sales Manager E—Sales Agent F—Travel Agent	V/T F—Buyer E—Office Manager E—Purchasing Agent C E—Banker F—Farm Manager G—Stock Broker	C G—Government Administrator E—Industrial Engineer G—Personnel Manager NA—President or other Major Officer of a Business G—Sales Engineer	Prestige Creativity Work with Mind Work with People Leadership Salary Variety Independence	Social Leadership Persuasive Language Computational Mathematical Scientific
Math-Science	V/T E—Computer Programmer Lab Technician C G—Actuary	C F—Architect G—Biologist G—Chemist E—Engineer G—Ecologist F—Forester E—Gcologist	C F—Mathematician E—Medical Technologist G—Pharmacist G—Physicist E—Statistician E—Surgeon	Security Leadership Creativity Work with Mind Independence Salary Variety Prestige	Mathematical Scientific Computational Language Spatial Mechanical

JOB/CAREER

Career Cluster Chart (Continued)

Cluster	Typical jobs			Job values	Required abilities
Medical-Dental	C G—Audiologist F—Chiropractor E—Dentist G—Optometrist	C E—Psychiatrist G—Speech Pathologist E—Physician E—Veterinarian		Prestige/Salary Leadership Creativity/Variety Work with People Security Work with Mind	Scientific Social Mathematical Language Spatial Manual
Social Services	APP/OJT E—Dental Assistant G—Teacher Aide V/T E—Dental Hygienist E—Emergency Medical Technician E—Nurse G—X-Ray Technologist	C F to E—Clergy F—Counselor G—Economist NA—Educational Administrator F—Historian F—Home Economist F—Librarian G—Occupational Therapist	C G—Physical Therapist F—Political Scientist NA—Probation Officer F—Professor, College F—Teacher, School G—Psychologist G—Social Worker F—Sociologist	Work with People Creativity Work with Mind Independence Leadership Variety Prestige Security Salary	Social Language Mathematical Scientific Teaching Persuasive
Skilled Crafts	APP/OJT G—Assembler G—Auto Mechanic G—Carpenter G—Construction Work E—Cook E—Dental Technician G—Electrician F—Farmer G—Lithographer	APP/OJT G—Machinist E—Military Service G—Miner E—Optician E—Plumber F—Printer G—Sewing Machine Operator G—Stock Clerk	APP/OJT E—TV Repairer G—Truck Driver V/T G—Aircraft Mechanic F—Radio/TV Technician	Work with Hands Physical Activity Routine Activity Supervised Work	Mechanical Manual Spatial Clerical Mathematical Computational
Technical Work	APP/OJT G—Air Traffic Controller E—Surveyor	V/T G—Airline Pilot E—Drafter E—Electronic Technician	V/T E—Quality Control Technician E—Scientific Helper NA—Technical Illustrator	Physical Activity Work with Mind Work with Hands Routine Activity Supervised Work	Mathematical Scientific Computational Mechanical Artistic Manual/Spatial

OBTAINING ADDITIONAL INFORMATION

There are several excellent Department of Labor publications that you will find in most libraries or that you can obtain relatively cheaply by writing to the Superintendent of Documents, U.S. Government Printing Office, Washington, DC 20402. One is the *Occupational Outlook Handbook,* which is revised every two years. It provides job descriptions, training requirements, up-to-date forecasts of job prospects, salaries, work conditions, and sources of additional information. A second valuable resource is the *Guide for Occupational Exploration*. It divides the 20,000 United States jobs into sixty-six work groups and provides information about the interests, aptitudes, adaptabilities, and other requirements for each work group. The *Guide* makes possible a comparison of these requirements with what you know about yourself from the Career Decision-Making® System and other career exploration activities.

SUGGESTIONS FOR FURTHER EXPLORATION

1. Continue to study those careers that especially interest you by:
   —talking with people in the careers
   —visiting them when possible at their places of work
   —seeking the advice of trained career counselors
   —reading as much as possible about the careers
   —trying to find related part-time jobs or volunteer experiences

THE HARRINGTON/O'SHEA SYSTEM FOR CAREER DECISION-MAKING®

2. Read through the eleven career clusters described in the chart on pages 221 and 222. If any interest you, study them in the same way you were instructed to study the clusters suggested to you by the Career-Decision-Making® System.
3. Remember that a final career choice is yours alone. Others can only suggest some reasonable options for you to explore.

HOW TO PARTICIPATE IN THE TOTAL CAREER DECISION-MAKING® SYSTEM

What you have just experienced is but a small sample of the total Career Decision-Making® System in which much more information is gathered about you—not just interests as was the case here, but values, abilities, and plans. In addition, there are eighteen clusters compared to the eleven here, and a significantly greater number of specific jobs. The total program
- —is a new and total approach to career planning incorporating self-estimates of ability, specification of job values, school subject preferences, and future plans
- —plus a career interest survey:
  - —widely used with young people and adults in schools, colleges, and agencies throughout the United States
  - —meets the National Institute of Education Standards for sex fairness
  - —based on sound psychological theory and research
- —provides extensive career information:
  - —includes jobs that employ 95 percent of the United States work force
  - —interpretive materials in the program describe for you job activities, job requirements, and a frequently updated employment outlook

?

Additional information on the total Career Decision-Making® System is available from
Career Planning Associates, Inc.
P.O. Box 273
Needham, MA 02192

Copyright © 1980, Career Planning Associates, Inc.

?

Does Your Job Have Good Growth Potential?

Is your job one you can stay with for the rest of your career, or is it only a stepping stone to another, more successful position? Do you have a realistic hope of promotion with your present company or are you locked into a stalemate with no prospect of advancement?

If you are sure that you are completely satisfied with your present position, read no further; but if you have your doubts, this test can help you resolve them. If you are stuck in a dead-end job, wouldn't it be best to find out as soon as possible?

In order to succeed, you must be well-qualified, but competence alone is not enough. In the best of organizations, you must make your abilities and accomplishments visible to your superiors. In the worst of organizations, no amount of corporate gamesmanship is enough, because there are built-in obstacles to promotion that are difficult or impossible to overcome. If you find yourself in such a company, the best thing to do is leave and find a job that will allow you to make the best use of your talents.

?

1. How would you describe your company's financial situation?
    a. Profits are down from last year.
    b. Profits are increasing slowly but steadily.
    c. The situation has been about the same for the last several years.
    d. Profits are very inconsistent; one year they're up, the next year they're down.

2. How would you describe the management of your company?
    a. Innovative and attuned to all the latest technical developments.
    b. Likes to wait and see whether a new idea works for other companies before adopting it.
    c. A bastion of conservatism.
    d. A fashionable, with-it trend-setter.

3. How can you find out about job openings in your company?
    a. They're posted on the bulletin board.
    b. Check the personnel department every week.
    c. Eavesdrop outside the executive suite.
    d. Ask your supervisor.

4. How would you describe your company's promotion policy?
    a. Capricious; there's no telling who will be promoted next.
    b. Predictable; if you're good, sooner or later you'll be promoted.
    c. Moth-eaten; the same elite group has been at the top for as long as anyone can remember.
    d. Unfair; only teacher's pets go to the head of the class.

5. Into which group do the top managers in your company fall?
    a. Young to middle-aged
    b. Elderly
    c. Mostly elderly, with a few youngsters in their thirties and forties
    d. All ages equally represented

DOES YOUR JOB HAVE GOOD GROWTH POTENTIAL?

6. Which of the following statements is true of your department?
   a. The same people have been there for years.
   b. It has more employees than it really needs to get the job done.
   c. There is frequent turnover.
   d. It's hard to find good people who can handle the work.

7. Which of the following descriptions best fits your immediate superior?
   a. Adequate, but you could do better.
   b. A nice person but a mediocre manager.
   c. Ambitious and bucking for promotion.
   d. Good at his or her job.

8. What's the best way to get promoted in your company?
   a. Be related to the boss.
   b. Make yourself visible by telling your superiors how good you are.
   c. Make some friends in the upper echelon.
   d. Be the best man or woman on the job.

9. What are you doing to protect your position?
   a. Creating a documentation system that no one but you can decipher.
   b. Currying favor with the higher-ups.
   c. Trying to learn about different aspects of the business.
   d. Just quietly doing the best job you can.

10. Your boss asks for your opinion
    a. when he or she is stumped by a problem.
    b. mainly to reinforce his or her own ideas.
    c. often, but you have the feeling that it's just for the sake of form.
    d. only on trivial matters.

11. Because you're interested in promotion, you want to find out something about your boss's background and how he or she got the job. What is the best way to do this?
    a. Ask your boss.
    b. Ask your boss's supervisor.
    c. Bribe someone in the personnel department to show you your boss's resume.
    d. Do some research in the library.

12. If you wanted to impress your boss with your competence, you would
    a. make some suggestions about things that he or she could be doing better.
    b. take on some extra work and hope the boss notices.
    c. take on some extra work and tell your boss about it after you're finished.

13. When you make a suggestion, your boss
    a. usually rejects it.
    b. follows your suggestion but pretends it was his or her idea.
    c. doesn't always follow it but encourages you to keep making suggestions.
    d. usually follows it.

14. Even though you already have a job, you want to keep informed about openings in your field. The best way to do this is to
    a. read the want ads.
    b. read professional journals.
    c. cultivate friends who work for competing firms.
    d. attend meetings of professional organizations.

15. What do you do if you're dissatisfied with something at work?
    a. Put an anonymous note in the suggestion box.
    b. Tell your supervisor.
    c. Tell your co-workers.
    d. Tell your best friend.

16. If you were offered a promotion to a very challenging spot, you would
    a. accept it if you thought you could handle it.
    b. accept it first, ask questions later.
    c. consider it for several weeks before deciding.
    d. probably decline.

17. What is your attitude towards "office politics"?
    a. You're above all that.
    b. You're always a member of the in-group.
    c. You try to please everybody, so neither the in-group nor the out-group can criticize you.
    d. You make sure you're on good terms with the people in power.

JOB/CAREER

18. Which statement best describes your progress so far in this company?
    a. The boss's brother-in-law was promoted over you.
    b. You have been passed over in favor of less-qualified people.
    c. Your boss has promised to recommend you the next time there's an opening.
    d. You haven't been with the company long enough to expect promotion.

19. You are considering going back to school for some further education that might help you in your work. Which of the following statements is true?
    a. You will only do it if your company pays for it.
    b. You're not so sure that you want to sacrifice your leisure time.
    c. You're not convinced that it would really be worth it; perhaps experience is the best teacher.
    d. The subject matter is interesting, so you'll probably do it even though there's no guarantee it will lead to promotion.

20. The best way to convince your superiors that you deserve a promotion is to
    a. let your actions speak for you.
    b. talk to them about your ambitions and goals.
    c. show them that you are just as good as they are by making suggestions that will help them improve their work.
    d. get to know them socially.

ANSWERS

Find the number of points next to the letter of each answer that you gave. Then add the points to determine your total score.

1. a—0; b—5; c—0; d—0
2. a—5; b—2; c—0; d—4
3. a—2; b—0; c—0; d—5
4. a—2; b—5; c—0; d—2
5. a—2; b—0; c—2; d—5
6. a—0; b—0; c—5; d—3
7. a—0; b—0; c—5; d—3
8. a—0; b—2; c—2; d—5
9. a—2; b—3; c—5; d—2
10. a—5; b—2; c—2; d—0
11. a—5; b—0; c—0; d—2
12. a—0; b—2; c—3; d—5
13. a—0; b—2; c—3; d—5
14. a—5; b—5; c—2; d—2
15. a—0; b—5; c—0; d—0
16. a—5; b—2; c—2; d—0
17. a—0; b—2; c—2; d—5
18. a—0; b—0; c—5; d—2
19. a—3; b—0; c—0; d—5
20. a—2; b—5; c—0; d—2

EVALUATION

90 to 100. *Stairway to the stars.* The sky's the limit! You're in a good spot, and you'd be wise to stay there.

80 to 89. *The road to success.* You're in a good position to succeed if you can make the most of your talents. Stay where you are, and try to make sure people notice you; a little public relations on your own behalf won't hurt.

70 to 79. *The path to oblivion.* You're in a rut, and you ought to consider how to dig yourself out. A job change might be a good way to do it.

69 or below. *Dead end.* Get out while the getting's good.

?

How Good Are Your Business Communications Skills?

???????????????????????????
???????????????????????????

Researchers have found that employers are increasingly concerned about the general communication skills of all employees; ineffective written and oral communications can lead to inefficiency and poor business relations. Strong communication abilities are thus essential to successful employment. Taking this test will show you if your business communications skills are an asset to your career.

Directions: These questions represent a small sample in a wide field of study called business communications. Record your answers in the space provided. Then check your answers with the key to find out how well you did. The answers are based on generally accepted communication principles, practices, or research.

???

1. Which sentence best represents the desired "you attitude" in business writing?
    a. "If you don't pay by March 10, your credit will be cancelled."
    b. "You no doubt realize that your error caused the delay in your shipment."
    c. "Your order was sent today and should arrive by UPS in time for Monday's needs."
    d. "While company policy prohibits credit sales, your merchandise can be sent C.O.D."

2. In a five-paragraph letter to credit union members, where should the following sentence be located: "By completing the questionnaire and mailing it in the attached envelope, you will be helping your credit union better serve you and other employees."
    a. In the first paragraph.
    b. In the second or third paragraph.
    c. In the fourth paragraph.
    d. In the last paragraph.

3. In a business letter, usually the best place to record unfavorable news is
    a. at the beginning.
    b. after some explanation but before the end.
    c. before some explanation but not at the beginning.
    d. at the end.

4. In a four-sentence business letter, which sentence usually delivers favorable news best?
    a. First sentence.
    b. Second sentence.
    c. Third sentence.
    d. Fourth sentence.

For Questions 5 through 9, select the one passage in each group of three sentences that most nearly meets the principles of effective business letter writing.

5. a. In regard to your request for credit, we are happy to grant it.
    b. Welcome as a credit customer. You may purchase up to $1,000 on credit at any one time.
    c. After examining the data provided in your application and checking with the credit bureau, your request for credit is approved.

227

JOB/CAREER

6. a. By circling the item you desire on the enclosed order form and returning it to us, we'll ship your order at once.
    b. By giving incomplete information, we could not mail the item; so as soon as we get the correct order number, we'll be happy to ship it right away.
    c. Did you forget to give the item number in your order? We'll hold your order until we get the missing information.

7. a. The size of the shipment is of the order of magnitude of 300 cases.
    b. It is my estimate that the shipment contains approximately 300 cases.
    c. The shipment contains about 300 cases.

8. a. We can't accept your admission to graduate school because your score on the admission test was too low. You may wish to take the test again.
    b. While your score on the admission test was too low for us to accept you into graduate school now, you may wish to take the test again and reapply.
    c. Because your score on the admission test was below our cutoff point, you are denied admission to graduate school. If you retake the test and raise your score, you may apply again.

9. a. As you can see from the attached resumé, I finished high school and then worked as a sales clerk at Minty's Department Store before getting my degree in marketing at the community college.
    b. I graduated from high school four years ago, worked for two years as a sales clerk, and then finished my degree in marketing at the local community college.
    c. My high school program in distributive education gave me the training and incentive to pursue sales work. After gaining two years of practical sales experience—and winning several sales awards—at a local department store, I pursued my career by earning a two-year degree in marketing at the community college.

10. Active voice is better than passive voice in most business writing situations. Select the sentence below that employs the active voice.
    a. The letters were mailed by him.
    b. She called the customer as soon as the order arrived.
    c. He was paid the sum owed by Mary immediately.
    d. While typing, the secretary was interrupted by a customer.

11. The desired average sentence length for most business writing is
    a. 10-15 words.
    b. 16-20 words.
    c. 21-25 words.
    d. 26-30 words.
    e. 30-plus words.

12. Is there agreement between the noun and verb in each of the following sentences?
    1. The criteria used to judge the quality of work is excellent.
    2. Your order, which contained seven suits and four wallets, are being sent today.
    a. 1 agreement; 2 agreement
    b. 1 agreement; 2 disagreement
    c. 1 disagreement; 2 agreement
    d. 1 disagreement; 2 disagreement

13. You have been asked to lead a meeting of co-workers for the purpose of discussing several office problems and to recommend solutions. Which of the following actions should you avoid?
    a. Prepare and distribute an agenda in advance.
    b. Create an atmosphere of ease.
    c. Encourage conflict for a healthy discussion.
    d. Arrange to start and end the meeting on time.

14. Linda Jones works in the Sales Department of Smith Corporation. Telephone calls are received by a central switchboard operator and then transferred to individuals or departments. When answering the phone, which greeting should Ms. Jones use?
    a. "Sales Department, Linda Jones."
    b. "Sales Department. May I help you?
    c. "Linda Jones; may I help you?"
    d. "May I help you?"

HOW GOOD ARE YOUR BUSINESS COMMUNICATIONS SKILLS?

15. About how much time does a typical business executive spend communicating each workday?
    a. 65 to 80 percent.
    b. 50 to 65 percent.
    c. 35 to 50 percent.
    d. 20 to 35 percent.

16. On which of the following communication activites does the average manager spend the most time?
    a. Speaking.
    b. Listening.
    c. Writing.
    d. Reading.

17. Most face-to-face business transactions occur between people who are not well acquainted with each other. The physical distance (space zone) between individuals conducting oral business transactions is usually
    a. 0 to 1½ feet.
    b. 1½ to 4 feet.
    c. 4 to 12 feet.
    d. 12 feet and beyond.

18. Body language (nonverbal messages) is most often communicated by which part of the body?
    a. Head.
    b. Arms.
    c. Legs.
    d. Torso.

19. Which physical setting would most encourage an honest, open discussion between a supervisor (S) and an employee (E)?

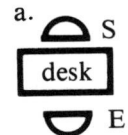

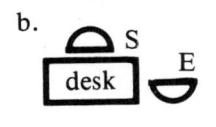

    a. [S at desk, E facing across desk]
    b. [S at desk, E beside desk]
    c. [desk with S and E sitting together on same side]

20. While ending an interview with a subordinate, a supervisor physically moves away, turns to face the exterior window, and says: "You're doing a fine job." In general, does the physical act agree with the spoken message?
    a. The physical act confirms the spoken message.
    b. The physical act is contradictory to the spoken message.
    c. The physical act neither confirms nor denies the spoken message.

21. In what order should the following parts of an inductive analytical report appear?
    a. Data, statement of problem, conclusions.
    b. Statement of problem, data, conclusions.
    c. Conclusions, statement of problems, data.
    d. Statement of problem, conclusions, data.

22. In a business report, what is the best way to refer to a statistical table?
    a. Make no reference to it since the reader will find it.
    b. "Table I shows the data pertaining to the problem."
    c. "Profits increased ten percent, as shown in Table I."
    d. "Table I, shown earlier, reveals that profit increased."

23. In reports, the primary use of headings is to
    a. simplify the preparation of the abstract.
    b. assist the writer in organizing the report.
    c. create a table of contents.
    d. aid the reader in digesting the report.

24. A major weakness of many report writers is that of
    a. being objective in drawing conclusions.
    b. preparing footnotes and bibliographies.
    c. stating recommendations.
    d. deciding about which topic to write.

25. The primary purpose for writing most analytical business reports is to
    a. provide data requested by government.
    b. condense large quantities of data.
    c. present information to decision-makers.
    d. examine and solve problems.

ANSWERS

1. c	10. b	19. c
2. d	11. b	20. b
3. b	12. d	21. b
4. a	13. c	22. c
5. b	14. a	23. d
6. a	15. a	24. a
7. c	16. b	25. d
8. b	17. c	
9. c	18. a	

JOB/CAREER

EVALUATION

Rate yourself on the number of correct answers by applying the following scale:

22 to 25. *Excellent.* You know communication principles. You have a fine blend of written and oral skills and are an asset to your business.

18 to 21. *Very Good.* You can improve, though. Having better skills will help you solve problems, direct information, eliminate confusion, and design better ways to approach problems. All this will, of course, make you a stronger participant in your company.

14 to 17. *Fair.* You need to take corrective measures because your skills are a hindrance to your career. Whether you take courses or seek help from your employers, learning to communicate better will help you to be a success in the marketplace. Learning the necessary skills will make you more confident and give your employer more reason to need you.

13 or below. *Poor.* You are in trouble and need help. Not the help you can get from friends or relatives, but from professionals in adult education courses or at colleges and universities. Take the time to find a course, and you'll work your way up the ladder to success.

Courtesy of Dr. Kenneth E. Everard, Business Communications Test, Trenton State College, Trenton, New Jersey.

?

??????????????????????????
Are You Ready for a Promotion?
??????????????????????????

Sooner or later every working person thinks about promotion. But no one gets a promotion unless the boss thinks he or she has what it takes. And superiors look for certain characteristics, such as a sense of responsibility, discipline, awareness, commitment, and an ability to motivate. If you think you're ready to ask for that raise and promotion, take this test and see if you're right.

?

1. I have demonstrated in my present position that I respond well to pressure.
   _____ True. _____ False.

2. I often take work home now, but I would have time to do even more work at home if I were promoted.
   _____ True. _____ False.

3. I am often the first one to suggest taking on a problem.
   _____ True. _____ False.

4. I often find myself trying to evade my boss when I haven't met a deadline.
   _____ True. _____ False.

5. I have proved that I can adapt quickly to change.
   _____ True. _____ False.

6. I sometimes have difficulty enforcing policies I don't believe in.
   _____ True. _____ False.

7. I can't always trust people to carry out my orders because they may not be as capable as I am.
   _____ True. _____ False.

8. My paperwork is detailed and well-organized.
   _____ True. _____ False.

9. I object to having to compromise when I know I'm right.
   _____ True. _____ False.

10. I have demonstrated that I can make decisions quickly.
    _____ True. _____ False.

11. My subordinates like working for me.
    _____ True. _____ False.

12. I am always available to help my subordinate make decisions.
    _____ True. _____ False.

13. I don't believe in office politics.
    _____ True. _____ False.

14. I know I am respected by my peers.
    _____ True. _____ False.

15. I believe that appearance and bearing are unimportant to success in business.
    _____ True. _____ False.

JOB/CAREER

16. If there is a split between two rival factions, I am usually on the winning side.
    _____ True.   _____ False.

17. Titles are not important; the only thing that matters is salary.
    _____ True.   _____ False.

18. I have no contact with the upper echelon in my company because I don't want to go over my boss's head.
    _____ True.   _____ False.

19. I would rather be respected than liked.
    _____ True.   _____ False.

20. The harder I work, the more likely I am to succeed.
    _____ True.   _____ False.

??

ANSWERS

The following answers indicate management potential. The number of answers you gave that coincide with these is your score.

1. True.	11. True.
2. True.	12. False.
3. True.	13. False.
4. False.	14. True.
5. True.	15. False.
6. False.	16. True.
7. False.	17. False.
8. True.	18. False.
9. False.	19. True.
10. True.	20. True.

EVALUATION

If your score was between 18 and 20, you will be a successful manager. You are capable, experienced, and possessed of mature judgment. You understand how to deal with subordinates, peers, and superiors. You know when to go out on a limb and when to compromise, and you know how to play the game without sacrificing your principles.

A score between 15 and 17 shows that you definitely have potential, but it is questionable whether you are ready for promotion to management. Perhaps the problem is your attitude; if you are too intransigent you will have difficulty getting others to go along with you, no matter how able or respected you are. Try to understand that office politics and the pursuit of status, which you may regard as petty games, have their place in the world of business. In order to succeed in that world you will have to deal with it as it is, not as you would like it to be.

If your scored below 15, you may be an able worker, but perhaps you should question whether you really want to assume the responsibility of a management position. Not everyone has to be constantly moving up; many businessmen and businesswomen find that the work load at their present level is as much as they can handle, and they make a conscious decision to stay where they are, rather than to pursue promotion. Perhaps this would be the best choice for you.

?

??????????????????????
Are You about to Be Fired?
??????????????????????

We're all afraid of being fired. Regardless of the reason—corporate takeover, cutback, layoff, reshuffling of the staff, superiors axed—getting fired is no picnic. Happily, you can do something to hold onto your job by being aware of office changes and office politics—hold on, that is, until *you're* ready to leave. Keeping your eyes open and your mouth shut can help you sense when a firing is imminent, and you can use this time to prepare. If you do so, your present job can be a steppingstone to something better, for it's much easier to get a job when you have one.

Take this test and find out who is a prime candidate for termination—and how soon it may happen.

?

1. My company has just been acquired by a large corporation.
   _____ True.   _____ False.

2. There seems to be a reorganization in the offing; I've been asked to give reports on all my subordinates.
   _____ True.   _____ False.

3. My boss has just been fired, and I am reporting to a new supervisor.
   _____ True.   _____ False.

4. Lately there have been several meetings to which I haven't been invited, although I formerly would have been.
   _____ True.   _____ False.

5. I never get copies of important memos anymore.
   _____ True.   _____ False.

6. A terrific promotion idea that I dreamed up seems to be fizzling.
   _____ True.   _____ False.

7. Top management has announced that all departments must cut their budgets.
   _____ True.   _____ False.

8. No budget cuts have been announced, but I happen to know that sales figures have been dropping steadily.
   _____ True.   _____ False.

9. The president has decided that it's time for a change; our company needs a fresh, new image.
   _____ True.   _____ False.

10. Some of my co-workers have either been fired or transferred to other departments.
    _____ True.   _____ False.

11. My boss and I often clash because we have very different business philosophies and personal styles.
    _____ True.   _____ False.

12. I am the most flamboyant, innovative person in my conservative company.
    _____ True.   _____ False.

13. My dress and manner are more casual than those of the rest of the company; my co-workers are rather stuffy.
    _____ True.   _____ False.

JOB/CAREER

14. I am neat and meticulous, whereas my co-workers are slobs.
    _____ True. _____ False.

15. My boss's mannerisms irritate me; we get on each other's nerves.
    _____ True. _____ False.

16. My boss is secretive, even sneaky; I never know what's on his mind.
    _____ True. _____ False.

17. My boss is always nice to *me* but makes cutting remarks about other employees behind their backs.
    _____ True. _____ False.

18. I never get involved in office politics; I don't believe in it.
    _____ True. _____ False.

19. There *are* factions in my company, and my boss is a member of the out-group.
    _____ True. _____ False.

20. My boss tends to play favorites, and I don't think I'm one of those favorites.
    _____ True. _____ False.

EVALUATION

If you answered *true* to five or more questions, you are in danger of being fired. In addition, your job is in danger if you answered true to even one of the following questions: 4, 5, 6, or 10. Don't despair, though; until you actually *are* fired there is hope, because there are several things that you can do to protect your job by making yourself indispensable, or at least extremely valuable, to your company. These techniques include being the best at your job and letting your superiors know it, learning as much as you can about different facets of the business, volunteering for the thankless jobs that nobody else wants, being an organizer of social events, making sure that you possess information or skills that few others have (possibly including trade secrets that your company will want to protect), coming up with ideas that will increase efficiency or profits, and, of course, making sure that the right people will go to bat for you when it is time to discuss layoffs. If you *do* get the ax, make the most of the interview in which you're fired: ask for more severance pay; ask for a favorable reference; ask for job leads; ask to use a desk and a telephone while you're job-hunting. Then go home, have a drink—but just one —and remember that most people who are fired eventually find jobs that are as good as or better than the ones they lost.

?

What Can You Expect as a Working Mother?

There is a new category in the work force—women who have raised families and are now entering or reentering the job market. Latest statistics show that there are over fifteen million working women (with children under eighteen) in the work force. Aside from the excitement and uncertainty involved in entering or reentering the job market, there are issues and problems to be discussed at home. Child care, domestic duties, and shared responsibilities must be considered—in addition to your outside work responsibilities.

?

1. Does your husband support your career plans?
   _____ Yes. _____ No.

2. Does your husband do his share of the housework?
   _____ Yes. _____ No.

3. If you and your husband together won't be able to do all the housework, is there a competent housekeeper or cleaning service available?
   _____ Yes. _____ No.

4. Does your husband accept equal responsiblity as a parent?
   _____ Yes. _____ No.

5. Is the job you are considering a fulfilling one that is right for you?
   _____ Yes. _____ No.

6. Does the job have good working conditions and reasonable hours?
   _____ Yes. _____ No.

7. Will transportation to your job be convenient?
   _____ Yes. _____ No.

8. Do you live close to your job?
   _____ Yes. _____ No.

9. Are you sure that you have time for a full-time (or part-time) job?
   _____ Yes. _____ No.

10. Have you arranged for the best possible baby-sitter or child-care facility?
    _____ Yes. _____ No.

11. Is the baby-sitter someone that your children, as well as you, like?
    _____ Yes. _____ No.

12. If you have been active in school or community affairs, are you easing yourself out of these commitments so that you will have time to devote to your job?
    _____ Yes. _____ No.

13. Have you prepared yourself to deal with guilt feelings?
    _____ Yes. _____ No.

JOB/CAREER

14. Have you braced yourself for the criticism of nonworking mothers who may feel the need to put you down?
    _____ Yes.   _____ No.

15. Do you take an active part in your children's school activities?
    _____ Yes.   _____ No.

16. Do you share your business day with your children?
    _____ Yes.   _____ No.

17. Do you talk to your children?
    _____ Yes.   _____ No.

18. Do you treat your children as independent persons whom you respect?
    _____ Yes.   _____ No.

19. Do your children know that they can count on you in an emergency?
    _____ Yes.   _____ No.

20. Do your children know that you love them?
    _____ Yes.   _____ No.

???

EVALUATION

If you answered 17 or more questions with "yes," go ahead! It's obvious that you've thought the conditions of the specific job you're considering, and it's equally obvious that your relationship with your children is a happy one. Don't let guilt feelings or the criticism of other dissuade you; if a career is what you want, you should have it, as long as you are satisfied that your children will be well taken care of. If you share experiences with them, your children will be proud of your achievements.

If you had between 14 and 17 "yes" answers, you may still be able to make a go of it, but give some serious thought to how you are going to handle everyday responsibilities. Explain to your husband and children why a job or career is so important to you. And if your children have problems, don't automatically assume that it's because you're a working mother. Remember that children of nonworking mothers can have problems too, and that the quality of the time you spend with your children is as important as its quantity.

If you answered less than 14 questions with "yes," don't go back to work until you have reconsidered your reasons for wanting a job. Perhaps you are so bored with your daily routine that you will snap up the first position available, whether or not it is right for you. You probably are not adequately prepared for the complications that taking a job outside the home will introduce into your life. Remember, you can always find a job later, when you are sure that both you and the children are ready.

?

??????????????????????????
Are You a Workaholic?
??????????????????????????

Do you drive yourself relentlessly at work? Are you unable to stop working? Do you abhor vacations and even weekends because you don't know what to do with yourself? When you are alone or with your family, do you compulsively try to impose structure on your free time? If so, you may be a workaholic.

Experts agree that what distinguishes a workaholic from the rest of us is not the amount of time he or she spends at work, but the compulsive character of his or her work habits and how well he or she handles leisure time. An efficient, well-adjusted person can leave the job behind when it's time to go home, while a workaholic usually can't. Are you a workaholic? Take this test and find out.

?

1. Do you always get to work early?
   _____ Yes.   _____ No.

2. Do you usually work late?
   _____ Yes.   _____ No.

3. Do you work even while you're eating lunch or taking a coffee break?
   _____ Yes.   _____ No.

4. Do you generally eat lunch in ten of fifteen minutes?
   _____ Yes.   _____ No.

5. Do you often realize at three o'clock that you've forgotten to eat lunch at all?
   _____ Yes.   _____ No.

6. Do you feel that you *must* finish all the work on your desk before you go home at night?
   _____ Yes.   _____ No.

7. Do you expect others to work as hard as you do?
   _____ True.   _____ No.

8. Is there so much work on your desk that you can't find things?
   _____ Yes.   _____ No.

9. Do you usually take work home at night?
   _____ Yes.   _____ No.

10. Do you hesitate to delegate work because you think no one else can do it as well as you?
    _____ Yes.   _____ No.

11. Are you always doing three or four things at once?
    _____ Yes.   _____ No.

12. Do you always accept phone calls no matter what you're doing?
    _____ Yes.   _____ No.

13. Are you working in a job that you don't really enjoy and that isn't what you originally planned to do?
    _____ Yes.   _____ No.

14. Do you put off taking a vacation?
    _____ Yes.   _____ No.

JOB/CAREER

15. Are you afraid that if you leave to take a vacation everything will fall apart at the office?
    _____ Yes.   _____ No.

16. Do you always hurry when walking and traveling from one place to another?
    _____ Yes.   _____ No.

17. Do you have interests that you don't have time to pursue and are putting off until retirement?
    _____ Yes.   _____ No.

18. Do you dread retirement because you fear thay you won't know what to do with yourself?
    _____ Yes.   _____ No.

19. Are you ignoring instructions from your doctor to slow down and reduce stress in your life?
    _____ Yes.   _____ No.

20. Do you feel that you could do anything if you only had enough time?
    _____ Yes.   _____ No.

EVALUATION

If you answered "yes" to at least ten questions, you are suffering from a classic case of workaholism. The cure requires learning to manage your time efficiently, learning to delegate authority, learning to deal with stress, learning to make the most of your leisure time without thinking about work, and especially gaining some insight into the reasons why you are driving yourself so hard. Many workaholics suffer from low self-esteem, which causes them to believe they must constantly prove themselves.

"Yes" answers to between five and ten questions show that you have symptoms of workaholism. You must learn how to work efficiently, how to deal with stress, and how to delegate authority. Keep in mind that no one is indispensable; if you take several weeks off for a vacation, your company will survive— and if you're afraid they will find they don't need you, forget it! You must be valuable to your company or you wouldn't be working for them. In many cases, you can get the best results by sharing your work load with your subordinates.

If you answered "yes" to fewer than five questions, you probably don't have a problem with workaholism, although it is difficult to generalize because even one "yes" answer, if the behavior is pursued compulsively, could be a danger signal.

?

??????????????????????????
Do You Have What It Takes to Start Your Own Business?
??????????????????????????

Owning your own business is risky. According to the United States Small Business Administration, about 1,000 small business firms fail every day, and more than half of the businesses that fail are less than five years old. In today's economy one might conclude that this is because it takes a lot of money to start a business, but Dun and Bradstreet says that almost 95 percent of all business failures are caused not by a lack of financing, but by poor management.

Obviously, it's important to know what you're doing. This test will help you measure how informed you are in your chosen field and how well-prepared you are to start your own business.

If you score well on the test, you may have the ability to be a good small business owner and manager. If you're score isn't as high as you'd hoped, however, don't be discouraged. The most important ingredient of success is usually the desire to succeed; sometimes a person whose prospects don't look promising on paper will achieve spectacular success simply because he or she wants it enough.

?

1. Presumably, you have a particular type of business in mind. Have you had extensive and varied experience in the type of business that you wish to open?
   _____ Yes. _____ No.

2. Are you willing to work long hours without seeing an immediate profit?
   _____ Yes. _____ No.

3. Are you a self-starter? Can you plan a project on your own and then see it through?
   _____ Yes. _____ No.

4. Can you persuade other people to go along with you?
   _____ Yes. _____ No.

5. Do you genuinely like people and enjoy meeting them every day?
   _____ Yes. _____ No.

6. Can you make a decision within a reasonable amount of time and then stick to it?
   _____ Yes. _____ No.

7. Can you accept responsibility? Do you like being in charge?
   _____ Yes. _____ No.

8. Do other people know that you mean what you say?
   _____ Yes. _____ No.

9. Are you in good physical health?
   _____ Yes. _____ No.

10. If you will be selling a product, have you found a likely location—a building that you can fix up without spending too much money, one that customers can get to easily?
    _____ Yes. _____ No.

11. Are you familiar with the kinds of paperwork that will be necessary—records of income and expenses, inventory and payroll records, and tax reports? If not, do you know where to get help with this?
    _____ Yes. _____ No.

JOB/CAREER

12. Is there a demand in your community for the product or service you're interested in selling?
    _____ Yes.   _____ No.

13. Are established businesses in your community doing well?
    _____ Yes.   _____ No.

14. Are other stores or businesses in your line, both in your community and in the rest of the country, doing well?
    _____ Yes.   _____ No.

15. Have you calculated the amount of money you will need to get your business started, including one-time expenditures such as furniture, equipment, and starting inventory, as well as monthly expenses such as salaries, rent, and utilities?
    _____ Yes.   _____ No.

16. Do you have enough financial assets to see you through the first year?
    _____ Yes.   _____ No.

17. If not, do you know where you can borrow the rest of the money you need?
    _____ Yes.   _____ No.

18. Do you know how much credit you can get from your potential suppliers?
    _____ Yes.   _____ No.

19. Calculate your expected net income per year—your own salary and your profit on the money you will have to put into the business. Will you be able to plow some of it back into the business to keep it growing?
    _____ Yes.   _____ No.

20. If you are lacking in some areas, such as capital or expertise, perhaps you will need a partner. Do you know someone who may fill the bill?
    _____ Yes.   _____ No.

? EVALUATION

Give yourself one point for each question to which you answered yes.

18 to 20. *Full speed ahead!* You will probably be an excellent business owner. Now that you have the knowledge, you have to sit down and seriously plan exactly the course of action you wish to pursue. Seek information from government offices, local authorities, and other small business owners.

15 to 17. *Proceed with caution!* You may have what it takes, but you need to do some homework before starting your own business. What looks simple on paper can cause tremendous problems. So, before you leave a secure job to strike out on your own, get all the facts and figures.

14 or below. *Whoa!* Consider seriously whether you really want your own business. Though everyone wants to be the boss, you might be happier in the long run by working for someone else. Take the time to see how your employer got to where he or she is and you'll learn a thing or two.

??????????????????????????
Women: Is Your Wardrobe Working for You?
??????????????????????????

Whether women like it or not, their appearance tells a lot about them. Clothes project an image, and in the business world women have to make that image work for them. Knowing what to wear will not make you a success, but it will give the business world the right impression. The following is not a test of high fashion; it is a test of your knowledge of clothes for the office businesswoman. Even though clothes are a matter of taste and even though a woman should wear styles flattering to her figure, there are certain styles of dress that are right in the world of business—and others that are wrong.

?

1. The best way for a woman who wants to succeed in business is to dress
    a. in the latest designer fashions.
    b. in tweeds, oxfords, and Supp-hose.
    c. simply and conservatively.
    d. in the styles that are most flattering to her.

2. Your favorite outfit for business is likely to be
    a. dress.
    b. pantsuit.
    c. skirted suit.
    d. skirt and blouse.

3. The best way for a woman to achieve an authoritative, businesslike look is to
    a. imitate her male colleagues' dress with a pinstripe suit and tie.
    b. try to look feminine without being sexy or immodest.
    c. wear conservative, well-made clothes that say she is more interested in being efficient than in looking attractive.

4. A dress is generally considered acceptable business wear, but not all dresses are suitable for the office. Which of the following would you wear to work?
    a. A floral print.
    b. A pastel-colored halter dress.
    c. A gray or brown plaid.
    d. A solid or pinstripe.

5. The most appropriate type of women's suit for business is
    a. a three-piece pantsuit.
    b. a two-piece pantsuit.
    c. a three-piece skirted suit.
    d. a two-piece skirted suit.

6. Your favorite color for a business suit or dress is
    a. gray or medium blue.
    b. maroon.
    c. brown or rust.
    d. pastel pink or yellow.
    e. red.

7. A female executive should
    a. often wear an outfit that includes a blazer jacket.
    b. avoid wearing blazers if possible.
    c. wear a blazer only if her office is cold.
    d. wear a sweater if her office is cold.

8. If you wear pantsuits, they are made of
    a. polyester knit.
    b. wool.
    c. tweed.
    d. corduroy.

JOB/CAREER

9. For an important business meeting, you would be likely to wear
    a. a denim skirt, a corduroy blazer, a turtleneck, and boots.
    b. a gray wool suit, a white blouse, and medium-heeled shoes.
    c. a floral-print dress, a designer scarf, and high-heeled shoes.
    d. a lime green polyester doubleknit pantsuit and sandals.

10. The best material for a blazer for business wear is
    a. wool.
    b. tweed.
    c. corduroy.
    d. velvet.

11. The coat that you wear to work is
    a. fur.
    b. leather.
    c. wool with a fur collar.
    d. wool.

12. Your raincoat is
    a. black.
    b. beige.
    c. navy.
    d. pink.
    e. green.
    f. white.
    g. red.

13. Most of your favorite shoes are
    a. platform shoes.
    b. spike heels.
    c. medium heels.
    d. flats.
    e. boots.

14. What type of stockings do you wear to work?
    a. Only natural or beige pantyhose.
    b. Usually regular pantyhose but occasionally patterned stockings.
    c. Knee socks.
    d. Pantyhose in winter, a suntan in summer.

15. In the summer, do you wear
    a. open-toed sandals with stockings?
    b. open-toed sandals without stockings?
    c. the same shoes you wear in winter?
    d. clogs or platform shoes?

16. In the winter, do you wear
    a. leather gloves?
    b. suede gloves?
    c. knitted gloves?
    d. mittens?

17. What is your attitude toward makeup?
    a. You don't believe in it.
    b. You never go out without your face on.
    c. You wear only lipstick, eye shadow, eyeliner, and mascara.
    d. You think makeup is best when nobody can tell you're wearing any.

18. When you need to take notes, do you
    a. rummage in your handbag unsuccessfully and often find yourself borrowing a pen or pencil?
    b. usually have a pen available even if it's only a ballpoint with a supplier's advertising slogan printed on it?
    c. always know exactly where your pen is because it's an expensive gold-filled one?

19. You are being interviewed for a job with a major corporation. Which outfit do you decide to wear?
    a. A tweed pantsuit with a turtleneck.
    b. A sweater, a midiskirt, and boots.
    c. A jacket dress with a prominent designer's signature and matching high-heeled shoes.
    d. A medium blue skirt with a pale blue blouse and navy blue shoes.

20. When you need to take work home, you
    a. simply put it in your attache case, since you always carry one whether you need it or not.
    b. stuff it in a manila envelope.
    c. use a canvas tote bag that you keep in your office just in case.

WOMEN: IS YOUR WARDROBE WORKING FOR YOU?

ANSWERS

1. a—0; b—2; c—5; d—0
2. a—4; b—3; c—5; d—1
3. a—0; b—0; c—5
4. a—0; b—0; c—5; d—5
5. a—0; b—3; c—0; d—5
6. a—5; b—4; c—4; d—0; e—0
7. a—5; b—0; c—0; d—0
8. a—0; b—5; c—4; d—0
9. a—2; b—5; c—2; d—0
10. a—5; b—2; c—0; d—0
11. a—0; b—0; c—2; d—5
12. a—5; b—5; c—5; d—0; e—0; f—0; g—0
13. a—0; b—0; c—5; d—2; e—0
14. a—5; b—0; c—0; d—0
15. a—0; b—0; c—5; d—0
16. a—5; b—3; c—0; d—0
17. a—5; b—0; c—0; d—5
18. a—0; b—2; c—5
19. a—2; b—1; c—3; d—5
20. a—5; b—0; c—0

EVALUATION

An impeccably dressed businesswoman would score 90 to 100. If this was your score, then you're obviously a well-dressed career woman. A score between 80 and 89 shows that you are also a successful dresser, but you've got to look around and see what the very successful are wearing. Being aware of the importance of the right clothes in the office can make the right image work for you. If you scored between 70 and 79 you're on your way, but you haven't made it yet into the world of business fashion. To be taken seriously in the office means making sure that you look like a career-oriented woman—it is dressing for success. Any score below 70 shows that you have a long way to go to get up the ladder of success. Your wardrobe is working against you and if you want to force people to notice and respect you, then you have to dress like the Chairperson of the Board. Watch what others wear, ask for advice, and shop in stores that cater to the businesswoman.

?

??????????????????????????
Men: Is Your Wardrobe Working for You?
??????????????????????????

"Clothes make the man." As superficial as it may sound, a businessman is judged by his office appearance. If you want to look successful, then you have to dress as though you are already a business success. Clothes can be made to work for you—if you know what to wear.

No matter how you feel about clothes, they do project a certain image. And this simple fact of life can be used to your advantage. This test will not determine how well you are dressed by the standards of high fashion; it is designed to tell you if your dress is right for the business world. For each question, choose the answer that comes closest to your dressing style, and see if you are really looking good.

?

1. When you shop for a suit, you should wear
    a. your best business suit and the same type of shirt, shoes, and accessories that you would wear to the office.
    b. just a shirt and slacks so that you can try on suits more conveniently.
    c. jeans and a T-shirt.
    d. It doesn't matter what you wear; you're only going to take it off anyway.

2. Your favorite suits are made of
    a. wool or wool and polyester.
    b. knitted fabrics.
    c. wool in winter, cotton in summer.
    d. velvet or corduroy.

3. Most of your suits are
    a. dark blue or dark gray.
    b. light blue or light gray.
    c. tan or beige.
    d. dark brown.

4. Your favorite suits are
    a. solids.
    b. pinstripes.
    c. plaids.
    d. chalk stripes.

5. The only shirt patterns acceptable in *all* business circles are
    a. solids, plaids, and paisleys.
    b. solids, stripes, and polka dots.
    c. solids, stripes, and plaids.
    d. solids, stripes, and some plaids.

6. Most of your shirts are
    a. white.
    b. solid pastel colors.
    c. stripes.
    d. plaids.

7. Which type of shirt do you prefer?
    a. Long-sleeved.
    b. Short-sleeved.
    c. Long-sleeved in winter, short-sleeved in summer.

MEN: IS YOUR WARDROBE WORKING FOR YOU?

8. The material of which most of your business shirts are made is
   a. silk.
   b. cotton.
   c. polyester.
   d. polyester and cotton.

9. Your favorite tie is a
   a. solid.
   b. club tie.
   c. rep tie.
   d. foulard.
   e. paisley.
   f. plaid.
   g. polka dot.
   h. bow tie.

10. Your most useful, all-around shoe for business wear is a
    a. wingtip oxford.
    b. plain-toe oxford.
    c. Gucci loafer.
    d. penny loafer.

11. The gloves you wear for business are
    a. black leather.
    b. brown leather.
    c. gray suede.
    d. black suede.

12. Your socks always match or cordinate with
    a. your suit.
    b. your shirt.
    c. your tie.
    d. your shoes.

13. Your attache case is
    a. dark brown leather.
    b. black leather.
    c. tan leather.
    d. canvas.

14. What color is your raincoat?
    a. Black.
    b. Navy blue.
    c. Beige.
    d. Green.

15. Which of the following is true of most of your business outfits?
    a. The shirt is light-colored, the tie is darker, and the suit is darkest of all.
    b. The shirt is dark, with a contrasting light-colored tie, and the suit is lighter than the shirt.
    c. The suit is dark, the shirt is bright-colored, and the tie is a pale or pastel shade.
    d. The suit is light-colored, the shirt is dark, and the tie is lighter than the shirt.

16. Which would be the most appropriate ensemble for a meeting with an older executive?
    a. A pinstripe suit, a blue shirt, and a solid tie.
    b. A dark suit, a white suit, and a foulard tie.
    c. A beige suit, a blue shirt, and a plaid or paisley tie.
    d. A pinstripe suit, a pinstripe shirt, and a striped tie.

17. If you want to look authoritative, you should wear
    a. bright, eye-catching colors and plaid or paisley ties.
    b. a dark, three-piece pinstripe suit, white shirt, and dark tie.
    c. unobtrusive beige or gray suits with striped ties.

18. If you are a large man, you should
    a. not be afraid to wear bright, contrasting colors or large patterns if they are properly coordinated.
    b. avoid dark solids and pinstripes so that you don't intimidate people by looking like an authority figure.
    c. wear plaid suits that will make you look shorter.

19. If you are a small man, you should
    a. wear inconspicuous clothing.
    b. wear elevator shoes.
    c. wear traditional, upper-middle-class executive garb with expensive accessories.
    d. sit down whenever you can.

JOB/CAREER

20. If you are traveling in a particular region such as the South, you should
    a. dress in the same style as the natives.
    b. play it safe (until you know the territory) by wearing something like a medium blue or beige suit, a white shirt, and a not-too-aristocratic tie.
    c. wear the traditional, executive-look pinstripe suit and polka-dot tie.

ANSWERS

The number of points for each answer is given below. Add the total number of points to determine you score.

1. a—5; b—2; c—0; d—0
2. a—5; b—0; c—2; d—0
3. a—5; b—3; c—2; d—0
4. a—3; b—5; c—2; d—2
5. a—0; b—0; c—2; d—5
6. a—5; b—3; c—2; d—2
7. a—5; b—0; c—2
8. a—2; b—5; c—2; d—3
9. a—5; b—5; c—5; d—5; e—2; f—2; g—5; h—0
10. a—3; b—5; c—2; d—2
11. a—2; b—5; c—3; d—0
12. a—2; b—0; c—5; d—2
13. a—5; b—2; c—3; d—0
14. a—0; b—2; c—5; d—0
15. a—5; b—0; c—2; d—0
16. a—2; b—5; c—0; d—0
17. a—0; b—5; c—0
18. a—0; b—5; c—0
19. a—0; b—0; c—5; d—0
20. a—0; b—5; c—0

EVALUATION

This test is designed for the businessman; those who work in an office and those who interact with people in offices. A score of 90 or better shows a successful dresser, someone who might not be Chairman of the Board but dresses as though he should be. Knowing what kind of suits, coats, and accessories to wear to give others the best impression is what will bring you to the top. Scoring 80 to 89 means that you know what to wear but you are not experimenting. Working your way up the ladder is commendable, and better clothes should help make the climb a little easier. If you scored between 70 and 79 you know that you *should* clean up your act, and you even know that you *could*. For those who scored lower than 70, investing a little time and money into a new wardrobe is the only way you'll make it—unless you hire a personal valet to help you select the clothes to make you a successful-looking executive.